TRADING AND INVESTING IN BOND OPTIONS

TRADING AND INVESTING IN BOND OPTIONS

Risk Management, Arbitrage, and Value Investing

M. Anthony Wong

Managing Director, BOT Securities, Inc.

in collaboration with
Robert High

JOHN WILEY & SONS

New York • Chichester • Brisbane • Toronto • Singapore

Library of Congress Cataloging-in-Publication Data

Wong, M. Anthony.
    Trading and investing in bond options : risk management,
  arbitrage, and value investing / M. Anthony Wong, in collaboration
  with Robert High.
        p.   cm.
    Includes index.
    ISBN 0-471-52560-X
    1. Options (Finance) 2. Bonds. 3. Government securities.
  I. High, Robert. II. Bond options. III. Title.
  HG6024.A3W66   1991   91-12216
  332.63′23—dc20

Printed in the United States of America

10 9 8 7 6 5 4 3 2 1

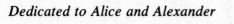

Dedicated to Alice and Alexander

Preface

Interest rate option markets have grown dramatically in the past five years, and many recently issued securities in the international capital markets contain option-like features. This book is intended for financial professionals who are preparing or beginning to become active participants in the bond option markets. These professionals include dealers and traders in banks and securities firms, interest-rate risk managers in insurance companies and industrial corporations, and investment officers in pension funds and unit trusts (mutual funds). To become successful in the bond option markets, it is important for these professionals to gain a practical, yet thorough, understanding of how options are priced, traded, and used in interest rate risk and fixed-income portfolio management.

This book assumes that the reader has some background in the financial markets, but mathematical sophistication is not a prerequisite. It attempts to provide practical answers to questions that new participants will ask as they become more sophisticated in the bond option market. This is not a theoretical treatise on bond options, but two chapters are included that describe in detail many of the widely used option pricing models, and there is a third chapter specifically addressing the question of how one chooses an appropriate pricing model in practice. To help move inexperienced option marketmakers along their learning curves, specific examples are given to illustrate how over-the-counter (OTC) option traders come up with their market quotes and hedge their positions. A related chapter is devoted to the discussion of risk management issues in options trading and of the important role played by advanced trader workstation technology. Instead of simply providing recipes for option investment strategies, this book addresses the various risk factors that arise when these strategies are used in practice.

HOW THIS BOOK IS STRUCTURED

This book describes the U.S. government bond option markets, and discusses how options pricing and computer technologies are used in marketmaking, strategic trading, and value investing in these options. It begins by introducing standard options terminology, with some specifics on the role of bond options, in Chapter 1. Chapter 2 provides some background information on U.S. Treasury bonds and the corresponding bond options markets, with a section devoted to the rapidly growing Japanese Government Bond (JGB) options market.

An introduction to bond options pricing models is given in Chapter 3, where Black-Scholes–type models and lattice-based models suitable for evaluating short-term options are described. Advanced pricing models, including those based on a changing term structure of interest rates, are discussed in Chapter 4. The question of how to choose the most appropriate pricing model for a specific application is addressed in Chapter 5.

Chapter 6 presents the fundamentals of bond options dealing. A computerized bond options trading and exposure management system is functionally specified in Chapter 7, to illustrate the importance of advanced workstation technology for participants in this market. The principles of relative-value analysis, and its application in strategic options trading are addressed in Chapter 8.

Options trading and investment strategies can be grouped into several categories. Delta-neutral option positions, which are often used to make bets on anticipated actual volatilities versus the traded, implied volatility, are described in Chapter 9. Strategies driven by interest rate forecasts are presented in Chapter 10, while the most widely used structured portfolio strategies involving options are given in Chapter 11.

The aim of this book is to bring the serious professional "up to speed" in the bond options market as quickly and painlessly as possible. Numerous examples, drawn from actual trading experience and portfolio mangement, are used to illustrate the strategic principles discussed. Practical issues frequently missing or lightly treated in standard option texts, including the criteria for selecting a particular options pricing model, the technological requirements of the bond options trader and risk manager, and the details of strategies such as relative-value trading, are examined in depth. References are presented at the end of each chapter, along with brief notes directing the reader to further readings.

Acknowledgments

I was fortunate to have Bob High's help in writing this book. He wrote most of the chapters on option pricing models, and was also responsible for Chapters 1 and 2. I would like to thank all my friends and former colleagues at Greenwich Capital Markets, Inc. (GCM), Greenwich Asset Management, Inc. (GAM), and The Long-Term Credit Bank of Japan (LTCB). Special thanks go to Tom Connor, Craig Nunez, Reza Anzari, David Lambert, Yichen Zhang, Jian Li, Michelle Beckwith, Margaret Jarris, Robert Fetter, and Richard Dziurzynski for reading early drafts of the manuscripts. I have benefited from discussions with Rick Garth, Tim Dann, Frank Duquette, Phil Lotz, Blake Drexler, Ray Diana, Dan Schmidt, Arthur Bass, Elliot Goldstein, Atsuo Imanishi, Satoshi Watanabe, Stephen Siu, Enlin Pan, and Elliot Detchon. GCM's Gary Holloway, Chip Kruger, Fumio Hayakawa, Masaharu Kuhara, and LTCB's Ryuji Konishi, Mitsuaki Kuze, and Masatoshi Shimizu suggested that I write this book, and I am grateful that they were so convincing. A very special thanks goes to Ted Knetzger, the President and CEO of Greenwich Capital Markets, Inc., for his continuous encouragement and enthusiasm throughout this writing project. Finally, I would like to thank LTCB's translation team, under Masatoshi Shimizu's superb leadership, for translating an earlier version of this book into Japanese, and to thank KINZAI (Institute for Financial Affairs, Inc.) for publishing the Japanese edition in 1989.

Contents

List of Tables and Figures

TABLES

FIGURES

TRADING AND INVESTING IN BOND OPTIONS

1

Introduction to Options

Newcomers to the options market naturally ask the following questions when they are first introduced to this market. What are options? What are their risk/return characteristics? Why does an options market exist? Who are the participants? This chapter addresses these questions, with a focus on the bond options market. The basic definitions and characteristics of options are given in the first section, and the role of bond options in financial markets is discussed in the second section.

WHAT ARE OPTIONS?

Once viewed primarily as an arena for speculation, options markets have in recent years assumed a key role in the financial world. While their highly leveraged character still makes options attractive to many speculators, their flexible risk/return characteristics have made options an essential tool for hedging more traditional investments, and a basic building block in the construction of new, derivative instruments, which have played an increasingly important role in the securities markets in the last few years.

Options markets in the United States, and the options market in cash bonds and bond futures in particular, have matured rapidly to the point where the traded volume in terms of the underlying securities, is frequently greater than that of the underlying securities themselves. Options on billions of dollars in Treasury bond futures trade daily on the Chicago

Board of Trade. There is also a thriving over-the-counter market in cash bond options. More complex derivative instruments such as interest rate caps and floors have also found a permanent role in contemporary financial life. In Japan, cash bond options started trading in 1989 and bond futures options will debut in 1990, and these markets can also be expected to grow very rapidly.

Definitions

A **call (put) option** is a contract granting the right to buy (sell) a fixed quantity of some underlying security, such as a stock, bond, or bond future, at a predetermined price, for a given period of time. The predetermined sale or purchase price of the underlying security is known as the **strike** or **exercise price.** An option contract is good only until its **expiration date.** If the buyer of the call (put) option can exercise his right to buy (sell) the underlying security on any date up to the expiration date, the option is said to be an **American** option; if it may only be exercised on the expiration date, it is said to be a **European** option. European options are easier to analyze, so theoretical treatments of options often take European contracts as their starting point; however, most traded options are American.

The principal determinants of an option contract are thus the following:

- Contract (settlement) date
- Expiration date
- The size or quantity of the contract
- The underlying security
- Strike price
- Whether the contract is a put or a call
- Whether the option is American or European

A typical cash bond option, for example, might be a $100,000 one-month American call option with a strike price of 96.00 on an 8% U.S. Treasury bond (T-bond) currently trading at 95.00. Such an option would normally have a price of around $^{25}/_{32}$nds, or $781.25 (= $100,000 $\times$ $^{25}/_{32}$%). (Chapter 3 will introduce the mathematical models necessary to calculate theoretical prices for such options from the contract terms.)

One of the most important features of an option contract is that it guarantees the call (put) buyer a *right*, the right to buy (sell) the underlying security at the agreed-upon strike price, but entails no *obligation* to do so. The seller of the option, also sometimes called the **option writer,** *does* have an obligation: to sell (in the case of a call) or buy (in the case of a put) the underlying security, at the agreed-upon strike price, upon demand (exercise) by the option holder. This asymmetry in the situations of option buyers and sellers is reflected in the risk/return characteristics of an options position, as illustrated below.

Since the option buyer has no obligation to exercise, he will do so only if and when it benefits him. Consider, for example, a buyer of the one-month call option on the 8% bond cited above. If the price of the underlying bond never rose above the strike price during the life of the option contract, the call would expire worthless, and the option buyer would have lost the cost of the option, *but never more than that*. If, on the other hand, the price of the underlying bond rose above the strike price, say to 100.00, the option holder could exercise, and profit by the difference between the prevailing price and the option strike. Upon exercise, the option holder would have made four points (100.00 − 96.00), or $4,000, for a net profit of $3,218.75 after deducting the cost of the option. (For simplicity we ignore all transaction costs.) Thus, the call buyer's potential loss is *always limited*, while his potential gains are theoretically unlimited. This situation is illustrated in Figure 1.1.

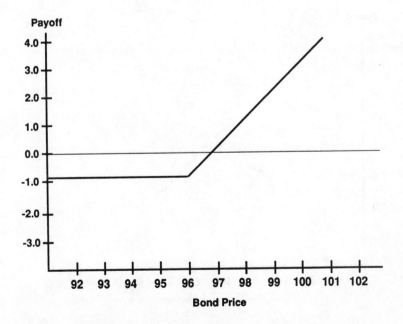

FIGURE 1.1   Call option payoff function.

The situation of the call seller depends to some extent on whether or not he actually holds the underlying security on which the option is written. A call seller who holds the underlying security is said to have written a **covered call,** whereas a call seller who does not hold the underlying security is said to have written a **naked call.** As the name would suggest, a naked call is riskier than a covered call. The writer of a covered call gives up any potential profit from appreciation in the price of the underlying security above the strike level; in exchange, he receives the option price as a premium. The writer of a naked call, however, is exposed to *unlimited* risk, because he must make good on his commitment to sell the underlying security at the agreed-upon price *regardless* of its market price if and when the option is exercised. (In practice, of course, the option writer doesn't just go to sleep until the option is exercised or expires, and will, if prudent, act to purchase the underlying security as soon as possible if its price threatens to soar. But illiquidity and other market factors can still squeeze such an option writer severely, so it is probably wise to continue to think of a naked call as exposing the writer to "unlimited" risk.) The payoff diagram of a written naked call is illustrated in Figure 1.2.

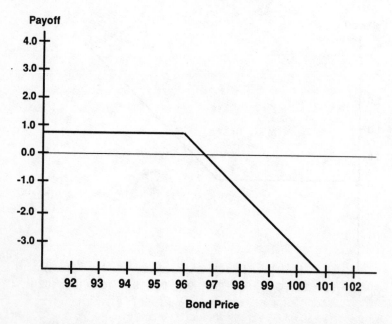

FIGURE 1.2   Written call option payoff function

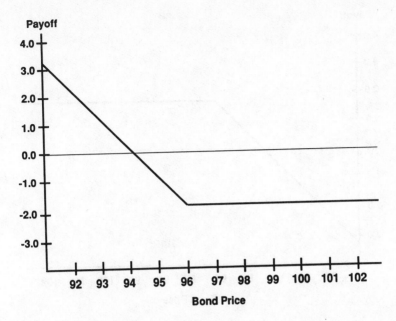

FIGURE 1.3 Put option payoff function.

The buyer of a put option has the right to *sell* the underlying security to the option writer at the strike price. He will do this only if the market price of the underlying security falls *below* the strike price. Holding a put is similar to shorting the underlying security—it is a bearish strategy; profit is associated with a fall in market price. But unlike a short position, the put holder is at no risk if the price of the underlying security *rises*; at worst, his put will expire worthless. As with a call, the option holder's risk is limited to the cost of the option. The risk/return characteristics of a put are shown in Figure 1.3, and those of a written put in Figure 1.4.

The key feature of option contracts is that they represent *contingent claims:* their value is contingent on the price of the underlying security at exercise (or expiration). If there were no uncertainty associated with the future price of the underlying security, an option would be just another kind of forward contract. Since there is usually considerable uncertainty about price movements, however, the value of an option contract incorporates a *risk premium* associated with that uncertainty. A call option will typically command a higher price the wider the market participants perceive the price fluctuations of the underlying security to be.

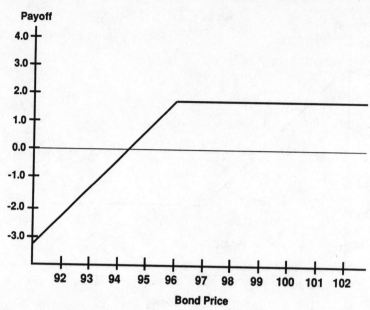

FIGURE 1.4   Written put option payoff function.

There is nothing new in the notion of a risk premium—there are premia associated with credit risk, liquidity risk, reinvestment risk, and the like. But option contracts allow market participants to conveniently package and transfer the risk associated with the uncertainty of future prices of specific securities over specific time spans. This is a major reason for their usefulness as risk management tools.

Qualitative Behavior of Option Prices

When the price of the underlying security is above (below) the strike price of a call (put), the option is said to be **in the money,** because it then has a definite, **intrinsic value** if exercised. When the reverse is true, the option is said to be **out of the money.** An option struck *at* the market price of the underlying security is said to be **at the money.** Option prices decrease as they get further out of the money.

The price of an in-the-money option is normally greater than its intrinsic value. The additional value placed on the option by the market is called its **time value,** and is a measure of how strongly market participants think the option may move (further) into the money before expiration.

This in turn is determined by the variability in the price of the underlying security—if the price of the underlying security changes very little from day to day an option is unlikely to move much (further) into the money, and hence will have little time value, whereas if the price is very volatile the underlying security will be much more likely to move (further) into the money, and the option's time value will, in general, be accordingly higher. The technical measure of this variability in the price of the underlying security is known as its **volatility;** the estimation and use of bond volatilities will be discussed in some detail in Chapter 5. The time to expiration is also a factor in determining the time value of an option. Since for each extra day to expiration the option owner has another opportunity for favorable price movements, the time value of an option will decrease as expiration approaches, all other factors remaining the same.

In general, one can make the following *qualitative* statements about the behavior of option prices:

1. Option price *increases* as the contract moves into the money, and *decreases* as the contract moves out of the money. Thus, call options *increase* in value as the price of the underlying security increases, while put options *decrease* in value as the price of the underlying security increases.
2. Time value, and hence option price, *decreases* as the term of the option decreases. This latter fact, which affects every option contract as it ages, is known as **time decay** (see Figure 1.5). Note that

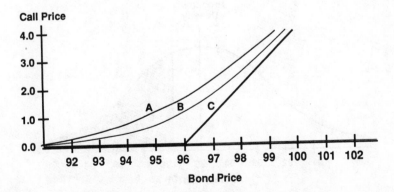

FIGURE 1.5 Time decay in option value. *A:* 60-day option. *B:* 30-day option. *C:* at expiration.

the time value of an option is *greatest* when it is exactly at the money.

3. Option price generally *increases* as the volatility of the underlying security increases. (Under certain circumstances, an increase in volatility may *not* lead to an increase in option price. For example, a deep-in-the-money bond option may actually have its price *decreased* by an increase in volatility, because the additional likelihood of ending up out of the money and worthless can outweigh any potential increase in value, since the underlying security, a bond, has an absolute cap on its price given by the sum of all future cash flows. But as a general rule, most options tend to increase in value with increased volatility.)

Options Pricing: A Probability Interpretation

The value of a European option contract will ultimately be determined by comparing its strike price with the price of the underlying security on the expiration date. Since we are uncertain about where the underlying security will be trading on that date, we can picture its price as having a range of possible values at option expiration—each with an associated option price. Some of these possible values will be more likely than others, and we can capture this fact by thinking in terms of a *probability distribution* of underlying prices on the expiration date (see Figure 1.6). An outcome with a price, P, less than the strike price, K, will have zero

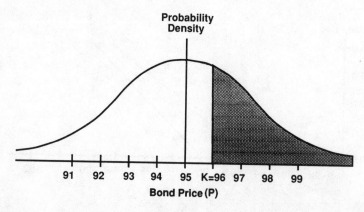

FIGURE 1.6 Probability distribution for bond prices at option expiration.

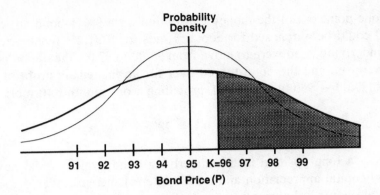

FIGURE 1.7 Probability distribution for bond prices at option expiration, with doubled volatility.

option value because the underlying issue is worth less than the strike price and the option expires worthless. The probability of having a zero option value is represented by the area under the probability curve to the left of the strike price K. An outcome with a price P in the shaded area to the right of the strike price K will have an option value of $P - K$. The probability-weighted average of these option values, discounted back to today's date by the appropriate risk-free interest rate, will be the fair value of the option today.

Let us now use this approach to illustrate why option prices generally increase as the volatility of the underlying security increases. The result of doubling the volatility of underlying prices given by Figure 1.6 is shown in Figure 1.7. It is clear that with a higher volatility, the distribution of underlying prices at option expiration is more diffuse and spread out. Since the fair value of the option today is the discounted probability-weighted average of the option values to the right of the strike price K, the option value will be higher for the higher volatility, because there is a much better chance of having extremely high prices at expiration. (Note that we are not comparing the *shaded areas* themselves in the two figures—the shaded area in Figure 1.7 is actually smaller than that in Figure 1.6. We are, however, comparing the *probability-weighted averages of* $P - K$ in the shaded areas; outcomes farther to the right will have higher values of $P - K$, and hence contribute more to the option value.)

Options as Leveraged Instruments

Because the cost of an option is small relative to its potential profit, options are highly leveraged instruments. For example, a $100,000 thirty-day one-point out-of-the-money call option on a 9% T-bond struck at 96.00 could be purchased for about $^{25}/_{32}$nds, or $781.25. If the price of the underlying bond were to move from 95.00 to 97.00, the option could be exercised and the bond turned over for an immediate profit of one point (97.00 − 96.00), or $1,000, providing a one-month return of:

$$\text{Return} = 100\% \left(\frac{1000.0}{781.25} - 1.0 \right) = 28\%$$

whereas a long position in the underlying bond, which would have a $2,000 capital appreciation and a $750 interest increase over the same interval, would only bring a one-month return of:

$$\text{Return} = 100\% \times \left(\frac{97,000 + 750}{95,000} - 1.0 \right) = 2.89\%$$

The down side of a highly leveraged position is, of course, the potential for dramatic negative returns. For example, if the bond in our example experienced *no* price movement over the 30-day life of the option, the option would expire worthless, and we would have lost 100% of our initial investment. Had we held the bond, we would still have experienced an interest increase of $750 for a one-month return of:

$$\text{Return} = 100\% \times \left(\frac{750}{95,000} - 1.0 \right) = 0.7895\%$$

Even if the bond experienced a price decline, a long position in the bond would show only a partial loss, as against the 100% loss on an option holding. The risk/return characteristics of an options position are indeed highly sensitive to the price dynamics of the underlying security. Those inclined to use options as speculative rather than hedging instruments should be well aware of the risks involved!

Exchange-Traded (Listed) and Over-the-Counter Options

Debt options contracts are commonly traded either on an exchange or over the counter (OTC). There is an important distinction between **exchange-listed options** and **over-the-counter options**. Exchange-listed options, as the name suggests, are traded through a centralized exchange. Options on T-bond and Treasury note (T-note) futures trade on the Chicago Board of Trade (CBT), while cash bond options trade on the American Stock Exchange (AMEX) and Chicago Board Options Exchange

(CBOE). CBT options on T-bond futures are traded on the nearest three futures contracts (see Chapter 2), and are struck at even-number prices centered around the current futures price. CBOE options on cash bonds come in fixed classes, typically with one-, two-, three-, or four-month terms, with a range of round-number or half-point strike prices (e.g., 99.50, 100.00, 100.50).

Over-the-counter options are available at whatever terms the parties involved agree to; for example, one could purchase a 19-day option on a particular T-bond struck at 99 and $12/_{32}$nds. Such options are typically for terms of less than six months; the majority are for terms under three months. Increasingly, however, some financial institutions have been offering European **long-dated options,** with terms up to several years. More complex "optionlike" contracts, such as interest rate caps and floors and interest rate swaps and options on these, are also available, and it has become important to develop techniques for pricing such longer term options and optionlike instruments. Some of the applications of such instruments are discussed below, and in succeeding chapters.

WHY IS AN OPTIONS MARKET NECESSARY?

Many observers have argued that options add little value to the financial markets. Certainly the fact that an option is held on a stock or a bond in no way changes the return characteristics of the underlying security itself; it neither reduces nor augments the principal value, dividends, or coupon income of that security. Moreover, as will be shown in Chapters 3 and 11, an option's price behavior can effectively be replicated (or synthesized) by a suitable position in the underlying security, dynamically adjusted as the security's price moves. What, then, are the reasons for the explosive growth in options markets?

First, the dynamic process of creating a synthetic option only works when the price of the underlying security evolves smoothly over time, without sudden, large jumps. As many U.S. institutional investors found out during the week of October 19, 1987, such a process can fail miserably in times of extremely high volatility. Owning an option is therefore the most convenient and effective way of taking advantage of these unique risk/return characteristics.

Second, the options market is not, as some observers have suggested, merely a casino for speculators. The bond options market brings together traders and investors with different goals. Some traders inevitably use options as a leveraged speculative instrument, hoping to profit hand-somely from their expectations on interest rate and volatility movements. However, options are also used by investment managers as a tool to hedge against portfolio losses during adverse market movements. Options therefore serve as a sort of insurance policy for investors; the option price can be viewed as a kind of insurance premium, with the option speculators playing the role of insurance carriers. Options are thus a vehicle for transferring risk from risk-averse investors (e.g., pension funds) to risk-seeking investors (speculators). Used in this way, options actually serve to *stabilize* the market. Options can also be used in com-bination with holdings in the underlying bonds to enhance the portfolio's current income, for example, by writing covered calls.

Third, traditional instruments, such as stocks and bonds, have very simple, and inflexible, risk/return characteristics. Their payoff functions are essentially straight lines, whereas options have a more flexible, dogleg payoff function (see Figures 1.1–1.4). By combining options with differ-ent strikes and/or expirations, it is possible to replicate *any* desired payoff function as closely as may be required. In theoretical terms, one says that options "complete the market," allowing investors to structure com-posite positions replicating any desired payoff profile. This ability to synthesize complex payoff functions has also become increasingly im-portant with the growth in the market for derived instruments such as interest rate caps and floors, which behave like a whole series of options with differing terms, or interest rate swaps and options on them, which are themselves complex contingent claims. The following sections outline the potential use of bond options for some of these purposes.

Creating Alternative Investment Vehicles

An investment manager's goal is to get the best return on the capital under given risk constraints. The manager keeps track of market devel-opments and continuously updates his or her market opinion using ana-lytical skills. When an investor is restricted to using only stocks and bonds themselves, there will be times when it may not be possible to construct a portfolio that will give an attractive return if the market pro-jections turn out to be right, but will at the same time limit any loss if the investor is wrong. Options are very useful in such circumstances because they can be used (*a*) to alter the risk/return characteristics of traditional instruments, and (*b*) to form new investment vehicles that provide genuine diversification of existing security classes.

EXAMPLE 1.1: T-BILLS PLUS OPTIONS

Consider the investor who wishes to invest in long-term bonds, but is not willing to take on the possible down-side risk involved in such an investment. Such an investor could instead purchase call options on T-bonds while investing the balance of his or her money in safer, short-term instruments, such as Treasury bills (T-bills). With such a position, the investor would participate in any significant bullish market movement, while his or her down-side exposure would be limited to the cost of the calls.

EXAMPLE 1.2: BUY-WRITE

For another use of options, consider the investor who wants higher current income, does not expect the market to fall, but is not particularly bullish either. One popular strategy for enhancing current income is the so-called **buy-write,** where the investor writes covered calls on the instruments in his or her portfolio. If the market doesn't move too far, income is enhanced by the option premium over the holding period (the life of the option). For example, if the investor bought $1 million in 30-year 8% bonds at a price of 95.00, and sold a 1-month at-the-money call option on the bond at a price of one and one half points, the annualized return over the 30-day holding period with no market movement would be:

$$\text{Return} = \frac{(\text{coupon income} + \text{option premium})}{\text{invoice price}} \times \frac{365}{30} \times 100\%$$

$$= \frac{(\$6{,}575.34 + \$15{,}000.00)}{\$950{,}000} \times 12.166 \times 100\%$$

$$= 0.0227 \times 12.166 \times 100\% = 27.63\%$$

(where for simplicity we have assumed there is no initial accrued interest.) This is a significant enhancement of the simple yield based on coupon income over the holding period, which, on an annualized basis, would be:

$$\text{Simple yield} = \frac{\text{Coupon income}}{\text{invoice price}} \times \frac{365}{30} \times 100\%$$

$$= \frac{\$6,575.34}{\$950,000.00} \times 12.166 \times 100\%$$

$$= 0.0069 \times 12.166 \times 100\% = 8.42\%$$

EXAMPLE 1.3: STRADDLE OR STRANGLE

Suppose that the bond market is volatile and expected to become more so. Without options, investors would see their portfolio values change drastically, and unpredictably, over time. With options, an investor can use a **straddle or strangle** strategy to exploit the anticipated volatility. This consists of simultaneously buying a put and a call on the bond, either both struck at the money **(straddle),** or equally out of the money **(strangle).** The result is that, if the bond price moves significantly *in either direction*, the investor will profit. The investor will break even if on the option expiration date the bond price is equal to the call strike price *plus* the total option premium paid, or to the put price *minus* the total option premium. Of course, if volatility is already high, options will be expensive, and the breakeven points will be farther away from the current market price of the underlying bond at the time the trade is put on.

EXAMPLE 1.4: SYNTHETIC FORWARD

Participants in the Japanese Government Bond (JGB) OTC options market have recently found a way to use JGB options to bypass one of their outstanding problems. For reasons to be discussed in Chapter 2, JGB traders and investors frequently find it difficult to establish forward positions required for cash-futures arbitrage trading. The lack of a true well-developed bond repurchase (borrowing/lending) market has meant that there are no real forward contracts available in the JGB market. With the opening of the JGB options market in June 1989, traders have found that they can construct *synthetic forwards* by combining a long call position with a short put at the same strike (or reversing the combination to construct a synthetic short). If cash bond prices rise the trader can exercise the call; if cash prices fall the trader will expect the put to be exercised against him or her. In either case, the effect is the same as having entered into a contract to buy a cash bond for a specific price at a certain future date—as in an actual forward contract.

Embedded Options and Derivative Securities

Options theory and technique are applicable to many securities that do not at first glance seem to have the characteristics of an option contract. Many standard securities have features that can be viewed and treated as *embedded options*—contingent claims the value of which can be separated out from the entire instrument and valued using standard option pricing techniques. Examples are the **call feature** of many government bonds—an embedded call option that is European until first call date and American thereafter; the **convertible feature** of some corporate bonds; and the use of **warrants** to enhance the attractiveness of some corporate bonds. Holding a convertible bond or warrant can be viewed as equivalent to being long on a long-dated call option on the underlying stock.

Embedded optionlike features are also present in bond futures and in mortgage-backed securities. In the case of bond futures, there is a whole cluster of embedded options related to delivery of the cheapest-to-deliver bond against the futures contract, including the choice of security, the choice of delivery date, and even the timing of delivery on the actual delivery date. These aspects of bond futures are discussed in more detail in Chapter 2. And in every mortgage-backed security, there are implied embedded long-term American options, because each mortgagor always has the option of *prepaying* his or her mortgage. This is a complex phenomenon, because its exercise is contingent on the movement of interest rates, and not directly on the price of the mortgage security. We will discuss the applicability of option pricing techniques to this and similar situations when we review advanced pricing models for long-dated options in Chapter 4.

Options also play a key role in the emerging field of **financial engineering**—the creation of new, synthetic financial instruments out of existing ones. Different investors have different constraints and needs, arising from different investment horizons, cash-flow requirements, willingness to face risk exposure, and legal and tax-related rules and regulations. Many institutional and investment banks have been working to create new "securities" that appeal to the particular needs of various investor groups.

One of the most popular capital market instruments issued recently in the Eurobond market has been the **Nikkei-linked Euro-yen bond.** The holder of this instrument receives coupon income regularly, but the return of principal at the end of three years is contingent on the performance of the Nikkei index. If at maturity the index has moved up, the holder receives the full face value, but if the index has moved down, the holder receives only a corresponding percentage of face. This essentially represents the sale by the investor of a three-year European put on the Nikkei index. Japanese institutional investors like to invest in these bonds because they believe that there is only a very small chance that the Nikkei index will go down significantly in value. Just as a convertible bond or warrant represents going long on a long-dated call, the Nikkei-linked Euro-yen bond represents going short on a long-dated put.

Other examples of this trend can be found in Ritchken (1987). Interest rate caps and floors, which guarantee to make up the difference between short-term interest rates and a fixed ceiling or floor on such rates for the duration of the contract, are representative examples.

Risk Management

Options are widely used by investment managers to hedge against losses during adverse market movements. They are also extensively used in various other risk management contexts, including currency risk hedging and asset-liability management.

EXAMPLE 1.5: PORTFOLIO INSURANCE USING PUTS

An investor or portfolio manager has a huge bond portfolio, and fears an adverse move in interest rates. It would not be practical to sell all the securities in the portfolio; transaction costs would be prohibitive, and the investor would still be faced with reinvestment risk. Moreover, such a move in interest rates may never take place. To protect against a *contingent* liability, the investor should resort to a *contingent instrument:* options. Most simply, by **buying puts** the investor can protect the portfolio against the effects of adverse interest rate movement: if bond prices *fall* the value of the puts will *rise* correspondingly. (Of course, there are many details as to just what proportion of options should be purchased, at what strikes and expirations. Many of these are explored in some detail in later chapters.) Exposure to currency risk can be similarly hedged by buying puts in the currency options market.

EXAMPLE 1.6: ASSET-LIABILITY MANAGEMENT

Banks, pension funds, and insurance companies all have to manage their asset and liability positions. Banks, for example, may have short-term liabilities and long-term assets. Pension funds may have a need to lock in rates within a certain range, for regulatory reasons. How can these institutions hedge away their yield curve risk (the danger that the shape of the yield curve—the spread from short- to long-term rates—may move against them)? One way is through the use of **interest rate swaps,** or options on swaps. (A swap allows one to exchange variable for fixed rates, for example.) Or the various assets and liabilities could be hedged separately, with a series of options on instruments of appropriate maturities. Another approach would be to use an **interest rate cap or floor** to limit the potential range within which effective short-term rates can vary. Again, by paying the price of an option, or an appropriate combination of options, as a sort of insurance premium, the investor can hedge away all or part of his or her risk exposure to interest rate movements.

As a final, topical example, consider the interest rate risk exposure inherent in the financing of any of the recent, multibillion dollar leveraged buyouts, such as the $24.88 billion takeover of RJR Nabisco Inc. by Kohlberg, Kravis, Roberts and Company (KKR). Under the terms of the deal, KKR was "required" to keep an interest rate hedge on half the outstanding bank debt until the total fell below $5 billion; this amounted to some $6 billion in hedges. Among the hedge instruments considered by KKR were Eurodollar futures contracts (the short-selling of which would make capital gains when interest rates rose); an interest rate swap, which would remove the uncertainty of floating interest rates; and an interest rate cap, which would limit the potential exposure to interest rate movement. Yet another possibility would have been to purchase a **caption,** or an option to buy a cap. This would reduce the cost of insurance if it were ever needed, because the option would be cheaper than the actual cap, but it would raise the total cost if rates ever actually exceeded the cap's ceiling.

REFERENCES

An overview of fixed-income options is given in Gartland et al. (1989). The basic definitions of options, and their risk/return characteristics, can

8 INTRODUCTION TO OPTIONS

be found in many standard texts, including Bookstaber (1987), Cox and Rubinstein (1985), and Ritchken (1987). Recipes for option investment strategies are detailed in McMillan (1986), while Ezell (1989) describes the various applications of debt options for banks and thrifts. An excellent introduction to the hedging uses of interest rate options is given in Brauer and Goodman (1989), while Bookstaber (1985) and Bookstaber and Clarke (1984), respectively, provide insights on how options are used in performance structuring and on how option strategies can be evaluated.

Bookstaber, R. M., "The Uses of Options in Performance Structuring," *Journal of Portfolio Management*, Summer 1985.
Bookstaber, R. M., *Options Pricing and Investment Strategies*, Probus Publishing Company, Chicago, 1987.
Bookstaber, R. M., and R. G. Clarke, "Option Portfolio Strategies: Measurement and Evaluation," *Journal of Business*, October 1984.
Brauer, J., and L. S. Goodman, "Hedging with Options and Option Products," in F. J. Fabozzi, ed., *Handbook of Fixed-Income Options: Pricing, Strategies & Applications*, Probus Publishing Company, Chicago, 1989, pp. 265–293.
Cox, J., and M. Rubinstein, *Options Markets*, Prentice-Hall, Englewood Cliffs N.J., 1985.
Ezell, J. M., "Applications of Debt Options for Banks and Thrifts," in F. J. Fabozzi, ed., *Handbook of Fixed-Income Options: Pricing, Strategies & Applications*, Probus Publishing Company, Chicago, 1989, pp. 421–437.
Gartland, W., T. Ritchford, and N. Letica, "Overview of Fixed Income Options," in F. J. Fabozzi, ed., *Handbook of Fixed-Income Options: Pricing, Strategies & Applications*, Probus Publishing Company, Chicago, 1989, pp. 3–45.
McMillan, L. G., *Options as a Strategic Investment*, Prentice-Hall, Englewood Cliffs, N.J., 1986.
Quint, M., "Talking Deals: Cutting Rate Risk on Buyout Debt," *The New York Times*, February 16, 1989.
Ritchken, P., *Options: Theory, Strategy and Applications*, Scott Foresman and Company, Glenview, Ill., 1987.

2
The Bond Option Market

This chapter analyzes the existing U.S. debt option markets, beginning with a brief description of the various U.S. Treasury securities and the participants in the primary and secondary Treasury markets. Following is a discussion of the different debt option products and their particular market structures and distinguishing characteristics. Finally, an overview of the Japanese Government Bond (JGB) market is presented, and this market is contrasted with its U.S. counterpart, with special emphasis on those differences most likely to affect the emerging JGB options market.

U.S. TREASURY SECURITIES: THE PRIMARY MARKET

The U.S. Treasury (UST) issues marketable securities, including Treasury bills, notes, and bonds, on a regular schedule to finance government spending and debt (budget deficits). These securities are backed by the full tax powers of the U.S. government. The Treasury issues short-term debt instruments (bills) in maturities from 30 days to 1 year on a regular basis. Issuing maturities for notes and bonds range from 1 to 30 years. All these securities are actively traded in the secondary market.

Treasury securities are widely held as investments because of the high credit of the U.S. government, the liquidity of their secondary market, their large outstanding volume, and the broad range of maturities. As of January 1988, the total volume of marketable U.S. government securities outstanding was about $1.7 trillion. Interest income from these instruments is not subject to state and local taxation, although it is subject to full taxation as ordinary income by the federal government. All these factors, and the fact that these securities represent a dollar-denominated stake in the U.S. economy, make Treasury securities extraordinarily attractive to many foreign and domestic institutional investors. Holders of these securities include foreign governments and agencies, domestic and foreign banks and other nonbanking financial institutions, industrial corporations, and pension and mutual funds.

Treasury **bills** (T-bills) are discount securities, with no coupon payments, issued by the Treasury with maturities of no more than one year. Securities with issuing maturities greater than one year are **coupon securities,** making semiannual coupon payments. The annual coupon (as a percentage of face value) is specified before the issue, and an amount equal to half the annual coupon is paid to the investor every six months. Treasury **notes** (T-notes) are coupon securities that are issued with a maturity of ten years or less, and Treasury **bonds** (T-bonds) are issued with a maturity of more than ten years.

The marketable Treasury securities are issued regularly on an auction basis with the assistance of the Federal Reserve System. For example, every Monday the Treasury auctions 91-day and 182-day T-bills and has them issued by the following Thursday, and every fourth Thursday it auctions a 52-week T-bill, making it available the following Thursday. T-bills are auctioned on a price basis, where the bids for the bills are ordered from highest price to lowest and then allocated from the highest price until the total issue is filled. T-bonds and T-notes are auctioned on a yield basis. Bids are ranked lowest to highest and then filled, starting from the lowest. The average yield of the successful bids is used to determine the coupon of the new bond; the annual coupon is set just below this average yield bid (the next lowest round $\frac{1}{8}\%$), so new bonds are issued at a slight discount to par.

Treasury Bills

With over \$200 billion brought to market annually, T-bills represent about 40% of the total marketable securities issued by the Treasury. They are negotiable, non-interest-bearing securities with an original maturity of either 13, 26, or 52 weeks. Bills are offered in denominations of \$10,000, \$15,000, \$100,000, \$500,000, and \$1 million, in book-entry form only.

Bills are always issued at a discount price, and this price is determined in auctions conducted by the Federal Reserve Bank. Investors in T-bills pay a discount price, but receive the full face value of the bill at maturity. This gain is treated as interest income for federal tax purposes, but is exempt from state and local taxation.

T-bill prices are quoted in **discount yields** to their maturity dates. Suppose a bill with N days to maturity is currently priced at $P\%$ of its face value, that is, at $\$P$ per $\$100$ face value. That bill has a discount yield D defined as:

$$D = \frac{360}{N} \times \frac{(100 - P)}{100} \tag{2.1}$$

To compute the actual price P in percentage of the face value, we use the formula:

$$P = 100 \times \left(1 - \frac{N \times D}{360}\right) \tag{2.2}$$

(Note that T-bill calculations always use a *360-day year*.)

The return on a bill held to maturity is also often stated in terms of its bond-equivalent yield Y. For bills with less than six months to maturity, this is just the *simple interest* on the bill:

$$Y = \frac{365}{N} \times \frac{(100 - P)}{P} \tag{2.3}$$

or equivalently,

$$Y = \frac{365}{[360 - (N \times D)] \times D} \tag{2.4}$$

For bills with more than six months to maturity ($N > 182$), a different formula is used to derive the bond-equivalent yield. Bond-equivalent means semiannual compounding. So, we solve for that rate Y that, for a starting principal of P, would yield 100 at the end of N days if a coupon of $P \times Y/2$ were paid after six months and reinvested to maturity along with the principal at the rate Y. The equation to be solved is:

$$100 = P \times \left(1 + \frac{Y}{2}\right) \times \left[1 + \frac{Y}{365}\left(N - \frac{365}{2} - 1\right)\right] \tag{2.5}$$

Expanding, we get a quadratic equation in Y, which can be solved to give:

$$Y = \frac{-\dfrac{2N}{365} + 2\sqrt{\left(\dfrac{N}{365}\right)^2 - \left[\left(\dfrac{2N}{365} - 1\right)\left(1 - \dfrac{100}{P}\right)\right]}}{\dfrac{2N}{365} - 1} \qquad (2.6)$$

EXAMPLE 2.1

Consider an 84-day $100,000 face value T-bill with a discount yield of 8.16%. Thus $N = 84$ days, $D = 0.0816$, and the price P in percentage of the face value is computed using Equation 2.2:

$$P = 100 \times \left(1 - \frac{84 \times 0.0816}{360}\right) = 98.096$$

The actual price of the bill will be $98,096. If the bill is held to maturity, its bond-equivalent yield, from Equation 2.3, is:

$$Y = \frac{365}{84} \times \frac{100 - 98.096}{98.096} = 0.0843 = 8.43\%$$

Treasury Bonds and Notes

Treasury notes are coupon-bearing securities with original maturity of not less than one year and not more than ten years, and T-bonds have an original maturity of more than ten years. Both are issued in bearer, registered, and book-entry form, and usually come in denominations of $1,000, $5,000, $10,000, $100,000, and $1 million. Some outstanding bonds are **callable**—redeemable at the issuer's will—five years before maturity, but no notes are callable. Currently the Treasury issues two- and four-year notes on a regular cycle, whereas other maturities are issued periodically depending on Treasury needs. For example, in the second week of February 1989, the Treasury issued $10.22 billion in 3-year notes, $9.7 billion in 10-year notes, and $9.5 billion in 30-year bonds in its regular refunding auction. Since Congress has imposed a 4.25% lid on the rate the Treasury may pay on bonds, and has recently granted only minor exemptions from this lid, the Treasury has not been issuing many new bonds; however, some bonds are typically offered at quarterly refunding dates, often by reopening an old issue. Because of past bond sales, there is a large volume of bonds outstanding, and the secondary markets for both bonds and notes are very liquid.

Bonds and notes are issued through auctions on a yield basis. The bids are ranked lowest to highest and then filled, starting from the lowest. The coupon rates of new notes and bonds are therefore determined by the interest rate market. Investors in these issues are entitled to a regular sequence of semiannual coupon payments, and to the principal (face) value of the issue at maturity. The ratio of the value of the coupon payments made in a year to the face value of the issue is called its **coupon rate.** The future income stream from these issues is fully specified by knowing the principal value, coupon rate, and maturity date, and these instruments are therefore known as **fixed-income** securities. For example, the owner of $1 million worth of the UST 9.125% coupon issue that matures on May 15, 2018 will receive $45,625 every May 15 and November 15 up to and including May 15, 2018; on that date, the owner will also receive the $1 million face value of the issue.

Treasury notes and bonds are quoted in secondary-market trading on a price basis in a special form. A quotation of [100.02] means that the price is 100 and $\frac{2}{32}$%, or 100.0625%, of the face value. The actual purchase price, or **invoice price,** of the bond is the quoted price plus the **accrued interest** since the last coupon payment. Accrued interest for Treasury notes and bonds is given by the formula:

$$\text{Accrued} = \frac{\text{Coupon} \times \text{Actual days}}{2 \times \text{Days in coupon period}} \qquad (2.7)$$

For example, the accrued interest on July 4, 1989, on the 9.125% issue of the bond maturing on May 15, 2018, mentioned above would be:

$$\text{Accrued} = \frac{9.125 \times 50}{2 \times 184} = 1.24$$

The **yield to maturity** of a bond or note is often quoted along with the market price; this yield is defined as that semiannually compounded discounting interest rate that makes the net present value of an issue's future income stream equal to its current market price. The formula connecting price and yield is:

$$IP = \frac{100}{(1 + y/2)^{N-1+(d/D)}} + \sum_{k=1}^{N} \frac{C/2}{(1 + y/2)^{k-1+(d/D)}} \qquad (2.8)$$

where IP is the invoice price (including accrued interest)

N is the number of remaining coupon payments

C is the annual coupon in percentage terms

d is the actual number of days to the next coupon payment

D is the number of days in the current coupon period

y is the annual yield in decimal terms

If this calculation is performed on a coupon date, it simplifies to:

$$IP = \frac{100}{(1 + y/2)^N} + \sum_{k=1}^{N} \frac{C/2}{(1 + y/2)^k} \qquad (2.9)$$

(In the terminology of financial theory, this yield is just the bond's internal rate of return.)

Note that unlike bill calculations, calculations for notes and bonds use a full 365-day year, and take into account variations in the actual length of coupon periods, which can be from 181 to 184 days, in computing fractional parts.

Treasury Yield Curve

In many ways, the state of the UST market at a given point in time can best be captured by plotting the **treasury yield curve.** This is the graph of **yield to maturity** against **term to maturity** for all current Treasury issues. (In the case of T-bills, the discount yield must be converted to a bond-equivalent yield for consistency, as in Equations 2.3 and 2.4 above.)

Treasury issues with longer maturities generally have higher yields. Because the prices of longer maturity bonds fluctuate more than the prices of shorter ones for the same change in interest rates, longer bonds have a greater price risk, and their investors accordingly demand a higher yield from these bonds. The treasury yield curve will thus normally be upward sloping; see Figure 2.1 for an example of a normal treasury yield curve, based on actual yields as of April 20, 1988. Yields on short-term issues do, however, at times rise above long-term bond yields, creating what is known as an **inverted yield curve.** This usually happens when most market participants anticipate that interest rates are going to *fall* in the future. Figure 2.2 shows an example of an inverted yield curve, based on actual yields for April 20, 1989.

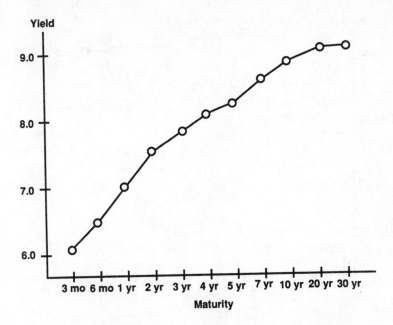

FIGURE 2.1   Yield curve for April 20, 1988.

The **current issue** treasury securities—the most recent issues at each maturity—are the determinants of the treasury yield curve most frequently referenced by traders. The yields of older issues (known as **off-the-run** issues) can be plotted along with the current issues; typically, they will trade at spreads to the current issues, because they are less liquid and hence command a yield premium (which is equivalent to a price concession). Occasionally a particular issue will face extraordinary demand and go **special;** its yield may then fall *below* the current yield curve, at least temporarily. By tracking the historical spreads of off-the-run issues to the current issues, traders get a sense of the relative richness or cheapness of specific issues in the various sectors of the yield curve.

The treasury yield curve contains within it an immense amount of information about the market. Because UST securities are considered essentially immune to default, the treasury yield curve gives us a good approximation of the market's perception of the **term structure of risk-free interest rates.** Comparison of current treasury yields at different maturities allows one to derive implied forward rates for given intervals; thus, the market's expectations for forward rates are implicit in the treasury yield curve. One can also derive a **term discount function** from the

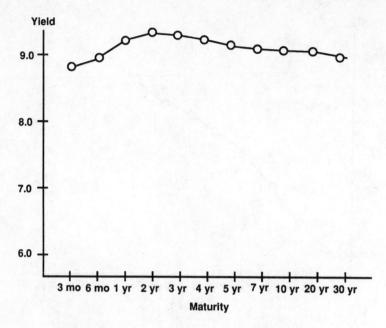

FIGURE 2.2 Yield curve for April 20, 1989.

treasury yield curve, giving the implied discounting factors for valuing future cash flows of any given maturity. This function is also known as the **zero-coupon bond (ZCB) price curve**; the present value of a ZCB, a bond with a single cash flow at maturity, is just the product of the bond's face value with the term discounting factor for that maturity.

To a very crude approximation, a fitted yield curve given by a particular functional form can be specified by its short-rate value (the 3-month yield), its slope (the spread of the long rate—30-year yield—to the short rate), and a curvature parameter. When traders and investors consider the sensitivity of their holdings to interest rate movements, they most often think in terms of *parallel shifts* in the yield curve—movements up or down by the entire yield curve that keep the spread between the long and short rates constant. When dealing with some of the more complex and long-term interest rate-sensitive instruments, such as interest rate caps and floors and options on swaps, however, the *slope* of the yield curve, and even its particular shape (curvature), become very important considerations. We will see in Chapter 4 how the more sophisticated option pricing models required to handle long-dated options on interest rate-sensitive instruments take into account potential changes in the term structure of interest rates.

Duration

In examining the price sensitivity of an individual bond or note to interest rate movements, traders often refer to its **duration,** a cash flow-weighted average maturity measure. For historical and technical reasons, the measure most frequently used is known as the **modified duration.** On a coupon date, modified duration is given by the formula:

$$D_{mod} = \left(\frac{1}{1 + y/2}\right) \frac{\text{sum of time-weighted discounted cash flows}}{\text{invoice price}} \tag{2.10}$$

$$= \left(\frac{1}{1 + y/2}\right) \frac{\sum_{t=1}^{M} \left[\dfrac{tC/2}{(1 + y/2)^t} + \dfrac{100M}{(1 + y/2)^M}\right]}{\sum_{t=1}^{M} \left[\dfrac{C/2}{(1 + y/2)^t} + \dfrac{100}{(1 + y/2)^M}\right]}$$

where D_{mod} is the modified duration

M is the number of coupon periods to maturity

C is the annual coupon in percentage terms

y is the annual yield in decimal terms

[D_{mod} is called the *modified duration* to distinguish it from the original definition of this measure by Macaulay (1938), which differed from modified duration by the factor $1/(1 + y/2)$.]

A bond's modified duration is, in fact, its percentage change in dollar price per basis-point change in yield:

$$\left(\frac{100}{P}\right)\left(\frac{\Delta P}{\Delta y}\right) = -D_{mod}$$

(Since price *decreases* as yield *increases*, the negative sign is required.) It is sometimes useful to refer to a duration-based yield curve, plotting yield to maturity against the duration of each Treasury security rather than against the maturity itself.

ROLE OF A PRIMARY DEALER IN THE SECONDARY MARKET

Requirements and Obligations

As of March 1989, there were 44 primary UST dealers in the United States. Primary dealers are required to actively compete in Treasury auctions, bidding on each new Treasury issue. Inventory acquired through purchases in the primary market is then resold in the secondary market to institutional customers and to other dealers.

Primary dealers are required to report their daily trading activities to the Federal Reserve Bank of New York, and to maintain their status they must have at least a 1% market share of overall trading volume. From the Federal Reserve's viewpoint, the primary dealer's principal reason for existence is to help the UST market its bonds. Primary dealers must also report their financial status monthly to the National Association of Securities Dealers (NASD), which ensures that each dealer complies with the $50 million minimum capital requirement.

A primary dealer's most important responsibility in the secondary market is to provide **market liquidity.** A primary dealer **makes a market,** providing continuous bid and offer quotes to potential customers. By assuring the liquidity of the secondary market, primary dealers also assist the Treasury in marketing its bonds. The Federal Reserve Bank (the Fed) also exercises its influence over the economy in part by buying securities from the primary dealers, and by controlling the Fed Funds rate, the rate of interest paid on overnight loans of federal funds, those banking reserves on deposit with the Federal Reserve System. This in turn has a direct influence on the repurchase agreement rates central to financing bond deals, as described below.

Dealing in the Secondary Market

Treasury securities are widely held as investments by domestic and foreign financial institutions and individual concerns. But they are also actively traded, as holders of such securities seek to change the makeup of their portfolios, whether for long-term or speculative purposes. The secondary Treasury market is very liquid; total average daily volume is about $100 billion. Liquidity is provided by the dealers, who are obliged to continuously make quotes.

Many institutions like to deal directly with primary dealers because they are better capitalized and are constantly monitored by the Fed. Most institutions transact two thirds of their business with just three dealers. In selecting these main dealers, they use the following criteria:

- Good execution of orders
- A continuous flow of accurate market information
- Appropriate trading strategy suggestions
- In-depth research, analysis, and reporting services

Primary dealers deal only with high-credit institutions; other institutions have to deal with the nonprimary dealers, who themselves, like other institutional investors and traders, trade with the primary dealers. Primary dealers do not trade directly with one another. They compete and trade with other dealers via the **brokers (screens)**, which provide instant market data—the current, second-by-second state of the market, with the best bid and offer prices available from any dealer. Nonprimary dealers do not have access to these broker screens; they are therefore less well informed and less competitive, with wider bid-ask spreads.

Brokers are not principals in trading bonds. They simply match buyers and sellers, for a commission. Apart from providing consolidated pricing information, brokers also provide the very important service of protecting the anonymity of their client dealers. They match trades between dealers, acting as intermediaries for the two sides, so that dealers can build up inventory and establish positions through brokered trades without revealing their trading strategies to other dealers, as they would have to if they were trading directly with each other.

This interdealer broker market in UST securities is very efficient, driven by the large volume of public order flow in these securities and the easy availability of dealer price quotes through the screen broker system. A dealer quoting prices away from the market will either be *hit* immediately and repeatedly, forcing the dealer to correct the quotes or assume disproportionate inventory risk, or simply excluded from the market until the quotes are more competitive. On the other hand, this efficient interdealer market allows dealers to count on relatively stable prices at which to adjust temporary inventory imbalances due to fluctuations in public order flow.

Most bond trades are known only to the two parties involved. Even a large-size trade may go unnoticed by most market participants if the primary dealer involved has the capability to distribute most of the trade to its other institutional customers. No single dealer sees the full breadth and depth of bond trading activity. Dealers that regularly execute large volumes of trades are in a much better competitive position than smaller dealers. The largest ones are privy to the most useful transaction flow information, and therefore can better distinguish momentary pricing fluctuations from more permanent market trends. This allows them to make better markets and gives them an edge in order execution, in pricing derivative products, including options and futures, and in providing their customers with more accurate market information. The top ten primary dealers control over 50% of the bond market. As pointed out succinctly in Feldman and Stephenson (1988), major nondealer financial institutions often receive much better information than many small primary dealers, because the largest dealers provide these institutions (but not their smaller dealer competitors) with research, analysis, and detailed market flow information.

Bond dealers have inventory risk. Their reward is in the bid-ask spread and changes in the market value of their inventory. The bid-ask spread on notes and bonds is normally about ⅔₂nds on notes and bonds, and one or two basis points on T-bills. Spreads are generally kept very narrow as a result of fierce dealer competition. Dealers may also make money on **carry,** the difference between the interest payment from the securities in inventory and the financing costs of these securities. When the interest return on the inventory securities exceeds the financing cost, a **positive carry** exists and the dealer will experience a profit if its inventory is long in securities. In the case of **negative carry,** dealers experience a loss from carrying inventory. Since dealer financing is of a very short maturity and the securities held are always of a longer maturity, the carry is positive when long-term rates are higher than short-term rates, that is, when the yield curve (yield versus maturity) has a positive slope.

How Dealers Finance Their Positions: The Repo Market

Primary dealers borrow and lend securities in the "repo" market to finance their trading positions. The repurchase agreement, or "repo," is essentially a collateralized loan wherein the Treasury securities owned by the dealer are used as collateral for monies received from a lender. Institutions can earn higher short-term interest in the repo market than in short-term Treasury securities. Repo agreements are typically of very short maturity, usually overnight. The repo market is similar in structure to the secondary Treasury market, with dealers trading with each other through broker screens. The total outstanding overnight repo financing by primary dealers on a typical day, January 11, 1988, was over $180 billion. The market for longer **term repos** becomes thin as the maturity lengthens. Total outstanding term repo financing by primary dealers for 121 days or more was only $4.2 billion on January 11, 1988.

EXAMPLE 2.2

Suppose a dealer wants to finance a long position of $50 million in a T-bond, with an invoice price (including accrued interest) of $50.5 million.

The current overnight repo rate is assumed to be 7.5%, so the interest due for one day would be:

$$\text{Repo interest} = 0.075 \times \$50,500,000.00 \times \frac{1}{360} = \$10,520.83$$

If the coupon on the bond were 10%, the dealer would have a daily coupon income of:

$$\text{Coupon income} = 0.10 \times \$50,000,000.00 \times \frac{1}{365} = \$13,698.63$$

(To be precise, we should multiply half the coupon by 1/181 or 1/184, depending on the exact number of days in the coupon period.) The daily *positive* carry would be:

Carry = $13,698.63 − $10,520.83 = $3,177.80

On the other hand, if the bond coupon were 6% we would be in a situation of *negative* carry, and would *lose:*

$$\$10,520.83 - \left(0.060 \times \$50,000,000.00 \times \frac{1}{365}\right)$$
$$= \$10,520.83 - \$8,219.18 = \$2,301.65$$

each day. Note that the overnight repo rate does *not* directly depend on the yield of the underlying bond; rather, the repo rate will be driven by (spread to) the overnight Fed funds rate.

Dealers may also do **reverse repo,** or simply **reverse** deals, in which a security is *borrowed* and money simultaneously *loaned.* Reverses are sometimes used to cover short positions. When a security is squeezed by demand to fill short positions (or for some other reason), the repo rate may fall, or "go special," for that security. Institutions may thus raise cheap money by borrowing (and lending bonds as collateral) in the reverse repo market.

THE U.S. DEBT FUTURES MARKET

The cash markets provide investors with opportunities to trade Treasury securities for same or next-day delivery and payment. The Treasury futures market exists so that T-bills, notes, and bonds can be traded for deferred delivery and payment. In practice, however, as little as 5% of futures contracts end up in actual delivery. The futures contracts in Treasury securities include the three-month T-bill, the two-year T-note, the five-year T-note, the ten-year T-note, and the T-bond future contract. The bill contract has a face value of $1 million per contract, while the others have a par value of $100,000.

Uses of Futures Contracts

Interest rate futures markets offer institutions that know their future funding needs or lending capabilities the opportunity to lock in attractive interest rates when they become available. Futures contracts provide fixed-income portfolio managers with a hedge against unfavorable interest rate movements. They also provide speculators with an easy, leveraged way to bet on future interest rate movements. The financial futures market has grown dramatically since its introduction in 1976. For example, in the first ten months of 1988, the cumulative volume for the T-bond futures was over 58 million contracts.

Futures and the corresponding cash price movements are closely related. However, because participants in the cash and futures markets may have different objectives, there are times when the cash bond and futures contracts are trading at prices contrary to their expected relationship. Fixed-income arbitrageurs often seek out these situations and establish trading positions from which they will profit when the expected relationship between the cash and futures prices is eventually reestablished.

T-Bill Futures

The standard T-bill futures contract traded on the International Monetary Market (IMM) of the Chicago Mercantile Exchange (CME) is $1 million face value of 90- to 92-day bills. The delivery months are March, June, September, and December, with the next eight delivery months traded at any point in time. Settlement occurs in the third week of the delivery month, usually on a Thursday.

Cash bills are traded on a discount basis, but the IMM decided to quote bill future prices according to the IMM index, which is

$$\text{IMM index} = 100 - \text{discount yield in } \% \qquad (2.11)$$

The bill future price P in percentage of the face value, using Equation 2.2, is therefore:

$$P = 100 \times \left[1 - \frac{N \times (100 - \text{IMM index})}{360 \times 100}\right] \qquad (2.12)$$

EXAMPLE 2.3

Suppose the IMM index for delivery of a 90-day bill in 6 months is 91.72. Its market price P, in percent, can be computed from Equation 2.12 as:

$$P = 100 \times \left[1 - \frac{90 \times (100 - 91.72)}{360 \times 100}\right] = 97.93$$

The futures price will be \$979,300 because the face value is \$1 million. If this contract is bought or sold, a margin of \$2,000 will be required, and the bill contract will be marked to market daily. Price fluctuations on a bill contract are in multiples of a basis point, or 0.01%, which has a value of $(0.01\%) \times (90/360) \times (\$1 \text{ million}) = \$25$.

Hedging with T-Bill Futures

Suppose that the T-bill yield curve has a positive slope. An investor who has funds to invest for three months has several alternatives. In addition to simply buying the three-month bill and holding it until maturity, the investor can **ride down the yield curve** by buying, for example, the six-month bill and selling it three months later. The latter strategy may give superior results if the yield curve stays the same after three months, but if the yield curve shifts upward, the simple buy-and-hold strategy will give better returns. In order to hedge against possible upward shifts in yields, the investor can buy the six-month bill and sell a T-bill futures contract that settles in three months.

EXAMPLE 2.4

A 3-month (91-day) bill is trading at 8.395%. From Equation 2.2 its price is:

$$100 \times \left(1 - \frac{91 \times 0.08395}{360}\right) = 97.878$$

Buying and holding it will provide a return of:

$$\frac{100.00 - 97.878}{97.878} = 2.168\%$$

A 6-month (181-day) T-bill trades at a discount yield of 8.48%. From Equation 2.2, the price of this bill is:

$$100 \times \left(1 - \frac{181 \times 0.0848}{360}\right) = 95.736$$

If we assume no change in the yield curve, the 6-month bill will become a 3-month (90-day) bill at our horizon date, and will then be worth:

$$100 \times \left(1 - \frac{90 \times 0.08395}{360}\right) = 97.90$$

so riding the yield curve would bring a return of:

$$\frac{97.90 - 95.736}{95.736} = 2.2604\%$$

which is better than the buy-and-hold strategy.

If yields rose by 40 basis points, however, the value of the three-month bill on the horizon date would be:

$$100 \times \left(1 - \frac{90 \times 0.08795}{360}\right) = 97.80$$

and the return for riding the yield curve would be:

$$\frac{97.80 - 95.736}{95.736} = 2.156\%$$

which is slightly worse than the buy-and-hold strategy.

If the three-month T-bill future is trading at an IMM index of 91.72, the delivery price, calculated from Equation 2.12, will be:

$$100 \times \left(1 - \frac{90 \times (100 - 91.72)}{360 \times 100}\right) = 97.93$$

The three-month return obtained by buying the six-month bill and three months later delivering against this contract is:

$$\frac{97.93 - 95.736}{95.736} = 2.292\%$$

which outperforms the buy-and-hold strategy without exposing the investor to the market-level risk of riding the yield curve.

Treasury Note and Bond Futures

Treasury note and bond futures contracts are traded with a face value of $100,000 and settlement dates in the months of March, June, September, and December. Ten-year note futures, which are traded on the Chicago Board of Trade (CBT), call for delivery of T-notes with maturities between six and one half and ten years from delivery date. Contracts can be traded for up to the next eight delivery months, but contracts beyond the nearest three are typically very illiquid. Prices are quoted in thirty-seconds, or **ticks;** one tick is worth $100,000 × 0.0003125 = $31.25. Five-year note futures are traded on the New York FINEX exchange. Deliverable securities are T-notes with four and one half to five and one half years original maturity and at least four and one quarter years remaining maturity on delivery date. Prices are quoted in sixty-fourths, with the value of one tick equal to $15.625. Two-year notes, which began trading in 1989, call for delivery of T-notes with remaining maturity between one year nine months and two years one month. Like the five-year note future, they are quoted in sixty-fourths. Treasury bond futures call for delivery of T-bonds with a maturity or call date no less than 15 years from the delivery date. Other features are similar to the ten-year note future contract. There are always several issues deliverable against a given contract.

Contract Short-Seller's Advantages on Delivery

A bond future contract holder taking delivery does not know in advance which bond will be delivered, and therefore how much he or she will have to pay, until just before delivery. Moreover, while there is no trading in the futures contracts during the last seven business days of the month, delivery can take place up until the last business day of the month, at the discretion of the party delivering against the futures contract. Since the seller determines which issue is delivered, and on what day delivery occurs, he or she has significant advantages over the contract holder.

Another advantage enjoyed by the futures contract seller is the so-called afternoon option. This refers to the fact that the bond contract stops trading at 2:00 P.M. Chicago time, but sellers have until 8:00 P.M. to tell the CBT what they will deliver. (Most clearing firms require indications by 6:00 or 7:00 P.M.) A bond future contract seller can take advantage of any drop in the price of the most deliverable issue after 2:00 P.M. to improve his or her position, since he or she will in any case be delivering against the 2:00 P.M. futures settlement price. This advantage exists even after the contract stops trading in the delivery month.

The Conversion Factor

The full invoice price actually paid on delivery is determined by the futures settlement price (FSP) times the contract size, adjusted by a *conversion factor* determined by the coupon and maturity characteristics of the particular bond being delivered, plus any accrued interest:

$$IP = (FSP \times \$100,000.00 \times CF) + \text{accrued}$$

The futures price times the conversion factor, without the accrued, is also known as the **converted price,** or **delivery-equivalent price.**

As shown in Example 2.5 below, the conversion factor is just that bond price that on a particular date would provide an effective yield of 8%, divided by 100.00.

EXAMPLE 2.5

On August 9, 1988 the September T-bond future contract closed at 86 and $\frac{7}{32}$nds, denoted by [86.07]. The UST 10.75% issue of August 15, 2005, was one of the bonds deliverable against this contract. To calculate the conversion factor for this bond, for example, against the September, 1988, T-bond futures contract, we take the next *quarterly* date in the bond's coupon cycle falling in or after the delivery month of the future contract—in this case, November 15, 1988—and calculate the bond price corresponding to a yield of 8% on that date, which for this bond is [125.03+], or 125.11 in decimal. The conversion factor for this deliverable bond is therefore 1.2511, and the delivery-equivalent price (DEP) for this bond, in decimal, is:

$$DEP = 86.22 \times 1.2511 = 107.87$$

Note that the conversion factor is always *relative to a particular futures contract.* For details on the precise formulas used in the calculation of conversion factors, see Schwarz et al. (1986). The CBT publishes tables of conversion factors based on these formulas, which are generally used for invoicing purposes.

The Cheapest-to-Deliver Bond

The difference between the cash bond price (BP) and the DEP (the future settlement price multiplied by the conversion factor) is known as the **bond basis:**

Basis $= BP - DEP = BP - (FSP \times CF)$

When it is necessary to deliver against a bond futures contract, the party delivering (the seller of the futures contract) will seek to deliver that bond that has the *highest invoice price* relative to the cash bond price, that is, the issue with the *smallest basis*. This is known as the **cheapest-to-deliver** issue. Consider a bond futures contract seller who decides to make delivery on the last trading day of that contract. Ideally, the short seller would like to deliver a bond that would cost *less* in the market than the invoice price he or she will receive upon delivery; that is, the seller would like to deliver a bond issue with *negative* basis. This is not likely to be possible, however, because arbitrage activity would quickly drive up the price of such a bond. Failing this, the short party will seek that bond with the smallest basis, because it is, literally, the cheapest to deliver *relative to the DEP* that the long party (the buyer of the futures contract) is obligated to pay. Familiarity with basis, and the ability to identify the cheapest-to-deliver issue, are essential to any futures trader, because they are the key to the relationship between the cash and futures markets.

Prior to the delivery month, many issues will be potentially deliverable against a given futures contract. If a trader wants to buy a cash bond and carry it to delivery date, locking up the trade, which bond should he or she buy and carry? Here, coupon accrual and financing costs become very real issues. The most desirable issue will generally be the one with the smallest **net basis** (= basis − carry), because this will be the issue that will cost the trader the least (or bring the greatest return) *based on today's prices*.

EXAMPLE 2.6

As noted in Example 2.5, the September 1988, T-bond future contract closed at a price of [86.07] Bonds with maturities ranging from August 2005 to May 2018 were deliverable against this contract. For some of the deliverable issues, Table 2.1 shows (*a*) coupon rate, (*b*) maturity or call date, (*c*) August 9, 1988, closing price, (*d*) conversion factor to the September 1988 T-bond future contract, (*e*) delivery-equivalent price,

Table 2.1 Issues Deliverable Against September 1988, Bond Future Contract

Coupon Rate (in %)	Maturity or Call (Mo/Yr)	Market Price	Conversion Factor	Delivery-Equivalent Price	Bond Basis (32nds)	Repo Rate (in %)	Carry (32nds)	Net Basis (32nds)
10.750	08/05	[111.14]	1.2511	[107.28]	114.23	7.250	10.97	103.25
12.000	08/08C	[122.13+]	1.3935	[120.04+]	72.84	7.000	14.29	58.54
9.250	02/16	[98.29+]	1.1376	[98.02+]	26.88	7.000	9.57	17.31
7.250	05/16	[79.11]	0.9171	[79.02]	8.74	7.180	5.77	2.97
9.125	05/18	[99.08]	1.1267	[97.04+]	67.37	7.370	6.59	60.79

(f) basis, (g) repo rate, (h) carrying cost, and (i) net basis from August 9, 1988 to the September T-bond contract's last delivery date (September 30, 1988). The bond prices are given in thirty-seconds, in brackets, with [98.02 +] representing a price of 98 and $2.5/32$nds, because this is how they are normally quoted in the marketplace. Basis, carrying cost, and net basis are all given in thirty-seconds as well—a basis of 26.88 represents $26.88/32$nds.

With a net basis of $2.97/32$nds, the most deliverable (buy-and-carry) issue on this date was the UST 7.25% issue of May 15, 2016. If a short seller of the September T-bond contract wanted to buy and carry a cash bond to deliver on the contract's last delivery day (September 30, 1988), he or she should select the 7.25% bond because the worst-case loss would be only $2.97/32$nds (assuming that the repo rate stays the same). The seller would be in a position to make some profits if this 7.25% bond becomes rich relative to the other deliverable issues.

The Effect of Carry

Because of the forward nature of futures contracts, their prices depend heavily on the cost of carry for the deliverable issues. For example, on April 21, 1980, and April 4, 1983, long-term rates were comparable— 10.9% and 10.68%, respectively. However, in 1980 the Federal Reserve Board was tightening credit in its effort to control inflation, and the short-term rate was 15% (a negatively sloping yield curve), whereas in April 1983, the short-term rate was 9% (a positively sloping yield curve). With negative carry, the September 1980 bond contract was trading at [77.15], while the September 1983 bond futures contract traded at [75.23] in a regime of positive carry. With negative carry, the market makes the investor pay more for bonds in the future, because he or she can earn a higher rate on short-term investments; with positive carry investors would rather own the bonds, and the futures price will be adjusted downward accordingly.

EXAMPLE 2.7: A BOND BASIS TRADE

Let us look at a slightly more complex example in some detail (see also Bass, 1987, and Goldstein, 1987). Suppose that on June 18, 1987, a trader purchased $1 million of the UST 12% issue of August 15, 2013, at a price of [131.28], and sold September 14, 1987, bond future contracts

Table 2.2 UST 12% Issue of August 15, 2013, Versus September
T-Bond Future

Today's date: 6/18/87; Settlement date: 6/19/87		
Buy: $1 million worth of UST 12% issue of 8/15/2013 at	[131.28]	
Sell: 9/14/87 T-bond contracts at	[92.19]	
a) Purchase cost of UST 12% issue of 8/15/2013	1,318,750.00	
b) Accrued interest	41,104.97	
c) Total cost	1,359,854.97	(a + b)
d) Delivery price of futures contract	1,297,701.41	(92.59 × 1.4015)
e) Accrued interest on 9/30/87	15,000.00	(45 days' coupon accrual)
f) Total proceeds from future sale	1,312,701.41	(d + e)
g) Coupon income on 8/15/87	60,000.00	
h) Interest on coupon income at 6% repo	450.00	(45 days to 9/30/87)
i) Total proceeds and income	1,373,151.41	(f + g + h)
j) **Basis** on 6/18/87 in 32nds	67.36	(a − d)/312.50
k) **Gross profit**	13,296.44	(i − c)
l) Financing costs of c at 6% repo	23,344.18	(103 days' repo interest)
m) Carry	11,000.85	(e + g + h − b − l) or 35.20/32nds
n) **Net basis** in 32nds	32.15	(j − m)
o) **Net profit**	− 10,047.44	(k − l) or − 32.15/32nds
p) **Implied (breakeven) repo**	3.418%	

at [92.19]. (The conversion factor is 1.4015.) Such a trade is known as **buying the basis** (Table 2.2).

The price of $1 million worth of the UST 12% issue of August 15, 2013, is $1,318,750 (a in Table 2.2). The accrued interest for June 19, 1987, settlement is $41,104.97 (b), giving a total purchase price of $1,359,854.97 (c). On September 30, 1987, the last delivery date, the trader received sale proceeds of $1,297,701.41 (d), and accrued interest of $15,000 (e). There was also coupon income of $60,000 (g) on August 15, 1987, which produced $450 (h) in interest at the 6% repo rate. Subtracting the total cost (c) from the total proceeds (i), the trader apparently had a profit of \$13,296.44 (k). (Note that the bond's basis was trading at $^{67.3}\!\%_{32}$nds on June 18, 1987.)

Financing cost at the time was 6%. Applying this rate to the total purchase price (c) gives a financing cost of \$23,344.18 (l), and the financed basis-buying trade shows a loss of \$10,047.44 (o). The net basis is thus worth $^{32.15}\!\%_{32}$nds. (Note that the financing cost of futures margin is ignored in this example.) A bond's net basis should always be positive because of the contract seller's advantages. In this example, those advantages are valued at $^{32.15}\!\%_{32}$nds, assuming that the UST 12% issue of August 15, 2013, is the most deliverable bond.

The **implied**, or **breakeven, repo** is the financing rate that, when applied to the \$1,359,854.97 purchase cost (c), would give a financing cost equal to the gross profit \$13,296.44 (k), and hence make this trade break even. In our example, this rate is 3.418%. The bond issue with the highest implied repo is also the most deliverable, so this rate is very useful for comparing the various deliverable bonds. Note, however, that the **net basis** is the number that most directly characterizes the deliverability of a bond issue.

Option-Adjusted Basis

As noted above, the bond futures contract seller enjoys a number of advantages implicit in his or her options on delivery against the futures contract. In fact, these advantages can be treated explicitly as *embedded options*. Such embedded options can be valued using option valuation techniques, and an **option-adjusted basis** can thereby be calculated. Such an adjusted basis can give the trader or investor valuable additional insight into the fair value of a futures position. There are circumstances when a straight examination of the unadjusted basis between the bond future contract and the cheapest-to-deliver issue may suggest that the future contract is cheap (or rich) relative to the cash market, while a closer examination of the option-adjusted basis may show that it is in fact fairly priced (or vice versa). Tang (1988) observed that "on March 6, 1987 the June 87 Treasury bond contract was seemingly cheap relative to the cash market using the conventional models in evaluating futures contracts. After adjusting for the effect of the options, however, the bond contract was actually fairly priced."

Each of the delivery-related embedded options has its own terms and value; these particulars must be taken into account when choosing which option pricing techniques it is appropriate to bring to bear. The most important of these embedded options are the following:

1. The **quality option:** This is the contract seller's option as to which qualified Treasury bond issue to deliver during the period that the bond contract is still trading. The contract seller will always seek to deliver that issue that is cheapest to deliver (has the smallest basis) at the time of delivery. In an environment of volatile interest rates, however, the cheapest-to-deliver issue may well change during the period that the future contract is trading. This will affect the invoice price to be paid by the long party. The value of this option is actually the maximum of a bundle of option values, one for each potentially deliverable issue.

2. The **end-of-month option:** This is the contract seller's option as to which issue to deliver *after trading in the bond contract has ceased.* At this point, the settlement price for the future contract will already have been set; small changes in interest rates can thus affect the choice of cheapest-to-deliver issue. This is a short-term but potentially very volatile American option.

3. The **wildcard** or **afternoon option:** This is the seller's option to declare intent to deliver at any time prior to 8 P.M. Eastern Standard Time during the first 15 days of the delivery month. Since the futures market closes by 2 P.M., while the case market trades actively into the afternoon, there is a window of opportunity for the seller to take advantage of favorable interest rate movements. This is an interesting option, because its strike is reset each day, with the repricing of the futures contract.

4. The **timing option:** This is the seller's option to deliver on any chosen day of the delivery month; the emphasis here is not on *which issue* is delivered, but rather on considerations of *carry.* In an environment of positive carry (upward-sloping yield curve), ignoring the possible effects of any of the other delivery-related options, delivery would normally be deferred to the last day. In an inverted yield curve environment, early delivery would be advantageous. The value of this option is thus contingent on the likelihood of a yield curve inversion.

5. The **new issue option:** This is the value associated with the possibility that a new Treasury issue may turn out to be the cheapest to deliver against the future contract. While rarely of much value, this option can play a role in environments of high but falling yields, where

new issues are likely to have both the lowest coupon and the longest maturity among deliverable issues, factors that combine to give them the longest duration, making them good candidates for the cheapest-to-deliver issue. It is of more significance for note futures than for bond futures, because T-note auctions are more frequent.

While many of these embedded options only rarely take on significant value, the quality and end-of-month options are frequently noteworthy, and the active futures trader ignores any of these factors at his or her own peril. The diversity of characteristics of these options, and the fact, for example, that they must generally be considered as European prior to the delivery period, but American thereafter (but possibly with varying strikes!) makes clear the value of some of the more sophisticated option pricing methodologies to be described in Chapters 3 and 4.

Differences Between Note and Bond futures

Contract terms for the T-bond and ten-year T-note futures contracts are identical except for the definitions of deliverable issues. This difference in deliverables has some important consequences, however. Deliverable notes have shorter maturities, and hence lower durations than deliverable bonds. Moreover, because the *range* of deliverable maturities is much narrower for note futures (3½ years as compared with 15 years for bond futures), the range of coupons on deliverable note issues also tends to be narrower, leading to a narrower range of durations. The absence of callable notes among the deliverable issues acts to further reduce the variability in duration. The end result is less sensitivity to market level in T-note futures contracts, and hence a smaller basis.

The lower volatility of note futures prices means that most of the delivery options are worth less than the corresponding options for the T-bond futures contract. The one exception is the *new issue* option, which tends to be potentially more significant for note futures than for bond futures, because note auctions are more frequent, and there is a higher probability of a new issue becoming the cheapest to deliver. These comments apply even more strongly to the five-year and two-year note futures. In the case of the two-year note futures, there is only a four-month range of deliverable maturities, and typically only four or five deliverable issues. These issues usually have very similar coupons and maturities, and hence nearly identical durations. There is essentially no quality option for these contracts. On the other hand, there is *always* a new issue that could potentially become the cheapest to deliver.

THE U.S. DEBT OPTIONS MARKET

Options on Treasury securities and Treasury futures are traded on three different markets. Options on T-bond futures are traded on the CBT. Options on cash bonds are traded on the American Stock Exchange (AMEX) and Chicago Board Options Exchange (CBOE). There is also a significant over-the-counter (OTC) market for cash bond options.

Role of Debt Options

Interest rate options provide a flexible tool for the investor or speculator in the fixed-income arena. In general terms, they represent a very convenient repackaging and reallocation of interest rate-related risk, and thus lend themselves to both hedging and speculation. As a speculative instrument, interest rate options are highly leveraged, and thus provide a high potential rate of return for the trader who wishes to gamble on trends in the market level. Options also lend themselves to so-called volatility plays, combining options at different strikes and/or expirations to take advantage of anticipated changes in the volatilities imputed by the market to the various options. As hedging instruments, puts provide a relatively cheap form of insurance against market-level risk that does not require the liquidation of an underlying position.

As explained below, the option market on interest rate futures is much larger and more liquid than that on cash bills, notes, and bonds. While there are certainly situations where an options position in the cash instrument is preferred, and profit opportunities exist in this market for marketmakers, strategic traders, and investors, the futures option market is a much more active arena for the interest rate options player.

Exchange-Traded Options on T-Bond Futures

The CBT bond futures option market, initiated in 1982, has been very successful. With the volume of trading in one options contract equal to about one third of the volume in the underlying futures contract, these have become the second most active exchange-traded options in the world (second only to the CBOE's OEX stock index option). Volume on the bond futures option in December 1988 was 1,193,987 contracts, or over $119 trillion. Open interest for the month was a little less than half that. Volume in options on the ten-year note future was 67,638 contracts, or $6.76 billion.

CBT bond (note) futures options are traded on the nearest three futures contracts, and are struck at even, round-number prices centered around the current futures price. Expiration is on the third Friday of the month preceding the futures contract delivery month. Option prices are quoted in sixty-fourths.

If an option buyer exercises a call (put), a long (short) position in the underlying futures contract is assigned. The option seller is assigned a corresponding short (long) position. If the strike price equals the futures contract price, the transaction is complete. If the strike price is lower (higher) than the futures price, the call (put) seller must pay the buyer the difference.

Exchange-Traded Options on Cash Bonds

The AMEX trades options on T-bills and notes. The bill contracts are for $1 million in principal value, while the note contracts are for $100,000. Options on T-bonds are traded on the CBOE with a principal value of $100,000.

The buyer of an AMEX T-bill call (put) option has the right to buy (sell) $1 million in face value of 91-day T-bills (measured from the exercise settlement date) at the strike price. This right exists up to the expiration date. Issues deliverable against this option contract must be 91-day bills on option settlement date. Exercise notices tendered on any business day are settled on the Thursday of the following week; this allows the deliverable bills to be purchased at the Thursday auctions regularly scheduled by the Treasury.

The buyer of a T-bond call (put) option has the right to buy (sell) $100,000 in face value of a *particular* bond issue (e.g., the UST 9.125% issue of May 15, 2018) at the specified strike price. This right is held up to the expiration date, but note that *no other issue* may be delivered. Strike prices are quoted in even points or half-points bracketing the market price of the underlying bond. Expiration is on the third Friday of each month, and CBOE options with expirations in the nearest six months are traded at any given point in time. The options themselves are quoted in points and thirty-seconds of a point, with each point representing 1% of the principal value of the option contract, or $1,000. The price paid at exercise is determined by multiplying strike price by principal value and adding any accrued interest.

The market in listed options on cash bonds is neither as large nor as liquid as that in bond future options. In the month of December 1988,

T-bond options volume on the CBOE was 46,540 contracts, or $4.65 billion; T-note options volume was only 240 contracts, or $24 million. In part, this is due to the enormous liquidity of the underlying bond futures market; CBT bond future options marketmakers can easily hedge themselves by taking positions in the futures traded on the same exchange. Cash bond option traders at the AMEX and CBOE generally have no such convenient opportunities for hedging directly in the underlying bonds, and even if they did have ready access to the cash bond market, the greater transaction costs entailed by wider spreads, the difficulty of shorting some cash bonds, and the capital requirements of the cash bond market would pose significant obstacles to effective hedging. For all these reasons, the CBT bond future options traders have been able to make a tighter, more liquid market than have the listed cash bond options traders at the other exchanges.

Over-the-Counter Options on Cash Bonds

As we have noted, exchange-traded options on cash Treasury notes and bonds are not very liquid. Institutional investors wishing to trade options on cash bonds often do so on an OTC basis. This is a market made by government securities dealers, who will often create options contracts tailored to the needs of the investor. Since the participants are not trading listed contracts, strike prices, expirations, and face value may be freely specified. OTC markets also currently have an advantage over the exchange-traded cash bond options market in that the dealers themselves maintain quotes on a variety of underlying notes and bonds at all times. They are thus in possession of up-to-the-minute pricing information, and are also usually able to directly hedge their options positions with positions in the underlying bonds. The average daily volume in OTC cash bond options is unofficially estimated to be $750 million to $1 billion.

Differences between Exchange-Traded and OTC Options

The most obvious difference between the exchange-traded and OTC options markets is that in the OTC market contract terms are set entirely by the two parties, whereas exchange-traded options have predetermined strikes, expirations, and contract sizes (see Bass, 1988). In the OTC market, options may also be European or American, whereas the exchange-traded options are always American. There are some other important differences, however, that the potential OTC options market participant should have well in mind. If an investor wants to hedge a cash bond position using options on futures, he or she will be exposed to **basis risk,** because option exercise results in the assignment of a long or short futures contract position. In the OTC.market, where all options are on specific securities, there is no such risk. On the other hand, because futures prices represent a cash transaction at a future date, positive or negative carry is already factored into the futures price, whereas in the OTC market changes in the yield curve or financing costs for a particular security can have a major impact on the option price.

As in the case of exchange-traded options on the cash bonds, the OTC market is not in general as liquid as is the bond futures option market. Spreads in the OTC market are accordingly wider, typically $\frac{3}{32}$nds to $\frac{5}{32}$nds, compared to $\frac{2}{64}$ths to $\frac{4}{64}$ths in the exchange-traded futures option market, although this can vary widely depending on the maturity of the underlying cash issues, the volatility of the market, and how far out of the money the options are struck.

THE JAPANESE GOVERNMENT BOND MARKET: AN OVERVIEW

The Japanese Government Bond (JGB) market is a relatively young, rapidly developing market. Its growth has coincided with the Japanese government's need to finance large budget deficits since the mid-1970s. Such government deficits began with the oil crisis of the 1970s and have continued through the 1980s, with the JGB market now representing the second largest government debt market in the world, after the UST market. As of August 1987, the total outstanding volume in Japanese government bonds was 92 trillion yen. Daily turnover in the JGB cash market has averaged around two to three trillion yen in recent years—as much as seven to eight trillion yen in a bull market. Up to 95% of this volume is in large OTC trades involving security houses and banks, with only about 5% on the public exchanges.

Japanese government bonds are issued in maturities ranging from short-term (under 1 year) discount bonds to the so-called super-long 20-year bonds, but the vast majority of outstanding JGB securities—over 80% of the total—are coupon bonds with a 10-year maturity at issue date. Medium-term coupon bonds with two- to four-year maturities and a small number of five-year discount bonds make up the rest of the JGB market.

JGBs are each identified by a unique trading number. For example, as of September 1989, the current benchmark ten-year issue, the 4.6% of June 1998, was JGB 111. All JGB securities have coupon dates on the 20th of the month, and their maturity dates are on the corresponding coupon date (the 20th of the maturity month) or on the next Japanese business day. Normally, JGBs are issued in denominations of 100,000 yen.

Auction and Syndicate Systems in the JGB Primary Market

Unlike the UST auction system, many JGBs are issued through a syndicate system, in which a syndicate of 788 financial firms (including about 50 foreign firms) negotiates coupon rate, issue size, and price terms with the Japanese Ministry of Finance (MOF). After negotiation, the MOF has the right to impose terms, and syndicate members must accept these terms or be expelled from the syndicate. Such negotiations can at times be very difficult; the October 1987 auction was cancelled because issuing terms could not be agreed upon. The MOF has since moved to auction a part (20%) of the issue of ten-year bonds, but only at the negotiated price terms, making the auction a means to reserve greater participation in a given issue. This is of particular interest to foreign syndicate participants. In September 1988, the MOF announced that it would start using an auction pricing method for government bond issuances in April 1989. The auctions cover only 40% of each issue, but the remaining 60% are now priced at the auction average price, meaning that market forces effectively set the cost of Japanese government debt.

Medium-term (2- to 4-year) coupon bonds and the super-long 20-year bond are issued through an auction system very similar to that used by the UST. Secret bids are entered through participating securities houses, and are used to set a reserve price; all bids at or above the reserve price are guaranteed to be met in full.

The dominant ten-year JGB issues are coupon bonds with interest paid semiannually. These bonds are quoted in the market in simple yield terms. They are issued monthly through the syndication process, although in the past couple of years, as noted, the MOF has begun to introduce an auction element into the issue of these bonds. Coupon rates are generally low by U.S. standards, rarely rising over 6% in recent years. The bonds have payment dates on the 20th of the month, and are listed on the Tokyo Stock Exchange 40 days after payment. Bond issues can be reopened for up to three months, as long as the coupon rate remains the same. Issue size can be quite variable; in 1986 and 1987 issues ranged from 300 to 1400 billion yen. Old and new ten-year issues make up over 80% of outstanding JGB volume.

The so-called super-long 20-year bond is also a coupon bond with semiannual interest payments. Such bonds are issued four or five times a year by auction, with no fixed schedule of issue dates. The first such issue was in 1986, and the total outstanding amount of such bonds is still relatively small.

Five-year discount bonds are issued quarterly through the government bond syndication process, mostly to private investors. The volume of these bonds issued is not large, amounting to no more than 2% of the total outstanding JGB volume. Shorter term discount issues (under one year maturity) are also underwritten by syndication and sold mostly to private investors, and make up another 2% of outstanding volume.

Bonds, with two-, three-, and four-year maturities are also issued irregularly, by auction. They are all coupon bonds, with semiannual interest payments. As of August 1987, such bonds made up about 7% of outstanding JGB volume.

Differences between the UST and JGB Secondary Markets

There are a number of important ways in which the UST and JGB secondary markets differ. The incompleteness of the JGB market, the lack of liquidity of many issues, the premium attached to high-coupon issues, and tax considerations make it difficult to construct a meaningful yield curve for the JGB market. The lack of a true repo market and the structure of Japanese settlement dates make it very difficult—or at any rate, very expensive—to short JGBs. The emphasis on speculation and the disproportionate market role of a few large securities houses lead to very high volatilities and to sustained apparent price distortions that initially can be quite misleading to the UST-oriented trader. There are also some technical differences in the way in which JGB and UST market calculations are performed, most notably in the fact the JGBs are quoted in **simple yield** terms.

Shorting and the Gensaki

One important difference between the UST and JGB markets is in the difficulty of shorting JGBs. Until June 1989, there was no organized system for borrowing bonds to cover short sales, and failure to deliver brings drastic sanctions. While it is possible to short for a span of a few days, because of the JGB market's delayed settlement system, it is very difficult to arrange to borrow bonds for longer periods. The super-liquid benchmark issue commands a hefty premium, while side issues are often unavailable. This situation entails significant inventory costs for market makers, making them even more reluctant to trade in side issues, particularly those with low coupons. This is one of the sources of illiquidity in such issues.

Until June 1989, the only way to borrow securities (to go short) was through a **gensaki** (bond repurchase) agreement, in which the requisite bonds are borrowed from an investor in exchange for the loan of cash. Most gensaki agreements, however, are used by securities houses to borrow cash, using their surplus inventory bonds as collateral. Moreover, there is essentially no gensaki secondary market, unlike the well-established repo market in the United States.

Gensaki yield is calculated on a 365-day basis:

$$\text{Gensaki yield} = \frac{\text{repurchase price} - \text{current price}}{\text{current price}}$$

$$\times \frac{365}{\text{holding period in days}}$$

In late 1988, the MOF announced its intentions of introducing a true repo market in the course of 1989, to facilitate short sales for more than a few days at a time. Dealers had been pressing for such more flexible bond borrowing arrangements to rationalize the cash-futures relationship and hedging. This market was in fact opened in June 1989, but its performance proved disappointing. A gap between the rates proposed by investors and those offered by bond dealers and a lack of clear accounting standards for marking to the market initially depressed the market, leading to a fall in trading volume from an opening daily level of around 10 billion yen to only 500 million yen within a few days. The opening of a JGB options market in June 1989 has provided traders with another approach to this problem—the **synthetic short** (see Example 1.4 in Chapter 1).

Settlement

Japanese government bonds settle every five trading days—on the 5th, 10th, 15th, 20th, 25th, and last day of the month. Prior to August 1987, there were only three settlement days per month. This situation of relatively infrequent settlement encourages speculation and contributes to the domination of the market by the largest trading houses. Combined with the lack of an efficient, liquid repo market, which discourages rolling over short positions, this creates the conditions for "bear squeezes" and other market maneuvers at settlement, when short positions generally must be covered.

Coupon Effects

Marketmakers have been very reluctant to trade bonds with low coupons, because of the difficulty of selling short in the JGB market. Moreover, in the past high coupons were also preferred by certain institutional investors, such as insurance companies, which by law were only allowed to distribute coupon income to their policyholders. Prices were therefore systematically distorted, with a premium associated with higher coupon issues. This changed in early 1989. Bond holdings are now marked to the market, as in the United States, and the high-coupon issues have fallen out of favor. Along with other factors, such considerations have made it difficult to construct a meaningful yield curve for JGBs.

The Benchmark Issue

Perhaps the single most important characteristic of the JGB market is the overwhelming concentration of trading at any one time in what is known as the ten-year **benchmark** issue. Up to 90% of cash market trading can take place in this one issue, and the benchmark issue has been known to turn over up to four times its total volume in a single day. As a result of this enormous liquidity, the benchmark issue will trade at a very significant premium to the other, side issues—sometimes as much as 70 to 80 basis points premium. Trading spreads for the benchmark issue can be as narrow as one to two basis points, while recent side issues and old benchmark issues tend to trade with a spread of two to five basis points, and other side issues at an even wider spread.

The benchmark issue at any given time is determined through a complex process of market interaction by the largest trading firms—principally the so-called big four trading houses. To qualify, an issue must be large, with a remaining maturity of at least nine years, and with a relatively high coupon. Benchmark issues thus are not necessarily the most recent issue, and may persist for up to a year or more. In the absence of good new candidate benchmark issues, an older issue may even persist when its remaining maturity is less than nine years.

Since the benchmark issue trades at such a premium, it is frequently held more for speculative reasons, for short-term gains, than as a long-term investment. Long-term investors are still driven by the benchmark issue, however, because it provides the leading indicator for the direction of the entire JGB market (as its name would suggest!) Moreover, the transition from one benchmark issue to another can be a painful source of market uncertainty and risk; when confidence in an old benchmark issue erodes, it can suffer a sudden market collapse, as was evident in 1986 when JGB 78 (the 6.2% issue of July 1995) suffered a rise of 60 basis points relative to the rest of the market within seven trading days. As of September 1989, the benchmark issue was JGB 111 (the 4.6% issue of June 1998), which became the benchmark in November 1988.

The Big Four

Unlike the UST market, the JGB market is subject to considerable influence by a few very large securities houses—notably, the so-called big four (Nomura, Daiwa, Nikko, and Yamaichi). These firms regularly take such large positions in the market that they have a significant effect on bond pricing, and in particular on the determination of the benchmark issue. Their participation also contributes to the much greater volatility of the JGB market compared to the UST market. Any trader or investor in the JGB market must be aware of the sensitivity of the market to the trading decisions of the biggest players.

Tax Effects

JGBs are subject to a **withholding tax;** for non-Japanese investors whose governments have not yet signed any tax treaty with Japan, the tax is 20%. For other foreign investors, the amount of the tax varies, depending on the investor's nationality and that country's tax agreements with Japan. For U.S. investors, the rate is 10%. A 16% one-time tax on the difference between face and purchase price is also levied on discount bonds at issue. These taxes directly affect the prices of bonds in the secondary market. There is also a **transfer tax** on all domestic sales of JGB securities; this is one of the factors making the maintenance of a short position so expensive, because the transfer tax would have to be paid each time the short position was rolled over (every five days, as settlement dates are currently structured).

JGB Yield Calculations

JGB yields are quoted as a **simple yield,** which is different from the yield to maturity used with UST securities. The formula is:

$$\text{Simple yield} = \frac{(\text{par} - \text{price})/(\text{remaining term}) + \text{coupon}}{\text{price}}$$

This is just coupon over price, with any capital gain or loss amortized over the life of the security according to a straight-line amortization. (For comparison with UST securities, one should calculate the yield to maturity of the JGB security starting from its coupon and maturity; there is no simple conversion from simple yield to yield to maturity.)

JGB Futures

As part of the rapid development of a more complete financial market, the Japanese government in October 1985 introduced trading on the Tokyo Stock Exchange (TSE) in futures on the ten-year long bond. Trading on the same contract opened on the London International Financial Futures Eschange (LIFFE) in July 1987. Contracts are based on a notional 6% ten-year government bond, with a standard contract size of 100 million yen, and contract expiration dates in March, June, September, and December, with the next two contracts trading at any time. Delivery is restricted to listed JGBs with a remaining maturity of at least seven years on delivery date, which is generally the 20th of the month. Delivery price is determined by multiplying the delivery settlement price of the futures contract by a conversion factor determined by the coupon and maturity characteristics of the bond being delivered, in a manner similar to that for UST futures. (Contracts traded on LIFFE are for cash settlement, at the delivery settlement price of the corresponding TSE contract.) Last contract trading day is nine Tokyo business days before the last delivery date. JGB futures contracts are marked to market daily and make use of a margin system similar to that used in the UST futures market.

The JGB futures market has been so successful that within its first year, trading volume surpassed that of the extraordinarily liquid UST bond futures market. In mid-1987, open interest on the TSE in the JGB future contract was $85.9 billion. In part this can be ascribed to speculation in a new, highly leveraged instrument, but in part it reflects the fact that with JGB futures contracts investors could for the first time hedge an open position or effectively sell short (since transfer taxes make shorting cash JGBs prohibitively expensive). By mid-1989, daily turnover in the JGB future contract was running at around 10 trillion yen, and at the end of August 1989 there were over 20 trillion yen in outstanding contracts for the benchmark December JGB future contract. Nevertheless, investors in the JGB futures market should exercise caution, because the lack of liquidity in most issues (excepting the benchmark issue) can create difficulties for the delivering party. Moreover, it is impossible to adequately track the basis of nonbenchmark issues on a day-to-day basis because of their illiquidity; most JGB futures traders use the benchmark issue to track basis, even though, because of its liquidity premium, it will never itself be the cheapest-to-deliver issue. Most frequently, futures positions are closed out prior to the last trading date, to avoid having to deliver (or take delivery of) highly illiquid nonbenchmark issues.

JGB Options Market

The opening of a JGB options market in June 1989 represented another significant step by the Japanese government and financial institutions toward a more complete financial market. Like the JGB futures market when it was introduced in the mid-1980, JGB options are rapidly becoming a major market, representing as they do a new, highly leveraged set of instruments for both speculation and hedging. Total OTC JGB option trading turnover exceeded 11 trillion yen in July 1989. Traders and investors in yen-denominated bonds should be prepared for the impact of this new market, and they should recognize and understand some of its special characteristics.

The introduction of a JGB options market adds further pressure on the Japanese government and financial industry to move toward continuous settlement and a more liquid repo market. The lack of these features has made the application of classic option pricing models (see Chapter 3) to the JGB market less certain, because the cost of carry, forward prices, and discounting rates are harder to specify accurately. Since it is difficult for dealers to delta hedge some of their options positions using the underlying bonds, they have tended to use the benchmark issue or the future contract to cross-hedge (see Chapter 6). In the early stages of the JGB options market, trading has been largely concentrated on the benchmark and a few side issues. As one would expect, there have been certain discontinuities in option pricing, including some inconsistencies in implied volatilities for options with different strikes and/or expiration dates, which should not necessarily be taken to imply the same relative rich/cheap relationships and arbitrage opportunities as in the UST options market (see Chapter 8).

Because of the affinity of Japanese financial institutions for current high yields, early trading in JGB options was dominated by selling, and especially by call-writing against cash JGB positions. The net effect was to push implied volatility in the JGB options market during its first few months to unrealistically low levels, around 2%. This created a real investment opportunity, since historical JGB volatilities have been around 5%. As the market absorbed this fact, implied volatility levels have begun to correct to more realistic average levels. Bid-ask spreads were also wide in the early going, but as the JGB market has developed they have settled down to competitive market levels.

There is a basic issue in measuring volatilities in the JGB market. Because of the very high turnover in the benchmark issue, and the sensitivity of the market to the trading behavior of a few very large securities houses, the benchmark JGB volatilities have historically been several times higher than those of the ten-year T-notes. Volatilities for side issues can be difficult to estimate because of discontinuities in the trading of these issues. Historical volatilities show such wide fluctuations over time that JGB options traders should be wary of imputing a particular projected volatility based on historical figures.

In the fall of 1989, JGB traders began to use the new JGB options market to create **synthetic forward bond contracts,** as described in Example 1.4 in Chapter 1. This facilitates cash-futures arbitrage trading in the absence of a true repo and forward market. The existence of such synthetic forward contracts in fact means that one can now speak of **implied repo rates** in the JGB market.

REFERENCES

This chapter in no way pretends to be a comprehensive introduction to the fixed-income financial markets. The interested reader will find a wealth of detail in Stigum (1983), Stigum and Fabozzi (1983), Schwarz et al. (1986), and Labuszewski and Nyhoff (1988). Garbade (1982) provides a solid background in the analysis of securities markets in general. Stigum (1981) is a standard reference for calculations dealing with Fed funds, repo rates, discount, and bond-equivalent yields. The repo market is covered in detail in Stigum (1989). McEnally (1987) and Douglas (1988) provide much more detail on the Treasury yield curve and the term structure of interest rates. Kopprasch (1987) or Bierwag (1987) explain duration. An introduction to the uses of bond futures and futures options can be found in Oberhofer (1989), which also provides a detailed description of the terms of the various futures contracts. Burghardt et al. (1989) give a good overview of cash-futures basis considerations. Our discussion of bond basis, and Example 2.6 in particular, draws on Bass (1987) and Goldstein (1987). Ritchken (1987) and Labuszewski and Nyhoff (1988) deal with different aspects of the debt options market. The Credit Suisse First Boston (CSFB) Guide (1988) is a good introduction to the JGB market.

Banque Paribas Capital Markets, *The Japanese Bond Market: An Overview*, London, 1987.

Bass, A., "A Practical Approach to Bond Basis," in *Seminar on U.S. Treasury Bond Futures*, Greenwich Capital Markets Inc., Greenwich, Conn., 1987.

Bass, A., "Differences Between Exchange-Traded and Over-The-Counter Options," *Intermarket*, July 1988.

Bierwag, G. O., *Duration Analysis: Managing Interest Rate Risk*, Ballinger Publishing Company, Cambridge, Mass., 1987.

Burghardt, G., M. Lane, and J. Papa, *The Treasury Bond Basis: An In-Depth Analysis for Hedgers, Speculators and Arbitrageurs*, Probus Publishing Company, Chicago, 1989.

Credit Suisse First Boston, *The CSFB Guide to The Yen Bond Markets: Structure, Trends, Analysis*, Probus Publishing Company, Chicago, 1988.

Douglas, L. G., *Yield Curve Analysis: The Fundamentals of Risk and Return*, New York Institute of Finance, New York, 1988.

Feldman, L., and J. Stephenson, "Stay Small or Get Huge—Lessons from Securities Trading," *Harvard Business Review*, May–June: 116–123, 1988.

Garbade, K. D., *Securities Markets*, McGraw-Hill, New York, 1982.

Goldstein, E. "A Theoretical Approach to Bond Basis," in *Seminar on U.S. Treasury Bond Futures*, Greenwich Capital Markets Inc., Greenwich, Conn., 1987.

Jones, F. J., and B. Wolkowitz, "The Determinants of Interest Rates on Fixed Income Securities," in Fabozzi, F., and I. Pollack, eds., *Handbook of Fixed-Income Securities*, 2nd edition, Dow Jones–Irwin, Homewood, Ill., 1987, pp. 121–170.

Kopprasch, R. W., "Understanding Duration and Volatility," in Fabozzi, F., and I. Pollack, eds., *Handbook of Fixed-Income Securities*, 2nd edition, Dow Jones–Irwin, Homewood, Ill., 1987, pp. 86–120.

Labuszewski, J. W., and J. E. Nyhoff, *Trading Options on Futures*, John Wiley & Sons, New York, 1988.

Macaulay, F., *Some Theoretical Problems Suggested by the Movements of Interest Rates, Bond Yields and Stock Prices in the United States Since 1856*, National Bureau of Economic Research, Cambridge, MA, 1938.

McEnally, R. W., "The Term Structure of Interest Rates," in Fabozzi, F., and I. Pollack, eds., *Handbook of Fixed-Income Securities*, 2nd edition, Dow Jones–Irwin, Homewood, Ill., 1987, pp. 1111–1150.

Oberhofer, G. D., *Rate Risk Management: Fixed Income Strategies Using Futures, Options and Swaps*, Probus Publishing Company, Chicago, 1989.

Ritchken, P., *Options: Theory, Strategy, and Applications*, Scott, Foresman and Company, Glenview, Ill., 1987.

Schwarz, E. W., J. M. Hill, and T. Schneeweis, *Financial Futures: Fundamentals, Strategies, and Applications*, Dow Jones–Irwin, Homewood, Ill., 1986.

Stigum, M., *Money-Market Calculations: Yields, Break-Evens and Arbitrage*, Dow Jones–Irwin, Homewood, Ill., 1981.

Stigum, M., *The Money Market*, Dow Jones–Irwin, Homewood, Ill., 1983.

Stigum, M., *The Repo and Reverse Markets*, Dow Jones–Irwin, Homewood, Ill., 1989.

Stigum, M., and F. Fabozzi, "U.S. Treasury Obligations," in Fabozzi, F., and I. Pollack, eds., *Handbook of Fixed-Income Securities*, Dow Jones–Irwin, Homewood, Ill., 1983, pp. 253–269.

Tang, E. M., *The Effect of Delivery Options on Interest Rate Futures and Option Contracts*, Portfolio Management Technology, San Francisco, 1988.

3
Pricing Models for Bond Options

Financial professionals wanting to become active participants in the bond option markets must first learn how to evaluate options in different market environments. This chapter and the next describe various option pricing models, while specific recommendations are made in Chapter 5 as to which models are most appropriate for evaluating short- and long-dated options on cash bonds and futures. This chapter contains an introduction to option pricing and put-call parity. It describes the essentials of Black-Scholes-type models and their underlying assumptions. Lattice-based (binomial) models suitable for evaluating short-dated American options and for handling some specific aspects of bond options are also described.

INTRODUCTION TO OPTION PRICING

An option pricing model provides the user with a formula for valuing an option contract, given the terms of the contract and other relevant market data, including, for example, the price of the underlying security and its anticipated price volatility. In general, the terms of the contract will be known, while other inputs, such as the price of the underlying security at expiration and its volatility, must be specified and/or estimated by the user.

The "knowns" in most option pricing formulas include the following:

- The contract settlement date
- The expiration date
- The strike price
- Whether the option is a put or a call
- Whether the option is American or European
- The current price of the underlying security
- Current risk-free and term repo rates

The "unknowns" may include:

- The price of the underlying security at expiration (for American options, the entire behavior of underlying prices between contract date and expiration date)
- The yield of the underlying bond at expiration and/or at all intervening dates (note that this yield will correspond to a different point on the yield curve for each date, as the underlying bond matures)
- Short-term interest rates at expiration and/or intervening dates
- Projected price or yield volatilities

Option pricing models also provide additional analytics, such as the *hedge ratio*, or *delta*, of the option and other such measures of sensitivity in the option price to changes in one or another of the parameters of the pricing formula. Such sensitivity measures are frequently of at least as much importance as the option pricing formula itself, because they allow the holder of an option to quantify the risk exposure to changes in the value of the holdings due to shifts in market variables, time decay, and the like, and to determine how such risk can be hedged away. In particular, if the price of the underlying security changes by a unit, the price of a call option will change by delta, the hedge ratio. Thus, a holding consisting of long one call and short delta of the underlying security will be **delta neutral:** for small changes in the price of the underlying security, the value of the holding will not change.

The hedge ratio, delta, and other sensitivity measures may be computed directly from analytical expressions very similar to the option pricing formula itself, or they may be calculated by varying the parameter in question by a small quantity and computing the resulting variation in the option price.

Put-Call Parity

Many option pricing models satisfy a very general relationship known as **put-call parity,** which allows us to derive the price of a European put option from that of a European call with the same strike price and expiration (or ice versa). For options on equities, zero-coupon bonds, or other instruments with no intervening cash flows (dividends or coupon payments), this relationship is stated as follows:

$$P = C - S + DF(K) \qquad (3.1)$$

where P is the price of the put option

   C is the price of the call option

   S is the current price of the underlying security

   $DF(.)$ is the discounting function that calculates the net present value of the variable (in parentheses) at expiration

   K is the strike price

This relationship is traditionally established by considering a simultaneous position in European puts and calls on the same underlying security consisting of writing one call, buying one put, buying one unit of the underlying bond, and borrowing $DF(K)$ in cash. At expiration, what is the value of this position? If we assume that the value of the underlying bond at expiration is S', there are two cases: either the call finishes in the money ($S' > K$), and the put out of the money, or the call finishes out of the money ($S' < K$), and the put in the money. Where coupon accrual isn't an issue, the values of the various components of the holding in each case are shown in Table 3.1.

Since the total value at expiration is zero in every case, the initial investment required to create this position must also have a value of

Table 3.1 Put-Call Parity

	At Expiration	
Now	$S' > K$	$S' < K$
C	$K - S'$	0
$-P$	0	$K - S'$
$-S$	S'	S'
$DF(K)$	$-K$	$-K$

S' is the value of the underlying instrument at expiration.

zero; otherwise, it would be possible to arrange a perfect arbitrage (something for nothing). Thus the put-call parity relationship is established.

When put-call parity holds, it is unnecessary to have separate pricing formulas for European puts and calls, because the put value can be *solved for* from put-call parity. Sometimes separate pricing formulas for puts and calls *are* developed, however, and the put-call parity relationship is used as a test for the accuracy of the model. The relationship in Equation 3.1 does *not* hold in general, however, for *American* options, where the possibility of early exercise introduces an asymmetry into the relationship of puts and calls. For options on coupon-bearing bonds, where coupon accrual must be taken into account, a reformulation is necessary. In general, the price of the option will depend on the *forward* price of the underlying bond at the expiration date (current price less carry), which takes into account financing costs and coupon accrual. For European options on coupon-bearing bonds, it can be shown that put and call values obey the following modified form of put-call parity:

$$P = C - DF(FWD - K) \tag{3.2}$$

where *FWD* is the forward price of the underlying bond on the expiration date and the other variables are as above. (Note that $P = C$ when the strike is equal to the forward price.)

For a general exposition of put-call parity and many other aspects of option pricing theory in an equities setting, see Cox and Rubinstein (1985); for an exposition including discussion of options on debt instruments, see Ritchken (1987).

Varieties of Option Pricing Models

What distinguishes one option pricing model from another is the way it captures (or models) the uncertainty in the values of its parameters. We will look at two classes of option pricing models in this chapter.

1. Simple **analytical models,** including the well-known Black-Scholes model and its variants, which provide closed analytical formulas for option prices and sensitivities.
2. Computation-intensive, **lattice-based models,** sometimes known as *binomial* models, which do not, in general, lead to closed analytical formulas.

These option pricing models assume in common that one or more of their parameters (e.g., underlying price) evolve through time according to some statistical rule, which is usually specified by giving the assumed probability distribution for that variable at expiration, or in general as a function of time. Such a parameter is known technically as a **stochastic variable,** and the associated models are known as **stochastic models.** Different assumptions about the ways in which variable values are distributed give rise to different pricing models. These are also differences in the mathematical techniques used to derive the actual option pricing formulas or algorithms based on these statistical assumptions.

A simple stochastic option pricing model assumes that there is a single driving variable—such as the price of the underlying security, or frequently, in the case of cash bond options, the yield of the underlying bond. The analytical pricing model provides a closed formula based on the values of known variables (such as strike price and time to expiration) and of parameters specifying the particular statistical distribution assumed for the driving variable (e.g., price volatility). This closed pricing formula will be an exact or approximate solution to the stochastic differential equations specifying the driving process. Such models are highly accurate when applied to short-term (under six months) European options. For options with features such as early exercise (American options) and intervening cash flows, lattice-based models are more accurate. Both classes of models are generally inadequate for longer dated options (over six months), where variations in interest rates over the life of the option become significant (see Chapter 4).

COMMON CLOSED-FORM OPTION PRICING MODELS

Normal Price Model

In pricing an option on a bond future, a trader's intuitions might lead to the belief that the price of the underlying bond future contract was equally likely to go up by a given amount, say from 98 to 99 or from 99 to 100, as to go down by that same amount, say from 98 to 97, or from 97 to 96, over any given time interval. It can be shown that this assumption of *uniform absolute variability* in the price of the underlying bond future is equivalent, for the purpose of option pricing, to assuming that the price of the bond future on the expiration date obeys a **normal probability distribution,** with **mean** (expected value) equal to the current traded future price, and **standard deviation** determined by the assumed variability (volatility) of the bond future, in absolute price terms, over the life of the option. (What we are doing here is specifying the *shape* of the probability distribution of underlying prices at option expiration, as described in Figure 1.6 in Chapter 1.) This leads to a **normal price model,** one of the simplest option pricing models analytically, which has been used with short-term options on bond futures and other forward instruments. While not theoretically strictly correct (it can be shown that bond and bond future prices do not actually follow a normal distribution), this model gives useful pricing data for restricted values of the parameters. The basic assumptions of the model are:

- That the underlying price at expiration is normally distributed
- That the distribution is centered on the specified future or forward price
- That the standard deviation of the distribution is the projected absolute price variability for the term of the option
- That the discounting rate is constant over the life of the option
- That the market is continuous (liquid), and transaction costs can be ignored

The pricing formula using this model for a European call option with strike price K and time to expiration in years t is:

$$C = DF \{\sigma[zN(z) + n(z)]\} \tag{3.3}$$

where C is the value of a European call option with strike K and t years to expiration

DF is the discounting function over the interval t

$z = (F - K)/\sigma$ is the normalized difference between strike K and forward (or future) price F (for cash bonds, the arbitrage-free forward price can be found by taking F = spot price − carry)

$n(z)$ and $N(z)$ represent the standard normal density function and the cumulative normal distribution function at z, respectively

σ is the absolute price standard deviation for the interval t (this can be derived from the annualized percentage price volatility, v, the definition and estimation procedures for which can be found in Chapter 5, by setting $\sigma = v \sqrt{t} \times F$)

The option's delta or hedge ratio, which is just the derivative of the call price with respect to the underlying bond price, is:

$$\delta C = DF[N(z)] \tag{3.4}$$

(The mathematical derivation of these pricing formulas can be found in Appendix A.)

The normal price model has the theoretical disadvantage of allowing the possibility of negative prices, since the projected future distribution of prices is assumed to spread out arbitrarily in *absolute* terms in *both* directions around the forward price. However, this is mainly a problem for longer dated options, and/or in regimes of extraordinary volatility. For widely traded short-term (up to six-month) options on bond futures and other forward instruments, and under usual volatility conditions, the normal price model is sufficiently accurate for most practical purposes. For similarly short-term American options, some adjustments must be made; for example, by taking the maximum of the European call value given by the above formula and the intrinsic value of the option as a lower bound for the actual American option value.

EXAMPLE 3.1: PRICING A CALL ON A BOND FUTURE

Assume that we are given a three-month call option on a bond future that is currently priced at 98.00. Let the option be struck at 100.00 (par), and let price volatility be given in annual percentage terms as 16%. Finally, let us assume a risk-free three-month discounting rate of 2%. What should be the price of this option, according to the normal price model?

The option term t is 0.25 years, so the absolute price volatility is:

$$\sigma = \text{(price volatility)} \times (\sqrt{t}) \times \text{(future price)}$$

or

$$\sigma = 0.16 \times 0.50 \times 98.00 = 7.84$$

The risk-free discounting rate is 2% for three months, so the discounting factor is 0.98. Since $K = 100.00$ and $F = 98.00$, the normalized variable z is computed to be:

$$z = \frac{(98.00 - 100.00)}{7.84} = -0.255$$

and the corresponding call value and delta are calculated to be:

$$C = 0.98 \times 7.84 \times [-0.255 \times N(-0.255) + n(-0.255)]$$
$$= 0.98 \times 7.84 \times (0.38617 - 0.255 \times 0.40083)$$
$$= 2.18$$

or 2 and ⁵⁄₃₂nds. Similarly:

$$\delta C = 0.98 \times [1 - N(-0.255)]$$
$$= 0.98 \times (1 - 0.59917)$$
$$= 0.392$$

Lognormal Price Model (Black-Scholes Model)

A popular alternative to the normal price model is the **lognormal price model,** in which the *log* of the underlying price is assumed to be normally distributed. Such a model arises naturally if one assumes that the price of the underlying bond is equally likely to move up or down by the same *proportion* in a given time interval; that is, up from 100.00 to 110.00, or from 110.00 to 121.00; or down from 100.0 to 90.90, or from 90.90 to 82.64. Many traders believe that this is a natural assumption for many markets—that the expected size of changes should be proportional to market level—and this assumption gives rise to the classical Black-Scholes option pricing model, the earliest and best known of all the closed-form option pricing models.

Undoubtedly, the Black-Scholes model has been a milestone in options pricing theory. In theoretical terms, this model first established that the expected cash flows of any continuously traded asset obeying a reasonable stochastic process can be replicated for a risk-neutral cost, laying the groundwork for a consistent theory of the pricing of contingent claims. Practically, the Black-Scholes model introduced the first closed analytical options pricing formula to gain wide currency in the financial industry. Introduced in the mid-1970s as an equity option pricing model (Black and Scholes, 1973), and subsequently extended and modified to handle a variety of other instruments (see Cox and Rubinstein, 1985), the Black-Scholes model has proven extraordinarily accurate and consistent in those markets where its basic assumptions are met, and has become a standard tool for all options traders. The classical Black-Scholes option pricing model is a lognormal price model. It assumes that the underlying price at expiration obeys a lognormal probability distribution—that the natural log of the price is normally distributed. This distribution is specified by a *price-relative* volatility, which might typically be quoted in average percentage annual price change terms. (The volatility tracking and estimation process is described in Chapter 5.)

The assumptions of this model are:

- That the underlying price follows a lognormal process—that is, that the log of the price obeys a normal distribution at expiration
- That volatility remains constant over the life of the option
- That the risk-free discounting rate is constant over the life of the option
- That the market is continuous (liquid), and that transaction costs can be ignored

The resulting option pricing formula for a European call option with strike price K and time to expiration t in years is:

$$C = SN(z) - Ke^{-rt}N(z - \sigma \sqrt{t}) \tag{3.5}$$

where:

$$z = [\log(S/K) + rt + \sigma^2 t/2]/(\sigma \sqrt{t})$$

and C is the value of a European call option with strike K and t years to expiration

S is the current price of the security

K is the strike price

σ is the annualized **relative** price volatility

$r = \log(1 + r_{rf})$ is the continuously compounding form of the risk-free rate r_{rf}

The option's hedge ratio is given, simply, by:

$$\delta C = N(z) \tag{3.6}$$

Despite the great success and familiarity of the Black-Scholes model in pricing equity options, and the convenience of its closed analytical form, there are some important qualifying assumptions in applying this model to bond options. Coupon accrual complicates matters, but can be accounted for (as can the payment of dividends in the equity option pricing case) by replacing the underlying price S by the present value of the forward price $e^{-rt}F$. F incorporates the coupon effect; note that r is the *continuously compounded* discounting rate.

As in the case of the normal price model, adjustments must be made to compensate for the undervaluation of American call options due to the failure of the Black-Scholes model to take into account the possibility of early exercise. However, the Black-Scholes model depends fundamentally on the assumption of a constant risk-free rate, and on the assumption that price volatility is not time dependent, neither of which assumptions can consistently be sustained in the world of cash bond options. It is certainly unreasonable to assume that T-bill yields, for example, follow a lognormal process while the short-term risk-free rate remains constant. Perhaps less obvious is the fact that bond volatilities, whether price or yield based, *must* be time dependent, since the price of the bond must ultimately converge to par. Nevertheless, for short-term options on bond futures and on longer maturity bonds, where there is a low correlation between the bond's yield (or price) levels and the short rate, suitable versions of the Black-Scholes model are applicable.

EXAMPLE 3.2: PRICING A CALL ON A CASH BOND

Assume that we are given a 3-month (90-day) call option on an 8% cash bond maturity in 20 years, which is currently priced at 98.00. Let the option be struck at the money—98.00—and assume an annual percentage volatility of 12%. Finally, assume a risk-free discounting rate of 6%, and a term (three-month) repo rate of 5% for the bond. What should be the price of the option, according to Black-Scholes?

The time interval, t, is 0.246 years, and $K = 98.00$. We have $\sigma = 0.12$, $r = \log(1 + 0.06) = 0.058269$, and $e^{-rt} = 0.985745$. The forward price of the bond, assuming the bond currently has no accrued interest, is given by:

$$F = \text{price} - \text{carry}$$

$$= 98.00 - \left(100 \times \frac{0.08}{365} - 98 \times \frac{0.05}{360} \right) \times 90 = 97.25$$

The replacement for S is:

$$e^{-rt}F = 0.9857 \times 97.25 = 95.861$$

and we have $\sigma = 0.12$ and $r = \log(1 + 0.06) = 0.0583$. Therefore:

$$z = \frac{\log(95.86/98.00) + (0.0583 \times 0.246) + (0.12^2 \times 0.246/2)}{0.12 \times \sqrt{0.246}}$$

$$= \frac{-0.0229 + 0.0144 + 0.0018}{0.0596} = -0.1136$$

so:

$$N(z) = N(-0.1136) = 0.4612$$

and

$$N(z - \sigma\sqrt{t}) = N[-0.1136 - (0.12 \times \sqrt{0.246})] = 0.4376$$

and we have:

$$C = [e^{-rt}F \times N(z)] - [K \times e^{-rt} \times N(z - \sigma\sqrt{t})]$$

$$= (95.812 \times 0.46119) - (98.00 \times 0.9857 \times 0.4376) = 1.9405$$

or 1 and $^{30}\!/_{32}$nds and:

$$\delta C = N(z) = N(0.46119) = 0.461$$

Note that if the option is struck at the forward price, 97.28, we have $C = 2.875$, or 2 and $^{28}\!/_{32}$nds, and $\delta C = 0.512$, which gives a hedge ratio closer to 0.500. From put-call parity, we would expect the hedge ratio of an option to be about 0.500 when struck at the money; but to be at the money, an option on a cash bond must be struck at the *forward* price. (Put-call parity also implies that at this strike level, the call and put options will have the same price.)

Yield-Based Models

As has been pointed out, one major difficulty with any price-based model is in the amoritzation toward par, and the concomitant reduction in variance over time. Normal and lognormal price dynamics fail to deal with this time dependence of variance, but yield dynamics reflect it automatically. One justification for using yield as the driving variable has been the empirical observation that yield volatilities are fairly uniform within a given region of the yield curve. A five-year bond will in time become a four and three-quarters-year bond, and will be subjected to changing price dynamics, but its yield dynamics will not change significantly. Yield-based dynamics are also of interest because they provide a more natural basis than do price dynamics for the analysis of long-dated options, although a simple one-parameter stochastic model, whether yield or price driven, is no longer appropriate for such options, as we will see in Chapter 4.

Of course, price and yield are linked by a deterministic relationship (given one of these and the standard bond characteristics—coupon and maturity—the other can be determined), but what is of significance for the option-pricing model is the *process* postulated for the evolution of bond price/yield through time. If bond *yields* are presumed to be normally or lognormally distributed, bond *prices cannot* obey any such simple distribution. In particular, the mean of the implied price distribution will not, in general, correspond to the mean of the yield distribution. Traders must therefore be careful, for example, in converting price volatility figures not to yield volatility figures too freely. Traders should be aware of the modeling assumptions underlying their own and others' figures; otherwise they may find themselves in the position of comparing apples and oranges!

If a yield-based process is assumed, it is most realistic to assume that rates move up or down in proportion to the current yield, rather than by absolute steps—that is, according to a lognormal rather than a normal process. This obviates the ugly possibility of negative rates, and gives rise to a rather interesting yield-based model, described in the following section. In general, yield-based models are somewhat more analytically involved than are the price-based models, and because we have not found wide applicability for such a model, we omit discussion here of the normal yield model.

Lognormal Yield Model

In pricing short-term options on cash bonds, we have used a proprietary lognormal yield model developed by Enlin Pan (1986). This model is governed by a *yield-relative* volatility, which can be derived from the more commonly quoted price volatility figures, or from empirical data on the variability of daily percentage changes in yield levels, and also depends on having a good analytical approximation of the price/yield relationship. Once such an analytical approximation has been chosen, it can be used to evaluate the expression for the option price that arises as a solution to the stochastic differential equation implied by the assumed lognormal yield process. The implied distribution of prices at expiration is simplified using the chosen analytical approximation for the price/yield relationship, and the expected value of the option can then be explicitly computed. The result is a closed analytical expression that is an *approximate* rather than exact solution of the equation—but a very good approximation, consistent over a wide range of yield levels and volatilities.

This model assumes:

- That bond yield is lognormally distributed at expiration
- That yield volatility is constant over the life of the option
- That the short-term risk-free rate is constant over the life of the option

EXAMPLE 3.3: OPTION PRICING USING A LOGNORMAL YIELD MODEL

This lognormal yield model gives option prices and hedge ratios that are generally comparable to those produced by a Black-Scholes model, although there are small but systematic differences. For the same call option on a cash bond cited in Example 3.2 above, for example, the corresponding yield is 8.205, and the corresponding option price and hedge ratio are calculated to be $C = 2.014$, or 2 and $\frac{1}{64}$th, and $\delta C = 0.458$.

The choice of a yield-based model over, say, the standard Black-Scholes price-based model may be determined in part by the user's intuitions about underlying market dynamics, or by a desire for consistency with the assumptions of a broader modeling and simulations context.

Other Simple Stochastic Models

There are also simple stochastic models that assume distributions other than the normal or lognormal for the driving variable, in an effort to take into account various empirical deviations from these idealized distributions. Some empirical studies have indicated that the tails of the price distribution at expiration date would have to be thicker than would be predicted by a normal or lognormal distribution, for example, to explain the way some options are priced by the market, but we will not go into these extensions here, because they are relatively rarely used in practice.

LATTICE-BASED (BINOMIAL) OPTION PRICING MODELS

While the closed-form option pricing models described above have the advantage of simplicity and are generally analytically tractable, they cannot handle certain features of many bond options contracts, such as the early exercise feature of American options. This is because the decision to exercise before expiration depends on the behavior of the price of the underlying security *throughout* the life of the option, and this cannot be reduced to a single parameter. While adjustments can be made to take into account the premium associated with early exercise, as discussed above, these adjustments are only approximations. These models are also increasingly inaccurate as the term of the option lengthens, because of their inability to take into account variations in short-term interest rates, and/or the time dependence of volatilities. To deal with such features, more discriminating pricing models have been developed, which are generally known as **binomial** or (more accurately) **lattice-based**, models.

Introduction to Lattice-Based Option Pricing Models

The key to a lattice-based model is the division of the span from settlement to expiration into discrete intervals or steps; for example, for a one-month option the step size might be a single day. The model then assumes that the key parameter, typically the price or yield of the underlying security, evolves through time on a step-by-step basis, moving up or down by a fixed amount or proportion in each interval. If one allows only two possible movements (up and down) at each step, the result is a doubly branched, or binomial, lattice; however, one can equally well allow three or more possible movements (e.g., up, flat, and down) at each step, giving rise to more complex lattices. (It is important to note that the price or yield movements must be such that successive up and down steps cancel, so that the result of up followed by down will be the same state as down followed by up. This allows the model to deal with a true lattice, and not a rapidly branching tree, which would be computationally much more demanding!)

The lattice-based model derives an option value by working backward through the lattice from the final step, the expiration date, at which the option value is known, to the initial step, the contract settlement date. It is assumed that the states achieved in the lattice are all arbitrage free, and on this assumption it is possible to solve backward for the implied value of the option contract at each previous step. Thus, a lattice-based model gives rise to an algorithm, rather than a closed formula, for determining the option value.

For example, assume that at any node in the lattice the price S of the

underlying security may go up by a factor u with probability q, or down
by a factor d with probability $(1 - q)$:

$$
S
\begin{cases}
uS \text{ with probability } q \\
\\
dS \text{ with probability } (1 - q)
\end{cases}
$$

We also assume a constant short-term interest rate r_0, and set $r = 1 + r_0$, with $u > r > d$ (to avoid riskless arbitrage opportunities), and a
coupon assumed to accrue at the rate of c per period. Finally, we assume
that we can value the option at the up and down nodes (which will be
true at the terminal nodes, because the option will be expiring, and will
be either worthless or **intrinsic,** that is, worth the difference between the
price of the underlying security and the strike price):

$$
C
\begin{cases}
C_u \text{ with probability } q \\
\\
C_d \text{ with probability } (1 - q)
\end{cases}
$$

where C_u and C_d are the option value at the up and down nodes, respectively.

Now, suppose we create a position consisting of some proportion of
the underlying security and cash (or a riskless bond): $S\Delta + H$. (Note
that H may be negative—that is, it may represent *borrowing*.) We will
choose Δ and H in such a way as to *replicate* the price behavior of the
option in both up and down scenarios. At the end of one step, this position
will have the value:

$$
S\Delta + H
\begin{cases}
uS\Delta + rH + \Delta c \text{ with probability } q \\
\\
dS\Delta + rH + \Delta c \text{ with probability } (1 - q)
\end{cases}
$$

We will choose Δ and H in such a way as to ensure that:

$$uS\Delta + rH + \Delta c = C_u \tag{3.7a}$$
$$dS\Delta + rH + \Delta c = C_d \tag{3.7b}$$

Solving for Δ and H, we have:

$$\Delta = \frac{C_u - C_d}{(u - d)S} \tag{3.8a}$$

$$H = \frac{uC_d - dC_u}{(u - d)r} - \frac{\Delta c}{r} \tag{3.8b}$$

If there is to be no perfect arbitrage available during the step in question, the value C of the option must be equal to $S\Delta + H$; otherwise we could make a riskless return by buying the option and selling the combination of underlying security and riskless bond (or vice versa). We have *replicated* the option contract by a properly leveraged position in the underlying security and cash. Our portfolio $S\Delta + H$ goes up (or down) precisely as much as the value of the option contract in the up and down scenarios (Δ is thus the *price sensitivity* or *hedge ratio* of the option).

The value of the option can thus be determined at a given node from the values at the up and down nodes by the formula:

$$C = S\Delta + H = \frac{C_u - C_d}{(u - d)} + \frac{uC_d - dC_u}{(u - d)r} - \frac{\Delta c}{r} \tag{3.9}$$

Now, the value of the option is known *precisely* at the terminal nodes of the lattice; it is zero if the option expires worthless (out of the money), and it is just the intrinsic value of the option (the amount it ends up in the money) otherwise. We can therefore apply the above argument at each node in the lattice, until we eventually work our way back to the value of the option at the initial node. Note that the values of Δ and H will in general be different at different nodes; this means that we must adjust the proportions of the underlying security and cash in our replicating portfolio as we move through the lattice. This is only to be expected, because the price sensitivity of the option naturally changes as it moves further in or out of the money. This pricing method is therefore commonly known as **dynamic replication** of the option value. (An application of this methodology is demonstrated in Example 3.4 below.)

The key binomial pricing formula (Equation 3.9) can be rewritten as:

$$C = \left[\left(\frac{r - d}{u - d} \right) C_u + \left(\frac{u - r}{u - d} \right) C_d - \Delta c \right] / r$$

or:

$$C = [pC_u + (1 - p)C_d - \Delta c] / r \tag{3.10}$$

where:

$$p = (r - d)/(u - d) \tag{3.11}$$

Note that Equations 3.9 and 3.10 *do not involve the transition probability q;* the value of the option is *independent* of investors' expectations about market trends! Nor does the option value depend on investors' attitudes toward risk; the formula gives the same option value whether the investor is bullish or bearish, risk averse or risk seeking.

In fact, it is easy to see that for p in Equation 3.11, $0 \le p \le 1$, so p can be treated as a kind of *probability.* Equation 3.10 then expresses the option value at a given node as the *expected present value* of the option one lattice step into the future (adjusted for coupon accrual). The probability p is in fact just that value of the transition probability q that would lead to the one-period riskless rate of return r as a return on S; that is, it is the solution of the equation:

$$q(uS) + (1 - q)(dS) = rS$$

Thus p is the **risk-neutral probability,** and Equation 3.10 can be interpreted as asserting that *the value of an option is just its risk-neutral expected present value.*

By iterating Equation 3.10, we can work out algebraically what the option value must be in terms of its values two lattice steps into the future, three steps into the future, and in general n steps into the future. Thus an explicit formula for the value of the option at the initial lattice node in terms of its values at the terminal nodes can be written. The algebra is cumbersome, but the final formula sheds some light on the relationship between the price-driven binomial lattice pricing model and the Black-Scholes closed-form analytical model. Ignoring coupon accrual, the full binomial formula is:

$$C = S\Phi(a,n,p') - Kr^{-n}\Phi(a,n,p) \tag{3.12}$$

where:

$$\Phi(a,n,q) = \sum_{i=a}^{n} \left(\frac{n!}{i!(n - i)!} \right) q^i (1 - q)^{n-i}$$

and K is the option strike price

p is given by $(r - d)/(u - d)$, as above

p' is $(u/r)p$

a is the smallest nonnegative integer greater than $\log(K/Sd^n)/\log(u/d)$

For a derivation of this formula, due originally to Sharpe (1979), see Cox and Rubinstein (1985), which contains a detailed and lucid exploration of the relationship between the binomial and Black-Scholes pricing models. The presentation of the price-driven lattice-based pricing model in this section is based on theirs.

Relationship between Binomial and Black-Scholes Formulas

The simplest binomial lattice models assume the same driving parameters and statistical rules for their distributions as do the closed-form models: either the price or the yield moves up or down by a fixed absolute or relative step. It can be shown, and should be expected, that such models in fact converge to the closed-form models for European options "in the limit," as the size of the lattice step is made smaller and smaller. (This is natural, because the lattice-based approach is really just a discrete approximation to the underlying stochastic differential equation solved or analytically approximated in the closed-form models.) In particular, for suitable specification of the limiting behavior of the parameters q, u, and d as n goes to infinity, the binomial pricing formula of Equation 3.12 converges to the Black-Scholes pricing formula (Equation 3.5). Recalling that the option delta, or hedge ratio, is expressed by $N(z)$ in Equation 3.6, we see that the first term on the right-hand side of Equation 3.5 (or Equation 3.12) represents just *the amount invested in the underlying security* in creating a position dynamically replicating, or hedging, the option payoffs; the second term then represents *the amount borrowed* to finance the replicating, or hedging, position.

Since the closed-form models seem to give the same result, one may question why lattice-based models are even necessary. For *American* options, however, lattice-based models allow for an accurate valuation of the early exercise option, something the simpler closed-form models cannot achieve. This is accomplished by checking the desirability of early exercise at each node, setting the American option value $C'_{s,t}$ at each node (s,t) to $MAX(C_{s,t}, S_{s,t} - K)$ for a call and $MIN(C_{s,t}, K - S_{s,t})$ for a put, where $S_{s,t}$ is the value of the underlying at node (s,t), and:

$$C_{s,t} = [pC'_u + (1 - p)C'_d - \Delta c]/r$$

as in Equation 3.10, with C'_u and C'_d the *American* call values at the up and down nodes, respectively. The lattice-based models are also capable of incorporating irregular and path-dependent intermediate cash flows during the life of the option into their calculations. Of course, when such additional features are taken into account, there is usually no closed algebraic expression such as Equation 3.10 associated with the model. In fact, Equation 3.12 is generally of greater theoretical than practical interest, because implementations of lattice-based models generally calculate the prices of options and other contingent claims by explicitly working backward through the lattice from the terminal nodes to the initial node.

Price-Driven Lattice-Based Option Pricing
EXAMPLE 3.4: PRICING A SIX-MONTH CALL ON A CASH BOND

Consider a bond with initial price par (100.00) and 12% coupon, and a six-month call option on it struck at par. Assume that the price of the bond will move up by a factor of 1.1, or down by a factor of $1/1.1 = .09091$ over the life of the option. (The fact that the up and down steps are inverse means that we asume there is no drift in the median bond price over the life of the option.) We will price the option using a three-step lattice, so that at each step the price goes up by a factor of $u = (1.1)^{1/3} = 1.0323$, or down by a corresponding (inverse) factor of $d = 0.9687$ with equal probability ($p = 0.5$). We also assume a six-month risk-free rate r_0 of 5%, giving a discounting factor for a single step of $r = (1.05)^{1/3} = 1.0164$. (In practice, many more steps would be used for greater accuracy.)

Bond prices will follow the lattice shown in Figure 3.1. Using Equations 3.8 and 3.9, call prices follow the corresponding lattice (Figure 3.2), and hedge ratios follow the lattice shown in Figure 3.3.

```
                              110.00
                                /
                             106.56
                             /     \
                       103.23       103.23
                      /      \      /
                100.00        100.00
                      \      /      \
                       96.87         96.87
                             \      /
                             93.84
                                  \
                                   90.91
```

FIGURE 3.1 Bond price lattice.

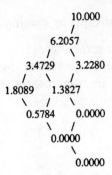

FIGURE 3.2 Call option price lattice.

For example, the call value of 1.3827 and its corresponding hedge ratio 0.5079 are obtained, using Equations 3.8 and 3.9, as follows:

$$\Delta = \frac{C_u - C_d}{(u - d)S}$$

$$= \frac{3.228 - 0.00}{(1.0323 - 0.9687) \times 100.00} = \frac{3.228}{6.360} = 0.5079$$

$$H = \frac{uC_d - dC_u}{(u - d)r} - \frac{\Delta c}{r}$$

$$= \frac{(1.0323 \times 0.00) - (0.9689 \times 3.228)}{0.0636 \times 1.0164} - \frac{0.5079 \times 2.00}{1.0164} = -49.412$$

and:

$$C = S\Delta + H = (0.5079 \times 100.00) - 49.412 = 1.3827$$

where $c = 2.0$ is the coupon accrual over a single step (two months).

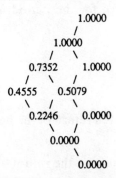

FIGURE 3.3 Hedge ratio lattice.

Rate-Driven Lattice-Based Option Pricing

To handle variations in short-term interest rates over the life of the option, we can let interest rates themselves drive the model; instead of moving the bond price or yield up and down through the lattice, we move the interest rate r through the lattice:

$$r_u \text{ with probability } p$$
$$r$$
$$r_d \text{ with probability } (1 - p)$$

The bond price at each node can then be determined from the assumed bond values at the succeeding nodes, but some additional assumptions are necessary. If we assume that the bond price should always be such that expected return over the next period will be that of a riskless bond (the so-called **expectations hypothesis**), we will have:

$$B = \frac{pB_u + (1 - p)B_d + c}{(1 + r)} \tag{3.13}$$

where B is the bond price

B_u, B_d are the up and down values of the bond price

p is the probability of an upward movement in the interest rate r

c is the coupon accrual for the period

On the other hand, we can price the bonds so that they provide a common risk-adjusted return for the period in question; all bonds will then be priced so that:

$$\frac{E(r_B) - r}{\sigma(r_B)} = \rho \tag{3.14}$$

where $E(r_B)$ is the expected return of the bond for the period in question

$\sigma(r_B)$ is the volatility of the return

ρ is a constant, the market price of risk

With this method we have:

$$E(r_B) = \frac{pB_u + (1 - p)B_d + c - B}{B}$$

and:

$$\sigma(r_B) = \frac{\sqrt{p(1 - p)}\,(B_u - B_d)}{B}$$

so:

$$\rho = \frac{pB_u + (1 - p)B_d + c - B - rB}{\sqrt{p(1 - p)}\,(B_u - B_d)}$$

and:

$$B = \frac{B_u[p - \rho\sqrt{p(1 - p)}] + B_d[(1 - p) - \rho\sqrt{p(1 - p)}] + c}{(1 + r)}$$

$$(3.15)$$

If $\rho = 0$, this latter equation reduces to the previous form (the bond pricing scheme derived from the expectations hypothesis). In any case, derivation of the lattice of bond prices from a given lattice of short-term interest rates requires some assumptions about investor attitudes toward risk. Finally, note that since we know the current price of the underlying bond, the up and down parameters u and d, together with the probability p and the assumed market price of risk ρ, must be constrained such that the bond price at the initial node coincides with the known price.

EXAMPLE 3.5: EVOLUTION OF INTEREST RATES AND BOND PRICES

Consider a bond maturing in five years, with a coupon of 10.00, and assume a current risk-free rate of 10%, and up and down parameters of 1.05 and 0.95. Using a probability $p = 0.5$, under the expectations hypothesis we have the lattice of rates and corresponding bond prices shown in Figures 3.4 and 3.5. (Note that the price B of a bond goes *up* when the interest rate at the corresponding node goes *down;* that is B_d is *greater* than B_u.)

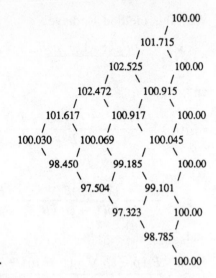

FIGURE 3.4 Lattice of interest rates.

For example, $7.738 = 8.145 \times 0.95$ and $8.552 = 8.145 \times 1.05$ in the interest rate lattice, and the bond price 100.917 is determined by:

$$B = \frac{(0.5 \times 100.915) + (0.5 \times 100.045) + 10.00}{(1 + 0.09476)} = 100.917$$

Note that the price of the bond at the initial node is 100.030, or 100 and $\frac{1}{32}$nd; if we were constrained to an initial bond price of par, for

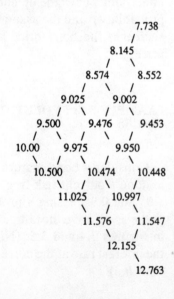

FIGURE 3.5 Lattice of bond prices.

example, we could determine that a probability $p = 0.504$ would give a tree of bond prices with an initial node bond price of almost exactly par.

We can now derive the price of a call at any point in the lattice similarly to the case of a bond price-driven lattice. Consider a holding consisting of a long position in the bond, and a short position of Δ calls. This position will have a current value of:

$$V = B - \Delta C$$

and a value in the up and down nodes of:

$$V_u = B_u - \Delta C_u + c$$
$$V_d = B_d - \Delta C_d + c$$

In order for this holding to be riskless—that is, independent of interest rate movements—these two values must be equal; we can then solve for Δ:

$$\Delta = \frac{B_u - B_d}{C_u - C_d} \tag{3.16}$$

(Note that here Δ is the *reciprocal* of the hedge ratio.)

Since we are assuming that this holding is riskless, it must have a rate of return over the next period equal to the riskless rate r for that period:

$$(1 + r)V = V_u = V_d$$

or:

$$(1 + r)(B - \Delta C) = B_u - \Delta C_u + c$$

Solving for C, we have:

$$C = \frac{\theta C_u + (1 - \theta)C_d}{(1 + r)} - \frac{c}{\Delta(1 + r)} \tag{3.17}$$

where:

$$\theta = \frac{B_d - B(1 + r)}{(B_d - B_u)} \tag{3.18}$$

As in the price-driven case, we work backward from the nodes at expiration, at which time the call prices are all known (they are either zero or intrinsic—that is, equal to $B - K$), to the initial node. Note that we derive the hedge ratio at the same time that we derive the call price.

FIGURE 3.6   Lattice of call option prices.

EXAMPLE 3.6: LATTICE-BASED PRICING OF A CALL OPTION ON A CASH BOND

We can now illustrate the pricing of an at-the-money call option on the above bond, which for simplicity we will assume to expire after exactly four lattice steps. The lattice of call prices generated according to the above algorithm is shown in Figure 3.6.

For example, the call price of 0.24526 at the initial node can be derived as follows. Since $B = 100.03$, $r = 10\%$ or 0.10 , $c = 10.0$, $B_u = 98.45$, $B_d = 101.617$, $C_u = 0.09867$, and $C_d = 0.44089$, using Equations 3.16 and 3.18 we get:

$$\theta = \frac{B_d - B(1 + r)}{(B_d - B_u)}$$

$$= \frac{101.617 - [100.030 \times (1 + 0.10)]}{(101.617 - 98.45)} = -2.657$$

and:

$$\Delta = \frac{B_u - B_d}{C_u - C_d}$$

$$= \frac{98.45 - 101.617}{0.09867 - 0.44089} = 9.2548$$

Therefore, from Equation 3.17:

$$
\begin{aligned}
C &= \frac{\theta C_u + (1 - \theta)C_d}{(1 + r)} - \frac{c}{\Delta(1 + r)} \\
&= \frac{(-2.657 \times 0.09867) + [(1 + 2.657) \times 0.44089]}{(1 + 0.10)} \\
&\quad - \frac{10.00}{(1 + 0.10) \times 9.2548} = 0.24526
\end{aligned}
$$

CONCLUSIONS

Lattice-based models can provide superior accuracy over the simpler closed-form models where intermediate cash flows and/or early exercise are an issue. Some such approach is required because there are no known simple closed-form analytical formulas for option prices in such contexts. Another approach, mentioned in Chapter 4, is to derive closed-form *analytical approximations* to options price and sensitivities. Lattice-based models have the advantage that they can be made arbitrarily precise by increasing the number of lattice steps, whereas analytical approximations generally have some irreducible margin of error. Other numerical methods, such as finite-difference techniques for approximating solutions to the underlying stochastic differential equations governing the evolution of the key parameters over time, are sometimes also feasible, and like the lattice-based models can be made arbitrarily precise, but at a cost.

While lattice-based models are essential for some applications, their accuracy is dependent on the number of lattice steps employed, and the computational demands of such models increase roughly as the square of the number of steps. There is thus an unavoidable tradeoff between increased accuracy and computational expense. Moreover, while some lattice-based models automatically generate the option delta, or hedge ratio, along with the option price, other sensitivities, such as the rate of time decay or the sensitivity to change in volatility, must be computed numerically, by recomputing the option price for slightly different values of the parameter in question. Sensitivity analysis may thus further increase the computational demands of such models.

As we have noted [and as is proven by Cox and Rubinstein (1985) and others], the option values calculated by lattice-based and closed-form models such as Black-Scholes will be *exactly the same* in the limit for

European options. Under some circumstances the difference between the values calculated by lattice-based and closed-form models will be small enough to be ignored for most practical applications. (It may be less than a pricing tick—the smallest pricing increment—for example, or at least within the market bid-ask spread.) The simpler, closed-form models should not therefore be scorned or discarded. For short-dated European options they are extremely accurate, and there are many other contexts, such as short-dated American options, where they may be perfectly adequate, and their cost and speed far superior to a lattice-based model.

The original exposition of the binomial lattice approach to option pricing, building on the ideas of Professor William Sharpe of Stanford University, can be found in Cox et al. (1979) and Cox and Rubinstein (1985). Certain modifications of the original models and arguments are necessary in dealing with bond options. Our exposition is based on that of Ritchken (1987), which includes a presentation of such models in a bond options context.

In any case, both the closed-form and lattice-based models discussed so far share some common limitations, the implications of which will be discussed in the next chapter, along with some of the more sophisticated models currently in use in the financial industry. These limitations have generally to do with the implicit assumptions about the behavior of interest rates and volatilities over the life of the option, and become particularly critical when dealing with *long-dated options*, those with terms of up to several years.

In Chapter 5 the various bond option pricing models are compared, and recommendations made as to the appropriateness of different models for different markets and types of securities. Familiarity with the more sophisticated models developed in Chapter 4 is *not* a prerequisite for understanding Chapter 5.

REFERENCES

For an excellent general introduction to options pricing theory, including a good exposition of the relationship between the simple binomial lattice approach and the Black-Scholes pricing model, see the book "Options Markets," by Cox and Rubinstein (1985). Their book, while thorough and clear, is written in the context of options on equities, and doesn't touch on bond options at all. For a survey of options pricing theory that includes bond options, see "Options: Theory, Strategy and Applications," by Ritchken (1987). Original research papers of Black and Scholes (1973), Merton (1973, 1977), Cox, Ross, and Rubinstein (1979), and Cox, Ingersoll, and Ross (1981) are cited because they have had a lasting impact on the literature and on the industry; the results cited in some of these older papers are for the most part available, often in more convenient form, in subsequent books and surveys, including the two cited above.

Black, F., and M. Scholes, "The Pricing of Options and Corporate Liabilities," *The Journal of Political Economy*, May–June:399–417, 1973.

Cox, J., J. Ingersoll, and S. Ross, "A Reexamination of Traditional Hypotheses about the Term Structure of Interest Rates," *The Journal of Finance*, September:769–799, 1981.

Cox, J., S. Ross, and M. Rubinstein, "Options Pricing: A Simplified Approach," *The Journal of Financial Economics*, 7:229–263, September 1979.

Cox, J., and M. Rubinstein. *Options Markets*, Prentice-Hall, Englewood Cliffs, N.J., 1985.

Merton, R., "Theory of Rational Option Pricing," *Bell Journal of Economics and Management Science*, 4:141–183, Spring 1973.

Merton, R., "On the Pricing of Contingent Claims and the Modigliani-Miller Theorem," *The Journal of Financial Economics*, 5:241–250, November 1977.

Pan, E., "Lognormal Yields and Options Pricing", Unpublished notes, Research Department, Greenwich Capital Markets Inc., Greenwich, Conn., July 1986.

Ritchken, P., *Options: Theory, Strategy and Applications*, Scott Foresman and Company, Glenview, Ill., 1987.

Sharpe, W., *Investments*, Prentice-Hall, Englewood Cliffs, N.J., 1979.

4
Advanced Pricing Models for Bond Options

This chapter begins by outlining some of the limitations of simple stochastic option pricing models—whether closed form or lattice based—and introduces some of the more sophisticated pricing models that have been developed over the past several years. Pricing models based on a lattice of changing term structures of interest rates are discussed, as are some alternative models, including one based on a continuous-time model of the term structure's evolution. Monte Carlo simulation methods and applications of these methods to options pricing are described, and some of the limitations of such methods are also pointed out. Alternative approaches to pricing options are surveyed in the final section. The question of how to choose the most appropriate pricing model for a specific application will be addressed in Chapter 5.

NEED FOR MORE SOPHISTICATED BOND OPTIONS PRICING MODELS

While the option pricing models described in Chapter 3 are adequate and appropriate for a wide variety of applications, including most short-dated bond options, they share some important limitations in the context of longer dated options and option-related contingent claims (embedded options).

Variable Interest Rates

Long-dated bond options prices will necessarily be highly sensitive to variations in interest rates over the life of the option. Both the closed-form analytical pricing models, such as Black-Scholes, and the simple price-driven binomial pricing models described in Chapter 3 explicitly assume a constant short-term rate over the life of the option. They are therefore inappropriate for pricing long-dated options, whether European or American. Even yield-driven binomial lattice pricing models of the sort described in Chapter 3 are in general inadequate, because they ignore any potential variation in the *relative* interest rates for differing terms during the life of the option—that is, they ignore changes in the *term structure* of interest rates.

Multistep Arbitrage Opportunities

It can be shown that while such simple models are arbitrage free over a single lattice step, they are susceptible to more subtle, multistep arbitrage relationships having to do precisely with relationships among implied forward interest rates for different terms at different nodes of the lattice. Bookstaber et al. (1986), for example, took as their point of departure an analysis of some of the often-overlooked sources of arbitrage in traditional binomial pricing models. They pointed out that while most such models are carefully designed to avoid the possibility of arbitrage "in the small" (locally, over a single lattice step), they are all susceptible to arbitrage "in the large" (globally, over multistep periods). The source of these arbitrage opportunities is the *overdetermination* of such binomial models when they have to deal with instruments of multiple maturities. They key local arbitrage neutrality argument common to most such models, which assume only *two possible states* in the succeeding step, solves a set of three equations in three unknowns:

$$C = S\Delta + H$$
$$C_u = S_u\Delta + rH$$
$$C_d = S_d\Delta + rH$$

where S is the price of the underlying security at the current node

r is the one-period discounting rate at the current node

S_u, S_d, C_u, C_d are the values of the underlying security and the contingent claim at the up and down modes

and the variables to be solved for are:

C: the price of the contingent claim at the current mode
Δ: the hedge ratio
H: the cash component of the replicating portfolio

Bookstaber et al. showed that if arbitrage possibilities over two or more periods are considered, the prices of the *two-period* (and in general *n*-period) bonds must also be taken into account, and that "in an arbitrage-free model, the number of independently priced instruments cannot be greater than the number of states." Therefore, **binomial models are exposed to multistep arbitrage opportunities**.

Bookstaber et al. initially proposed resolving this difficulty by moving to a **multinomial model,** in which there would be $N + 1$ possible states of the world when there are N remaining periods. However, this leads to a lattice in which, as they noted, "the number of paths will grow factorially, and the size of the equation system will be quadratic in the number of periods." Noting that the source of the difficulty is the existence of N *independently priced* instruments, the discount bonds of term 1, . . . , N, the authors observed that by imposing certain restrictions on the yield curve, it is possible to resurrect a binomial lattice framework. While the authors did not completely specify an arbitrage-free model in their paper (they were mainly concerned with illustrating the multiple sources of arbitrage inconsistencies in the simpler binomial option pricing models in common use), the constraints they were led to impose on the yield curve look a lot like those introduced by Ho and Lee (1986) and by Dattatreya and Fabozzi (1989) in the models to be discussed below.

Variable Volatilities

The price-based models presented in Chapter 3 are also inadequate where the term of the option is significant in relation to the maturity of the underlying bond, because the *amortization to par* in the price of the underlying bond implies that *price volatilities cannot be constant over the life of the option.* For example, the range of possible outcomes at expiration (payoff scenarios) for a three-year option on a bond with three and one half years to maturity is *narrower* than for a one-year option on the same bond, since the price of the bond must approach par as it nears maturity.

Path Dependence

Another important limitation of the models presented in Chapter 3 is their inability to handle *path-dependent* effects. The values of certain kinds of options depend critically on the path followed by the price of the underlying security over the life of the option. For example, **down-and-out** options, which have been in existence since the mid-1960s, behave like ordinary European options except that a call (put) contract is cancelled, possibly with a rebate payment, if the underlying security price ever falls below (rises above) a certain level (see Cox and Rubinstein, 1985, for details). More recently, so-called **look-back** and **average-strike** options have been introduced. These option contracts have *uncertain strike prices*: a look-back call (put) option is European, but the strike price is the *minimum (maximum)* daily closing price of the underlying security over the life of the option. The strike price of an average-strike option is the *average* of the daily closing prices over its life. Clearly, evaluating the fair price of such an option requires examination of the path followed by prices over the entire life of the option.

There are a number of possible techniques for overcoming these limitations. Perhaps the most popular approach in recent years has been to adapt the lattice-based approach to take into account variations in the term structure, at the same time constraining interest rates at the various lattice nodes so as to avoid any arbitrage relationship. Two such classes of models are outlined and contrasted below. Of course, such models are more technically involved and computationally intensive than simpler models, but they are also more powerful. Properly applied, they allow the accurate pricing of a very wide range of complex options and other contingent claims. We will also describe the continuous-time term structure model of Cox et al. (1985), which attempts to model the evolution of interest rates in such a fashion that, at least for European options, an exact (albeit rather complicated) analytical solution is possible.

Simulation techniques have been used where it is necessary to fully capture *path-dependent* effects, although such methods are expensive computationally and are themselves subject to certain theoretical limitations. Such techniques are discussed later in this chapter. Finally, a variety of alternative models based on different assumptions about the driving price or yield dynamics have also been proposed to handle one or another of the limitations we have pointed out. We briefly survey some of these approaches in the last part of the chapter.

TERM STRUCTURE-BASED OPTION PRICING MODELS

Overview

To adequately handle long-dated options, including interest rate caps and floors, and other more complex bond and interest rate options, the potential variability among interest rates at different maturities must be taken into account. Instead of simply tracking the evolution of a single parameter, such as price or short-term interest rates, the *entire term structure of interest rates* is tracked, either continuously or by specifying a term structure at each node of a lattice, with appropriate up and down shifts. This allows the model to take into account the subtler dependencies of option value on variations in short-term interest rates as well as in the actual price or yield of the underlying security, the maturity of which, in the case of options on cash bonds, for example, may change significantly during the life of the option.

To facilitate comparison of the salient features, strengths, and weaknesses of the term structure-based models discussed here, we have attempted to present each in a common format, giving model assumptions, the methodology underlying each model's basic option valuation algorithm, some of the noteworthy properties of the model, and important limitations. Readers are urged to go to the original expositions, and to test the various models carefully in the context of their own particular needs, perhaps with the assistance of the Monte Carlo simulation techniques to be discussed later, before selecting one or another as most appropriate for their use.

Lattice-Based Term Structure Models

In general, this class of models requires as input the current yield curve (term structure). The model then specifies a stochastic process for shifting these rates up or down at successive nodes in the lattice. The rates themselves, the lattice transition probabilities, and/or the volatilities (step size) at each level are adjusted to ensure that the lattice is arbitrage free, and that the relevant underlying instruments are properly priced at the initial

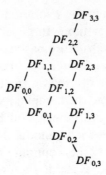

FIGURE 4.1 Lattice of discount functions.

node. Option prices are then calculated by working backward through the lattice very much as in the simpler binomial models.

All these models share certain common assumptions, which Ho and Lee (1986) aptly described as "the standard perfect capital market assumptions in a discrete state-time framework":

1. The market is *continuous* and *frictionless*, with no transaction costs.
2. The market is *discrete*, clearing at regular intervals or periods 1, . . . , T in time.
3. The market is *complete*, with riskless discount bonds of every maturity T.
4. The market has only a *finite number of states* at a given time period t. The market at state s and time t is completely characterized by a vector of interest rates $r_{s,t}(T)$ [the **yield curve** at node (s,t)], or by the equivalent **discount function** $DF_{s,t}(T)$ at node (s,t). [$DF_{s,t}(T)$ is just the price of a zero-coupon bond of maturity T. It tells us the value today of a dollar T periods in the future. Given a complete yield curve $r_{s,t}(T)$, we can solve for the discount function $DF_{s,t}(T)$ and vice versa.]

The general scheme of such a model is given in Figure 4.1. Note that $DF_{i,j}$ stands for the entire discount function $DF_{i,j}(T)$ at node (i,j), not just a single rate.

Continuous-Time Term Structure Models

Continuous-time term structure models, of which we discuss only that of Cox et al. (1985), seek an analytical solution to the stochastic differential equation characterizing the evolution of the price of an option, or other contingent claim, over time. In general, such models specify the *functional form* of the term structure based on certain model parameters. These parameters must be *estimated* based on empirical data, and a yield curve or term structure *fitted* based on the chosen functional form. The choice of functional form, and the complexity and economic intuitiveness of the model parameters, are determined by the larger framework of economic theory underlying such a model. Many idealizing assumptions are made about the market, the economy, and economic agents. The relative strengths and weaknesses of such models are briefly discussed below.

Ho and Lee's Arbitrage-Free Rate Movement Model

Dr. Thomas Ho has been one of the pioneers in the development of lattice-based term structure option pricing models. Over the past several years, he and his collaborators have developed a class of what they call AR (for **arbitrage-free rate movement**) models for pricing long-term contingent claims. In these models, an initial term structure is determined from a set of benchmark bonds covering all relevant maturities, and the evolution of the term structure as it moves through the lattice is then constrained in such a way that all the bonds so used are themselves automatically properly priced at the initial node. Such models have the property that they can simultaneously and consistently price a wide range of bonds and bond options in a *common* arbitrage-free universe.

Methodology

Ho and Lee (1986) presented a simplified version of the general AR model that makes clear the general principles on which this class of models are based. The central features of the methodology employed are as follows.

Estimation of the Initial Term Structure. First, a starting specification of the term structure of interest rates, or the corresponding discount function, must be determined. This can be accomplished in a number of ways (see, e.g., Vasicek and Fong, 1982). Typically, what is involved in choosing a universe or basket of bonds covering the relevant range of maturities for which good empirical pricing data are readily available; moreover, a particular *functional form* for the discount function or yield curve must be specified. (Vasicek and Fong used **exponential splines**.)

Estimates of the unknown parameter values for the specified functional form are obtained from empirical data using standard statistical techniques. The empirically determined discount function is thus one of the important inputs to the model.

Arbitrage Constraints on Rate Movements. The term structure of interest rates is assumed to evolve through time in such a way as to sastisfy certain natural constraints. Ho and Lee (1986) gave the term structure at a node (s,t) of the lattice by specifying the discount function $DF_{s,t}(T)$ at that node. (In the notation of their paper, this discount function is given by $P_i^{(n)}(T)$, at the i-th state of the n-th period in the lattice.) They assumed that the discount function evolves through time according to the rules:

$$DF_{s+1,t+1}(T) = \frac{DF_{s,t}(T + 1)}{DF_{s,t}(1)} h_u(T) \qquad \text{(up)}$$

and:

$$DF_{s,t+1}(T) = \frac{DF_{s,t}(T + 1)}{DF_{s,t}(1)} h_d(T) \qquad \text{(down)}$$

for all nodes (s,t) and all periods $T = 1, \ldots, N$ (see Figure 4.1). The functions $h_u(T)$ and $h_d(T)$ [$h(T)$ and $h^*(T)$ in Ho and Lee's terminology] are called the **perturbation functions**.

Note that $DF_{s,t}(T + 1)/DF_{s,t}(1)$ is just the T-period *forward rate* that would be implied at the node (s,t) in a *risk-free* (certain) universe. The perturbation functions $h_u(T)$ and $h_d(T)$, respectively, measure how the up and down states of the term structure differ from these implied forward rates. The *volatility* of the term structure is therefore embedded in these perturbation functions. [In general, $h_u(T)$ and $h_d(T)$ could depend on the node (s,t), but for simplicity Ho and Lee assumed in their paper that these functions are independent of s and t.]

In order for a lattice to be arbitrage free, we must first of all have:

$$DF_{s,t}(0) = 1, \quad \text{and} \quad DF_{s,t}(T - 1) > DF_{s,t}(T) \qquad (4.1a)$$

at all nodes (s,t) and for all periods T. (That is, the value of a dollar today must be a dollar, and a dollar tomorrow must never be worth *more* than its value today!) In addition, any *portfolio* of fairly priced bonds must itself be fairly priced. It can be shown [Ho and Lee (1986) included an appendix to this effect] that this implies that there must exist at each node (s,t) a parameter $\pi_{s,t}$ such that the prices $DF_{s,t}(T)$ of the T-period discount bonds at (s,t) are all equal to π-weighted linear combinations of the bond values one period forward, suitably discounted at the one-period rate for (s,t), *independent of T*. That is:

$$DF_{s,t}(T + 1)/DF_{s,t}(1)$$
$$= \pi_{s,t}DF_{s,t+1}(T) + (1 - \pi_{s,t})DF_{s+1,t+1}(T) \qquad (4.1b)$$

for all T.

To ensure the arbitrage-free character of the lattice of term structures, Ho and Lee therefore assumed that the perturbation functions obey the relationship:

$$\pi h_u(T) + (1 - \pi)h_d(T) = 1 \qquad (4.2)$$

for some constant π independent of time T and the initial discount function $DF_{0,0}(T)$. From the up and down equations defining $DF_{s,t}$ in terms of the perturbation functions, Equation 4.2 clearly implies that Equation 4.1b will be satisfied. (Again, while π could depend on s and t, for simplicity Ho and Lee assumed it does not.)

Path Independence Constraints on Rate Movements. To ensure **path independence**—that is, to ensure that the term structure resulting from an up step followed by a down step is the same as that resulting from a down step followed by an up step—we must have:

$$DF_{s+1,t+2}(T) = \left(\frac{DF_{s,t}(T + 2)}{DF_{s,t}(2)}\right)\left(\frac{h_u(T + 1)h_d(T)}{h_u(1)}\right)$$

$$= \left(\frac{DF_{s,t}(T + 2)}{DF_{s,t}(2)}\right)\left(\frac{h_d(T + 1)h_u(T)}{h_d(1)}\right)$$

and hence:

$$h_u(T + 1)h_d(T)h_d(1) = h_d(T + 1)h_u(T)h_u(1)$$

It can be shown that together with the condition in Equation 4.2, this implies that there must exist a parameter δ [again assumed for simplicity to be independent of the node (s,t)] such that:

$$h_u(T) = \frac{1}{\pi + (1 + \pi)\delta^T} \quad \text{for } T \geq 0 \qquad (4.3a)$$

and:

$$h_d(T) = \frac{\delta^T}{\pi + (1 + \pi)\delta^T} \qquad (4.3b)$$

Together with the initial discount function $DF_{0,0}(t)$, the parameters π and δ completely specify the evolution of the term structure. (More complex AR models may have π and δ dependent on state s and time t as well, as we have noted.) Ho and Lee showed in their paper that under these assumptions, an interest rate-contingent claim $C_{s,t}$ can then be evaluated by working backward through the lattice using the following relationship:

$$C_{s,t} = [\pi C_{s,t+1} + (1 - \pi)C_{s+1,t+1}] DF_{s,t}(1) \qquad (4.4)$$

Interpretation of Parameters

The parameter π in Ho and Lee's AR model can be interpreted as a kind of "risk-neutral probability"—it is precisely that "probability" at which the price of a T-period bond today is equal to the present value of its expected value in one period. Equation 4.1 can be interpreted as stating that:

$$\pi = (r - d)/(u - d)$$

where r is the one-period riskless return, and u and d are the one-period returns in the up and down scenarios. This relationship should be familiar from our discussion of the simpler binomial lattice models in Chapter 3 (see Equation 3.11). Equation 4.4 thus says that, as in those simpler models, the value of the option or contingent claim in state $(s,t), C_{s,t}$, is just as its *expected present value* in a risk-neutral universe.

The interpretation of the parameter δ is slightly less straightforward. As Ho and Lee noted, δ determines the *spread* between the two perturbation functions, $h_u(T)$ and $h_d(T)$. The larger the spread, the greater the variability in the term structures. Thus, δ is connected with the *volatility of the term structure*. Note, however, that this volatility varies *inversely* with δ.

Estimation of Parameters

Ho and Lee noted that one must "use a nonlinear estimation procedure to determe π and δ such that the theoretical prices of a sample of contingent claims can best fit their observed prices. The estimated values of π and δ are then used to price other contingent claims." This is not a trivial procedure. A very simplified approach would be to take two securities, for example, a two-year option on a five-year bond and a three-year option on a ten-year bond, and calculate their values according to the model using some initial best guess at values for π and δ. The resulting theoretical values will in general differ from the observed market values for both securities, so π and δ must then be modified to give new theoretical values better fitting the observed market prices. This process is repeated until the theoretical prices are close enough to the market prices, or until further improvement becomes impossible. At least two different securities are required, because there will in general be a range of pairs of values for π and δ giving the *same* price for any single given security. In general, a basket of several securities would be used. As Ho and Lee noted, this process is similar to the estimation of implied volatilities for bonds or bond futures from market prices of options on those securities.

Properties of the Model

The Ho and Lee AR model allows one to model the variability in the term structure of interest rates with time in a relatively straightforward and satisfactory fashion, driven by the two parameters π and δ, which can be estimated from market data. It provides consistent, arbitrage-free prices for a specific universe of bonds and options. Since it is driven off an initial term structure that is empirically derived, it is a *relative* pricing model. The initial term structure is specified *exogenously*. This differs from some other models that generate *endogenous* yield curves driven, for example, by a short-rate stochastic process. This can be a strength where what is required is a measure of the relative richness or cheapness of securities within the given universe.

Because of the way in which the term structures are constrained, this model automatically accounts for the amortization to par experienced by all bonds. A T-period bond will initially have a price determined by the initial, empirically determined term structure; as it matures, it will show greater price variability up to a certain point—that is, there will be a considerable range of implied prices for $T/2$-period bonds at time $t = T/2$, for example. But as the bond approaches its maturity, its price variability will decline again; there will be very little price variability among one-period bonds at time $t = T - 1$. What this says is that the assumed dynamic for term structures (or discount functions) implies a price distribution for bonds that *automatically* converges to par as the bonds approach their maturity. Of course, this also implies that implied *price volatilities* for individual bonds are time dependent in these models.

Limitations of the Model

These AR models do have some limitations. The term structure process imposed by the constraints and initial conditions can sometimes lead to implied negative forward rates, at least in the simplified version specified in Ho and Lee (1986). It has also been pointed out that Ho and Lee's model implies a common volatility for all interest rates (see Hull, 1989). In practice long-term interest rates are normally less volatile than short-term rates.

Estimation of model parameters is not always easy; it is assumed that the parameters π and δ are properties of the term structure of interest rates, rather than of any one bond or class of bonds. It is therefore assumed that one can back out appropriate values for these parameters by adjusting their values until some appropriately chosen class of securities for which market prices are readily available is properly priced by the model. It is assumed that this estimation process is stable with respect to changes in the choice of reference securities used in the estimation process, and that the parameter values will not change rapidly with time. All these assumptions require further testing and verification.

Moreover, like all lattice-based models, these AR models are computation-intensive. The production versions of these models, as marketed by Global Advanced Technology Corporation, make use of a customized vector processor board, making them dependent on proprietary hardware (as well as software) technology. Nevertheless, their power and theoretical consistency has led to wide use by many financial firms.

Dattatreya and Fabozzi's Rate Movement Model

Dattatreya and Fabozzi (1989) presented a "simplified" debt options valuation model that is essentially a one-parameter, binomial model driven off an initial yield curve, with the resulting moving term structure adjusted and constrained to avoid arbitrage relationships and properly price a selected universe of bonds at the initial lattice mode. Variants of this model have been in common use in the securities industry for some years.

Methodology

Dattatreya and Fabozzi broke their approach down into four separate methodological steps: (a) determination of the initial yield curve; (b) generation of the basic interest rate process; (c) assurance of *internal consistency* in the basic valuation algorithm; and (d) calibration of the model to ensure *external consistency*.

Determination of the Initial Yield Curve. As in Ho and Lee's AR model, the initial yield curve is defined as a *discount function*, derived from the prices of current-coupon Treasury securities, statistically fitted and interpolated to give a smooth curve for all intermediate maturities.

Generation of the Basic Interest Rate Process. Dattatreya and Fabozzi assumed that the evolution of the term structure through their lattice is driven *explicitly* by the short rate. They pointed out that their model framework can accommodate a variety of choices for the stochastic process governing the evolution of the short rate. In their exposition, they chose a lognormal process, with a fixed volatility (independent of time). A preliminary lattice of short-rate values was then generated according to the specified process.

Assurance of Internal Consistency: The Basic Valuation Algorithm. Dattatreya and Fabozzi's basic valuation algorithm defined the value of any security to be the *path average* of its values over all possible paths through the lattice to the terminal level. This is shown to be equivalent to the result of **sequential backward averaging:** working backward through the lattice, calculating the *expected present value* of the security at each node. That is, the value $C_{s,t}$ of a security at node (s,t) is given by:

$$C_{s,t} = [pC_{s+1,t+1} + (1 - p)C_{s,t+1}]/1 + r_{s,t}/100 \qquad (4.5)$$

where p is the probability of an up step in the lattice

$r_{s,t}$ is the short rate at node (s,t) in percentage terms

(This formula can be suitably adjusted to take into account intermediate cash flows, such as coupon payments.)

Calibration for External Consistency. Given the initial lattice of short rates, theoretical prices can be calculated for the zero-coupon bonds of varying maturities using this process of backward averaging through the resulting lattice. The resulting prices will *not* in general correspond to those in the initial discount function fitted to empirical data. To ensure consistency with the empirically given external data, the rates in the lattice are modified to meet the given constraints. The rates at each level

FIGURE 4.2 Lattice of short rates (ZCB_1 = 96.15; ZCB_2 = 92.86).

t in the lattice are successively adjusted by a level-specific *drift* parameter, chosen to ensure that the (t + 1)-period zero-coupon bond is
properly priced by the backward averaging process.

Consider the initial lattice of short rates shown in Figure 4.2. Suppose
that the one- and two-period zero-coupon bonds are priced, respectively,
at 96.15 and 92.86 (decimal). The one-period zero-coupon bond is already
properly priced, since the unique discounting rate for the first period,
$r_{0,0}$, is *defined* by the one-period zero-coupon bond. To ensure that the
two-period zero-coupon bond is properly priced, the rates at level 1 in
the lattice are adjusted. For example, using the initial lattice of rates, we
find that the *theoretical* price of the two-period zero-coupon bond (ZCB)
is:

$$ZCB_2 = \left(\frac{100}{1.044} + \frac{100}{1.03635} \right) \Big/ (2 \times 1.04)$$

$$= \frac{95.7854 + 96.4925}{2.08} = 92.4412$$

which is different from the actual price of 92.86. It is therefore necessary
to add a drift constant of -0.938 at level 1, so that the theoretical price
is the same as the actual price (see Figure 4.3):

$$ZCB_2 = \left(\frac{100}{1.03931} + \frac{100}{1.03166} \right) \Big/ (2 \times 1.04)$$

$$= \frac{96.2177 + 96.9312}{2.08} = 92.8600$$

Next, to ensure that the three-period zero-coupon bond is properly

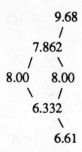

FIGURE 4.3 Lattice of short rates after adding drift term at level 1.

priced, the rates at level 2 are adjusted, and so forth. Note that *we use the one-period rates just calculated to discount over the first period*; only the rates at a single level are adjusted at each step.

Dattatreya and Fabozzi noted that the model could also be calibrated by modifying the *transition probabilities*, but that this would also change the volatility and lognormal distribution assumptions. By adjusting the rates by an additive drift constant, the volatility and distribution assumptions are preserved.

Once the lattice of rates has been properly adjusted and calibrated, options—or any other security with clearly defined contingent cash flows—may be priced using the by now familiar backward averaging approach (always discounting at the appropriate local short rate, of course!) The essential pricing algorithm is given in Equation 4.5, iterated through the lattice back to the initial node.

Interpretation of Parameters

The Dattatreya and Fabozzi model has the advantage that its parameters are quite intuitive—the short rate is governed by a lognormal process with a specified volatility. The moving term structure generated by this process is, however, initially *endogenous* rather than exogenous—it is entirely determined by the short-rate stochastic process. The empirical yield curve enters in only through the somewhat ad-hoc calibration process, and it is hence somewhat less explicit than in the Ho and Lee model just how the entire term structure of interest rates evolves with time. (What is the implied volatility of *long*-term rates, for example?) In this respect, Dattatreya and Fabozzi's model is closer to the simple rate-driven lattice-based models of Chapter 3.

The transition probabilities also play an explicit role in this model, through the backward averaging process, and a different choice of transition probabilities may, in general, lead to different prices. Dattatreya and Fabozzi assumed transition probabilities of 1:2 throughout in their exposition, but it is unclear why other probabilities might not be chosen. (A choice of transition probabilities other than 1:2 would imply a market drift, and hence a bullish or bearish view on the market.) Of course, this would imply a different rate distribution and would lead to different calibrated rates. Calibration guarantees that the universe of zero-coupon bonds is always properly priced, but it is unclear whether the resulting prices of other contingent claims would still be the same.

Properties of the Model

The Dattatreya and Fabozzi model provides a relatively simple and straightforward approach to pricing long-term and path-dependent interest rate–contingent claims. Like the Ho and Lee AR models, this approach guarantees proper pricing of the initial universe of bonds used to specify the empirical yield curve—the calibration process forces such pricing. Parameter estimation is likely to be simpler than in the Ho and Lee models, if only because the short rate is more immediately accessible than supposed structural properties of the term structure as a whole.

As the authors of this model pointed out, it can also be used to calculate an **option-adjusted spread (OAS)** for non-Treasury securities. Such a spread arises from the fact that higher discount rates must generally be used in discounting cash flows from lower quality (riskier) non-Treasury securities, else the resulting prices will be too high. By solving iteratively for the appropriate spread to the short rate to be added uniformly throughout the lattice in order to generate observed market prices for such securities, an implied OAS can be calculated. (Note that such an OAS is spread to the *short rate*, and may be somewhat different from OAS values as defined by some other models. It will have much the same qualitative behavior and significance, however.)

These authors also noted in their paper that one of the consequences of the arbitrage-free constraints is that "the average or expected return from all securities for any horizon is the same."

Limitations of the Model

As noted above, this model is similar in many ways to the simpler lattice-based models of Chapter 3, and it shares some of their limitations. Volatilities are assumed to be constant through time. The evolution of the term structure of interest rates is driven directly by the short-rate stochastic process. It is unclear how some traditional measures of sensitivity (to changes in the price or yield of the underlying security, for example, or to changes in the volatility of the underlying security) could be evaluated. (The authors addressed this problem by introducing a new sensitivy measure called the **stochastic duration**, defined as the *price sensitivity to variations in the level of short-term rates*. This is an interesting measure, but lacks the intuitive appeal of traditional duration, and is unlikely to replace the option delta in most traders' minds!)

Cox et al.'s Equilibrium Term Structure Model

In an influential theoretical paper, Cox et al. (1985) have presented a continuous-time analytical model of the evolution of the term structure of interest rates. This model, which draws on the author's earlier work on a general equilibrium theory of a continuous-time competitive economy, allows for exact analytical solution of the stochastic differential equations governing the price of European bond options, and provides a very general framework for the analysis of other interest rate–dependent securities.

Methodology

The model takes as its starting point a specialization of the earlier equilibrium theory developed by these researchers. As they stated in the introduction to their paper, "we consider the problem of determining the term structure as being a problem in general equilibrium theory, and our approach contains elements of all the previous theories. Anticipation of future events is important, as are risk preferences and the characteristics of other investment alternatives. Also, individuals can have specific preferences about the timing of their consumption, and thus have, in that sense, a preferred habitat. Our model thus permits detailed predictions about how changes in a wide range of underlying variables will affect the term structure."

The authors formulated a stochastic differential equation governing the evolution of an equilibrium interest rate, r:

$$dr = \kappa(\theta - r)dt + \sigma\sqrt{r}\,dz \tag{4.6}$$

where σ is the volatility

θ is a long-term central value of the rate r

κ is a parameter governing the rate of autoregression toward θ

z is a stochastic variable the behavior of which is determined by the assumptions of the authors' general economic theory

From Equation 4.6, the authors derived an equation for the evolution of the price of a discount bond of maturity T at time t:

$$P(r,t,T) = (\tfrac{1}{2}\, \sigma^2 r P_{rr} + \kappa(\theta - r)P_r + P_t - \lambda r P_t)/r \qquad (4.7)$$

where $P(r,t,T)$ is the price of a discount bond of term T at time t for rate r

σ, θ, and κ are as above

λ is a measure of the market price of risk

(The subscripts denote partial derivatives. For example, P_t is $\partial P/\partial t$, the derivative of P, *viewed as a function of time t*, with respect to t.) This equation has as its solution the expression:

$$P(r,t,T) = A(t,T)e^{-B(t,T)r} \qquad (4.8)$$

where:

$$A(t,T) = \left[\frac{2\gamma e^{(t\kappa + \lambda + \gamma)(T-t)/2}}{(\kappa + \lambda + \gamma)(e^{\gamma(T-t)} - 1) + 2\gamma} \right]^{2\kappa\theta/\sigma^2}$$

$$B(t,T) = \frac{2(e^{\gamma(T-t)} - 1)}{(\kappa + \lambda + \gamma)(e^{\gamma(T-t)} - 1) + 2\gamma}$$

and:

$$\gamma = [(\kappa + \lambda)^2 + 2\sigma^2]^{1/2}$$

Note that the market risk parameter, λ, here plays a role in determining bond prices.

The corresponding formula for the yield to maturity of a discount bond of maturity T at time t is:

$$R(r,t,T) = \frac{rB(t,T) - \log A(t,T)}{(T - t)} \qquad (4.9)$$

Finally, as an illustration of the applicability of their model to the pricing of contingent claims, the authors determined the value of a European call option:

$$C(r,t,T,s,K) = P(r,t,s)\chi^2 \left[2r^*[\phi + \psi + B(T,s)]; \frac{4\kappa\theta}{\sigma^2}, \frac{2\phi^2 re^{\gamma(T-t)}}{\phi + \psi + B(T,s)} \right]$$

$$- KP(r,t,T)\chi^2 \left[2r^*[\phi + \psi]; \frac{4\kappa\theta}{\sigma^2}, \frac{2\phi^2 re^{\gamma(T-t)}}{\phi + \psi} \right] \quad (4.10)$$

where:

$$\phi = \frac{2\gamma}{\sigma^2(e^{\gamma(T-t)} - 1)}$$

$$\psi = (\kappa + \lambda + \gamma)/\sigma^2$$

$$r^* = \left[\log\left(\frac{A(T,s)}{K}\right) \right] \Big/ B(T,s)$$

and $\chi^2(.)$ is the noncentral chi-square distribution

γ is the interest rate parameter

t is the time of evaluation

T is the term of the option

s is the maturity of the underlying bond

K is the strike price

Other parameters are as above [r^* is the interest rate below which exercise will occur; that is, $K = P(r^*,T,s)$.]

Properties of the Model

One of the obvious, interesting properties of this model is that interest rates, and hence bond and option prices, depend on the market price of risk. Cox et al. pointed out that "risk aversion will cause forward rates to be systematically greater than expected spot rates, usually by an amount increasing with maturity. The term premium is the increment

required to induce investors to hold longer-term ("riskier") securities."
Their model also implies that "as we consider longer and longer maturities, the yield approaches a limit which is independent of the current
interest rate." This limiting long-term rate is expressed, from Equation
4.9, by:

$$R(r,t,\infty) = \frac{2\kappa\theta}{\gamma + \kappa + \lambda} \qquad (4.11)$$

When the spot rate is below this long-term yield, the term structure is
upward sloping. When rates are above $\kappa\theta/(\kappa + \lambda)$, the term structure is
downward sloping. For intermediate values, the yield curve is humped.
In his discussion of the Cox et al. model, Hull (1989) pointed out that,
whereas the Ho and Lee model implies *equal* volatility rates for interest
rates of all maturities, the Cox et al. model assumes that the long-term
rate has *zero* volatility!

The Cox et al. model is very much an *endogenous* term structure
model, because the shape of the yield curve is determined by the parametric functional form imposed by the authors' theoretical assumptions.
The model parameters, κ, θ, σ, and λ, must be estimated from market
data, but the resulting yield curve will always only approximately fit the
empirical yield curve at any given point in time.

Although the pricing formula given by this model may appear formid-
able, it is a closed analytical formula, and therefore computationally very
efficient. Option sensitivies, including sensitivities to all model parameters, are also straightfoward to compute, and the authors in fact discussed the qualitative behavior of bond prices with respect to changes
in the model parameters, based on Equation 4.8, in their paper.

Limitations of the Model

The ideas introduced by Cox et al. in their model have been seminal in
a number of ways in the development of term structure-driven models.
Some practicing professionals may find the dependence of the Cox et al.
model on the assumptions of their general equilibrium theory disturbing,
because, like all economic theories, this represents a considerable ideal-
ization of reality. Most of the theoretical assumptions are quite general,
however, and are shared by many other econometric models. The gen-
erality of the model, and the way its dependence on key economic parameters is made explicit, are, if anything, to be counted as strengths.

The accuracy and stability of parameter estimation, however, are real issues.

Of somewhat more concern is the fact that the parametric functional form of the term structure will rarely exactly fit current empirical market data. This means that model parameters would have to be tuned, or some adjustment made, such as adding an appropriate spread, to bring the price of specific underlying securities in line with reality when pricing options on them. Internal theoretical consistency is bought at the price of some dissonance with empirical market data.

Some readers may be unhappy with the zero volatility of very long-term rates implied by this model, but it is questionable whether this is any more troublesome than the constant volatility across maturities implied by the Ho and Lee model. Any model that does not explicitly introduce time- and term-dependent volatilities as parameters will suffer from some such distortions.

Equation 4.10 as it stands is incapable of adequately handling the early exercise feature of American-style options. This is a serious limitation, because many traded long-dated options are in fact American, and the premium for early exercise can be significant, particularly for puts. It is possible to apply the general theoretical framework of this model in a discrete (lattice-based) framework, however, to take into account features such as early exercise. In fact, the authors noted that a discrete-time equivalent of their model has been tested by Wood (1964), although not in an option pricing context.

SIMULATION METHODS

There are times when an option contract (or some other contingent claim) depends on one or more parameters in a way that is intrinsically path dependent; that is, in such a fashion that we *cannot* assume that up and down steps cancel out. This will be true, for example, when we deal with **look-back options,** the strike prices of which are based on the *minimum* or *maximum* daily closing price of the underlying security over the life of the option. In such a case, the lattice opens out into a tree of possibilities, and we must resort to simulation techniques.

Description of Simulation Methodology

Simulation methods, like all pricing models, make certain assumptions about how key parameters evolve through time. Like the lattice-based models, a simulation method will typically break time (the term to option expiration, or to maturity of a mortgage, for example) into some number N of discrete steps. At each step, the key parameter or parameters (price, yield, short term rate, etc.) are assumed to move as random variables, according to certain specified probability distributions. If we were to proceed as in the lattice-based models, the parameters would move up or down (or possibly to one of three or more states) at each step. Were we to attempt to evaluate all possible paths through such a tree, however, we would be faced with evaluating at least 2^N terminal states, since we cannot in general assume that any two sequences of up and down steps bring us to a common node. For even relatively small values of N, this is computationally prohibitive; for $N = 20$ there are over a million terminal nodes, and for $N = 30$ over a billion.

Simulation models get around this exponential proliferation of paths by sampling the set of all possible paths—they compute some large but manageable subset of paths through the tree, called *runs*, and statistically average the results of whatever calculations are to be performed over the given set of paths. Any two runs are completely independent, and each represents a different possible realization of the random model parameters over this time. Each run is like playing out a self-contained scenario in time. For example, if we know the history of interest rate levels at each step in time, we can determine even path-dependent interest rate-contingent cash flows, and hence, by appropriately discounting back (using the discounting rates generated at each step of our scenario), the current value of a security. Each run will generate a *different* price for such securities. Some of these runs may produce highly unlikely results, but the great majority, and hence the average, will tend toward the most likely outcome. The more runs are used the more accurate will be the convergence of the simulation average to the "true" price of the security in question.

Conceptually, this methodology is *estimating* the *expected value* of some quantity, such as an option value, over all possible future scenarios, given some probabilistic assumptions about how key variables will evolve through time. General statistical principles assure that for a sufficiently large sample size (number of runs), the resulting estimate can be made as stable and exact as we desire. More precisely, for a given number of steps N, tolerance ϵ, and probability p, we can find a number M such that the result of averaging M or more runs will be within ϵ of the "true" expected value with probability at least p. (Note that this is *not* a guarantee that the resulting value will be within ϵ of the real-world value of the security in question; this depends critically on other factors, such as the correctness of our assumptions about the processes governing the evolution of key parameters, and the accuracy of any initial inputs.

In practice, this scheme is modified in several ways. Since we are no longer constrained to follow the branches in a binomial (or multinomial) lattice, the stochastic model variables are often allowed to evolve from step to step as *continuous* random variables, taking on any permissible value according to the probability distribution specifying their process. This allows for smoother modeling of the evolution of key parameters through time. Additional constraints may be placed on the allowable paths—negative or very large interest rates may be disallowed. And for some applications, the parameter values generated for a given set of runs may be *normalized* to meet certain initial conditions or constraints—for example, the interest rates generated in a rate-driven simulation might be adjusted to ensure that the model properly prices certain benchmark securities, such as the current-issue Treasury securities.

Simulation methods permit extraction of important additional information along with the primary output (usually a security price). For example, the variance of individual prices over the set of all runs gives a measure of reliability, or confidence interval, for the resulting price. Extreme values among the runs can be valuable as the kind of worst case scenario analysis. Statistics can also be accumulated on the behavior of model parameters over the course of the runs, so, for example, we could get a sense of just how likely it is, given modeling assumptions, that interest rates will rise above, or fall below, some critical outlying levels (such as levels at which the user might begin to question the applicability of the modeling assumptions!).

Simulation Methods and Model Evaluation

In a novel application, Bookstaber (1989) pointed out that simulation methods can be used to validate other option pricing models *even when the detailed assumptions of the model to be evaluated are unknown!* As Bookstaber noted, the key to such an evaluation methodology is the fact that an option position can be *dynamically hedged* by an appropriately leveraged position in the underlying security and cash. That is, it should always be possible to construct a position:

$$S\Delta + H \tag{4.12}$$

where Δ is the option delta or hedge ratio

S is a unit of the underlying security

H is a (possibly negative) cash amount

which is equivalent in value to the option; and, as an option hedge, this position should be *self-financing* over the life of the option. For a call option, for example, this would mean that we could initially *sell* the call, receiving C dollars (the presumed fair price of the option), and *buy* $S\Delta$ of the underlying security, which might require borrowing some quantity H in addition to the proceeds from the written call. As time passed, we should always be able to adjust our position in the underlying security, possibly financing any purchases required by increased borrowing, in such a way that *at option expiration we should at least break even.* (Transaction costs are ignored in this argument, but interest on borrowed money—or on invested proceeds from the written call—is taken into account; it is calculated at each step at the current short rate.) This is the heart of the **arbitrage neutrality** argument behind all lattice pricing models, as explained in Chapter 3. Given *any* option pricing model, even a black box, which produces option prices *and sensitivities* (at least hedge ratios), we can simulate many interest rate scenarios (or paths driven by other stochastic model parameters) and simply play out our dynamic hedging strategy along each path. We construct an initial position:

$$S\Delta + H = C$$

using the option price C and hedge ratio Δ provided by the model to be tested, adjust the position at each lattice step using the model-generated value of Δ at that step, and measure how far our final position differs from the option value at expiration (which will *not* depend on the model, because we will know with certainty in each scenario how far in or out of the money we end up!). We can then compute the average final hedging error over all runs, as well as other statistics, such as the average *maximum* hedging error over the life of the option (the amount by which the hedge position $S\Delta + H$ differs from the model-generated option price C at any given lattice step). This allows us to evaluate any pricing model *on its own terms.*

Note that with this approach, we are simultaneously evaluating the prices and sensitivities given by the model. This is quite natural; as we will see in Chapter 6, hedge ratios are as important as prices to most options traders. Bookstaber also suggested ways in which the simulation paths generated can be driven off empirical market data, so as to avoid any biases introduced by assuming a particular theoretical distribution of the driving stochastic variable. For many of the more complicated option pricing models, and particularly for those where the dependence on parameters and parameter estimation is complex and/or poorly understood, such applications of simulation methodology could be extremely valuable.

Limitations of Simulation Methodology

Simulation models do have certain limitations. For example, they are not generally applicable for calculating the values of American options, which require a comparison of intrinsic value (value if exercised immediately) and option value (value if *not* exercised) at each step. To compute the value of the unexercised (American) option at step k, we would have to spawn another entire simulation, "rooted" at this step, because the option value cannot be calculated based only on the known parameter values for the current run. The recursive nature of this bootstrapping process would quickly make the number of calculations required grow prohibitively!

Since each run of a simulation model is a straightforward calculation of option (or other) values given certain hypothetical values of the parameters at each step, it can be simpler conceptually than many lattice-based models. However, since a large number (hundreds, often thousands) of runs are required to produce stable, reliable results, simulation models can be highly computation intensive. For this reason, simulation models are sometimes most useful in confirming the accuracy and robustness of other, of necessity more approximate pricing models, or in quantifying the ways in which such models appear to deviate from exact values, rather than in day-to-day production.

EXAMPLE 4.1: LOOK-BACK AND AVERAGE-STRIKE OPTIONS

One situation in which simulation techniques would be appropriate is in the evaluation of look-back and average-strike options. A **look-back option** is a European option with an initially indeterminate strike; at expiration, the contract holder has the option to exercise at a strike price equal to *the minimum (for calls) or maximum (for puts) of the daily closing prices* of the underlying security over the life of the option. Clearly, the strike price, and hence the value of the option, is *path dependent*: even on the expiration date, it is necessary to know the entire history of the security price over the life of the option in order to determine its value.

A lattice-based approach would be inappropriate, because the lattice would not be *closed*; it would open out into a tree with 2^N nodes at the N-th level. A simulation approach is clearly more appropriate; at the end of each run we will know the strike price, and hence the option value, which can then be discounted back at the appropriate rates to give a present value to be averaged with that from other runs.

An **average-strike option** is one for which the strike price is set to the *average of all daily closing prices* over the life of the option, rather than the maximum or minimum of these. Again, the strike, and hence the option value at expiration, are unavoidably path dependent, and a simulation approach is indicated.

EXAMPLE 4.2: MORTGAGE OAS MODELING

This book is not primarily addressed to those working with mortgage-backed securities, and we have made no effort to lay the groundwork necessary to understand these complex instruments. Because some of the techniques required for long-term option pricing, and particularly simulation techniques, are widely used with these securities, however, an example is not out of place. The material in this section is not intended as a full introduction to mortgage-backed securities, nor to the associated option-related pricing techniques, and some readers may wish to omit it.

Mortgage-backed securities are, as the name suggests, securities backed by a pool of government agency-guaranteed mortgages. Principal and interest payments from the mortgages in the pool are passed through to the security holder. Mortgages themselves are very heterogeneous as to face amount, issue date, terms of interest payments, and the like. Only by pooling many individual mortgages, and thus homogenizing them to some extent, can mortgage-backed securities with a definite coupon and maturity be created. Nevertheless, they remain more complex than U.S. Treasury securities and many other securities in many respects. For background on mortgage-backed securities, including the uses of option pricing techniques, see Fabozzi (1988).

One of the key ways in which mortgage-backed securities differ from other bonds is in their prepayment risk. This is the risk that, as interest rates fall, a significant proportion of homeowners will chose to refinance their mortgages, paying off existing mortgages at higher interest terms in exchange for lower current rates. This in turn can lead to sudden, unexpectedly large cash flows to the holders of mortgage-backed securities at precisely the wrong time for profitable reinvestment (because rates are assumed to have fallen). Thus, prepayment risk is a form of reinvestment risk.

Prepayment risk can be viewed as a kind of *option*: the homeowner has the option to prepay the mortgage at any time. However, home-owners will sometimes exercise this option even when it is not advantageous—for example, when they must sell their home for some reason. The amount of principal prepayment to date is clearly a *path dependent* feature of mortgage-backed securities—it will be sharply higher if interest rates have dipped significantly in the course of the security's life than if they have remained flat.

Estimation of yields on mortgage-backed securities is thus complicated by uncertainty about future cash flows as a result of prepayment considerations. Static cash flow yield calculations, based on coupon, remaining term, scheduled amortization, and prepayment assumptions, are relatively straightforward but exhibit extreme sensitivity to changes in prepayment assumptions. Because of prepayment uncertainty and other factors, mortgage instruments trade at a *yield spread* to Treasury instruments. Rather than calculating mortgage yields directly, we can seek to evaluate the yield spread instead. This can be accomplished by simulating the evolution of the term structure of interest rates, driven off the current Treasury yield curve. For example, the short rate might be assumed to obey a random process given by:

$$r_{t+1} = r_t + \sigma_1 x \tag{4.13}$$

where r_t is the short rate at step t

σ_1 is the short rate volatility

x is a normally or lognormally distributed random variable

and the spread of the long rate to the short rate might be modeled by a mean-reverting process given by:

$$s_{t+1} = s_t + \sigma_2 y - \alpha(s_t - s_0) \tag{4.14}$$

where s_t is the spread from long to short rate at step t

σ_2 is the volatility of this spread

α governs the severity of mean reversion

s_0 is the mean to which the spread reverts

y is a normally or lognormally distributed random variable

Rates determined by such a process for a set of simulation runs could then be normalized to the discount function implied by the current Treasury yield curve in much the same way as was done in some of the models presented earlier.

Prepayment assumptions can then be applied with considerable precision *at each step*, because current interest rates are assumed to be known. The resulting cash flows in each simulation run are then discounted back to give a hypothetical price for the mortgage-backed security at the initial step, and these hypothetical prices are averaged over all simulation runs, giving a theoretical (model) price for the security in question. The resulting theoretical price will, in general, differ from the observed market price. The theoretical price can be brought in line with the market price by adding an appropriate *spread* to the rates used in discounting the cash flows back at each step. This spread would be solved for iteratively in a fashion similar to that used to solve for the *additive drift* values in Dattatreya and Fabozzi's model, although the calculations involved here are more intricate. Because it is determined by optionlike features of the mortgage, such as the prepayment risk, this spread is known as the **option-adjusted spread (OAS)** for the security.

(Some readers may wonder why simulation techniques can be applied to an option that, on the face of it, looks American in character. Objections to the use of such techniques do not apply here because the prepayment function, which specifies the expected level of prepayments at a given level of interest rates, is determined *exogenously*; it is not calculated as part of the modeling process.)

It should be observed that an actual *option price* is not computed in the process of calculating the OAS; instead, a yield spread corresponding to an embedded option-related feature of the given mortgage-backed security is calculated. Many of the details of parameter estimation, normalization, and the like have deliberately been omitted; what we wish to emphasize with this example is the wide applicability of option pricing techniques to the related issue of valuing interest rate-contingent features of many securities.

OTHER OPTION PRICING MODELS

There are a wealth of alternative option pricing models, each with certain special features that may recommend it in special circumstances. These include models where more than one stochastic variable is assumed to drive interest rates and prices (so-called two-factor and multiple-factor models), others where the driving variables are assumed to satisfy more complex probability distributions than the normal or lognormal distributions, and combinations of these. There are also differences in the numerical methods used to approximate option values where no exact analytical solution is possible.

Multiple Factors and Variant Distributions

Brennan and Schwartz (1982) developed a model driven by two interest rates (long term and short term) rather than one; the two rates are assumed to obey a bivariate lognormal distribution. Other investigators have proposed similar models driven, for example, by the short rate and inflation rate. Merton (1977), and subsequently Ball and Torous (1983), investigated models incorporating time-dependent volatilities—in the case of Ball and Torous, by postulating a so-called Brownian Bridge process, a stochastic process conditioned by the constraint that both beginning and ending values be fixed (thus explicitly recognizing the convergence of bond prices to par). Merton (1976) and others also investigated models incorporating discontinuous jump processes. Courtadon (1982), building on the work of Cox et al. (1981) and others, developed models assuming a mean-reverting process (another way of handling convergence to par), using finite difference methods to solve the resulting stochastic differential equations.

Analytical Approximations

In another direction, Barone-Adesi and Whaley (1987) developed a fast, accurate analytical approximation for American option values that is of considerable value when more exact lattice-based methods would be prohibitively computation intensive. They derived the stochastic differential equation for American option values in a form in which one term, which can be shown to be very small most of the time, can be dropped, giving rise to a simpler equation that can be solved explicitly. Their method is demonstrably more efficient than other finite-difference and binomial algorithms. Geske and Johnson (1984) took another approach to approximating the value of an American put option, viewing it as the limiting value of a series of *compound options* that can be exercised only at a finite number of points in time. For example, if the term of an American put option is T, we can consider the options P_1, which is the corresponding European option; P_2, an option exercisable only at time $T/2$ and at expiration; P_3, an option exercisable only at time $T/3$, $2T/3$, and at expiration; and so forth. These compound European options can be valued analytically, albeit by formulas somewhat more complex than those presented in Chapter 3, and the value of the original American put is then the limit of this sequence. It should be noted, however, that analytical approximations for option *sensitivities* (delta, time decay, etc.) in these models are often considerably less accurate than are the approximations of the options prices themselves.

Hull (1989) surveyed a range of alternative pricing models from the point of view of how well they correct for what are frequently seen as biases in the pricing distribution for stocks given by the most popular, lognormal price process (which underlies Black-Scholes as well as a number of other pricing models.) Empirical distributions of stock prices have frequently been observed to have fatter tails and other deviations from the theoretical lognormal distribution. This is of some relevance to us, because empirical bond prices and yields also deviate from ideal theoretical distributions. Hull concluded that "No single alternative to the Black-Scholes model seems superior . . . . The best strategy appears to be to use an extension of the Black-Scholes model which captures the effects of dividends and early exercise opportunities." (Of course, we have seen that the Black-Scholes model is also inadequate for at least longer dated bond options.)

Research continues on a wealth of more sophisticated options pricing models. A few of these will undoubtedly eventually make their way into the practical world of finance, but for most practitioners the models outlined here and in Chapter 3 will serve more than adequately. As noted in Chapter 5, internal consistency, ease of parameter estimation and stability of dependence on parameters, availability of sensitivities, and ease and efficiency of implementation will often be of greater importance for the majority of practical applications than is squeezing one more decimal point of accuracy under possibly exceptional circumstances. It is only when pricing those options that are extraordinarily sensitive to interest rate fluctuations, path-dependent effects, or other exotic factors that recourse to these more arcane approaches is necessary.

REFERENCES

The more sophisticated option pricing techniques discussed in this chapter are just beginning to appear in texts and reference works on the subject; Hull (1989) is a good, recent reference. For the most part, the interested reader will still have to go to the original research papers. Cox and Rubinstein (1985), Jarrow and Rudd (1983), and Dyer and Jacob (1989) each contain brief discussions of some of the more advanced pricing techniques (mean-reverting and jump-diffusion processes, analytical approximations for American option prices, and so forth), but not in enough detail for practical application. Ritchken (1987) contains a valuable discussion of techniques for modeling interest rate-sensitive options, and bond options in particular, as well as background on the necessary mathematical skills. Hull (1989) also provides mathematical background, in an attempt to make his presentation of some of the more advanced pricing models self-contained. Herskovitz (1989) and Jacob and Toevs (1988) provide an introduction to mortgage-backed security OAS models. Askin et al. (1988) and Fong et al. (1988) discuss other applications of option pricing techniques to mortgage-backed securities. Research papers such as those of Barone-Adesi and Whaley (1987), Ho and Lee (1986), and Ho and Abrahamson (1988) are cited because there are currently no more conveniently available references for these important approaches to options pricing techniques.

Askin, D. J., W. C. Hoffman, and S. D. Meyer, "Evaluation of the Option Component of Mortgage Securities," in Fabozzi, F., ed., *The Handbook of Mortgage-Backed Securities*, revised edition, Probus Publishing Company, Chicago, 1988, pp. 743–786.

Ball, C., and W. Torous, "Bond Price Dynamics and Options," *Journal of Financial and Quantitative Analysis*, 18:517–531, December 1983.

Barone-Adesi, G., and R. E. Whaley, "Efficient Analytic Approximation of American Option Values," *The Journal of Finance*, June:301–320, 1987.

Bookstaber, R., *Simulation Methods for the Evaluation of Option Models*, Morgan Stanley, New York, October 1989.

Bookstaber, R., D. Jacob, and J. Langsam, *Pitfalls in Debt Option Models*, Morgan Stanley, New York, February 1986.

Brennan, M., and E. Schwartz, "Alternative Methods for Valuing Debt Options," Working Paper 888, University of British Columbia, Vancouver, B.C., 1982.

Courtadon, G., "The Pricing of Options on Default-Free Bonds," *The Journal of Financial and Quantitative Analysis*, March:75–100, 1982.

Courtadon, G., "An Introduction to Numerical Methods in Option Pricing," in *Financial Options: From Theory to Practice*, Proceedings of a conference at the Salomon Brothers Center, New York University, December 1988.

Cox, J., J. Ingersoll Jr., and S. Ross, "A Reexamination of Traditional Hypotheses about the Term Structure of Interest Rates," *The Journal of Finance*, September:769–799, 1981.

Cox, J., J. Ingersoll Jr., and S. Ross, "A Theory of the Term Structure of Interest Rates," *Econometrica*, March:385–407, 1985.

Cox, J., and M. Rubinstein, *Options Markets*, Prentice-Hall, Englewood Cliffs, N.J., 1985.

Dattatreya, R. E., and F. Fabozzi, "A Simplified Model for Valuing Debt Options," *The Journal of Portfolio Management*, Spring:64–72, 1989.

Dyer, L., and D. P. Jacob, "Guide to Fixed Income Option Pricing Models," in Fabozzi F., ed., *Handbook of Fixed-Income Options: Pricing, Strategies & Applications*, Probus Publishing Company, Chicago, 1989, pp. 63–109.

Fabozzi, F., ed., *The Handbook of Mortgage-Backed Securities*, revised edition, Probus Publishing Company, Chicago, 1988.

Fong, G., K-Y. Chung, and E. M. P. Tang, "The Valuation of Mortgage-Backed Securities: A Contingent Claims Approach," in Fabozzi, F., ed., *The Handbook of Mortgage-Backed Securities*, revised edition, Probus Publishing Company, Chicago, 1988, pp. 833–854.

Geske, R., and H. E. Johnson, "The American Put Valued Analytically," *Journal of Finance*, December:1511–1524, 1984.

Herskovitz, M. D., "Option Adjusted Spread Analysis for Mortgage-Backed Securities," in Fabozzi, F., ed., *Handbook of Fixed-Income Options: Pricing, Strategies & Applications*, Probus Publishing Company, Chicago, 1989, pp. 627–647.

Ho, T., and A. Abrahamson, "Interest Rate Options," in *Financial Options: From Theory to Practice*, Proceedings of a conference at the Salomon Brothers Center, New York University, December 1988.

Ho, T., and S. B. Lee, "Term Structure Movements and Pricing Interest Rate Contingent Claims," *The Journal of Finance*, December:1011–1029, 1986.

Hull, J., *Options, Futures and Other Derivative Securities*, Prentice-Hall, Englewood Cliffs, N.J., 1989.

Jacob, D. P., and A. L. Toevs, "An Analysis of the New Valuation, Duration and Convexity Models for Mortgage-Backed Securities," in Fabozzi, F., ed., *Handbook of Mortgage-Backed Securities*, revised edition, Probus Publishing Company, Chicago, 1988, pp. 667–710.

Jarrow, R. A., and A. Rudd, *Option Pricing*, Dow Jones–Irwin, Homewood, Ill., 1983.

Merton, R., "Options Pricing When Underlying Stock Returns are Discontinuous," *The Journal of Financial Economics*, 3:125–144, January-March 1976.

Merton, R., "On the Pricing of Contingent Claims and the Modigliani-Miller Theorem," *The Journal of Financial Economics*, 5:241–250, November 1977.

Ritchken, P., *Options: Theory, Strategy and Applications*, Scott Foresman and Company, Glenview, Ill., 1987.

Vasicek, O. A., and H. G. Fong, "Term Structure Modeling Using Exponential Splines," *The Journal of Finance*, XXXVII:339–348, May 1982.

Wood, J. H., "The Expectations Hypothesis, the Yield Curve and Monetary Policy," *Quarterly Journal of Economics*, 2:457–470, 1964.

5

Model Selection, Evaluation, and Parameter Estimation

The wealth of possible option pricing models presented in the two previous chapters may have left some readers wondering: Why so many different models? Which one should *I* use? In this chapter, we address some of the practical concerns of the financial professional choosing an options pricing model. First, we present some general criteria and recommendations for choosing an appropriate option pricing model, based on the particular characteristics of the class of options to be valued. How a model depends on its parameters, and how the user determines what values to assign to those model parameters, have a great deal to do with the practical usefulness of any pricing model. The critical use of volatility estimation, and other issues of parameter estimation and model robustness, are treated later in the chapter.

CHOOSING AN APPROPRIATE BOND OPTION PRICING MODEL

Which pricing model should be used in practice? The choice of an appropriate model will, in general, be influenced by option features, including the character of the underlying instrument (cash or future), the term of the option (short or long term), and whether the option is European or American, as well as by available technology and efficiency considerations. In this section, we present our suggestions, based on experience with the models in both research and applied settings.

Before presenting our specific recommendations, we would like to make some general observations on the choice of an option pricing model. Such a choice should not be made, or changed, lightly. Many financial professionals keep historical pricing and sensitivity data, and a change of models may devalue such historical data. A practicing professional should have a thorough understanding of his or her chosen pricing model, including the interpretation of the model's parameters, inputs, and outputs.

The user should be convinced that the model is **robust** for the range of market conditions the professional expects to encounter—the validity of the model should not depend on the market trading within some narrow range of prices or yields, nor on the particular shape of the yield curve. (It is undesirable to have to change models when the yield curve inverts!) The professional should also be aware of which models are in use by (*a*) others who may be providing them with key market data, and (*b*) market counter-parties with whom prices, hedging factors, and implied volatilities may frequently be compared. For a model to be useful, it must not only be theoretically sound, but also be appropriate for the instruments being priced and the environment in which it is to be used.

Most of the models documented in Chapters 3 and 4 are in wide professional use, and meet the general criteria of accuracy, stability, and robustness *when the given modeling assumptions hold true*. In this section, we attempt to sum up the *practical* considerations that might lead a professional trader, investor, or analyst to choose one model over another under specific circumstances.

For the convenience of the reader, we have divided our suggestions into four major categories: by underlying instrument (futures or cash bonds), and by term (where we have used the somewhat arbitrary rule of thumb that an option is long dated if its term is greater than six months). Under each category, we distinguish the handling of European versus American options. Our recommendations are made in full awareness that other considerations (such as available technology) may often weigh more heavily.

Options on Bond Futures

Traded options on bond futures are all American, but many practitioners treat them as European because early exercises of these options are very rare. Our discussion will therefore start with short-dated European options.

Short-Dated European Options: Use Black-Scholes (Lognormal Price) or Normal Price Models

The choice between normal and lognormal (or some other) distribution is influenced by the historical behavior of actual, observed market price distributions, and by trader intuitions as to how the security in question is likely to move in the market. A normal distribution implies equal probability of *absolute* up or down steps (so that a bond trading at 110.00 would be seen as equally likely to move to 109.00 or to 111.00 under a normal price model), whereas a lognormal distribution implies equal likelihood of *relative* up or down steps (so that the same bond would be seen as equally likely to gain or lose 1% of its value). The normal distribution has the disadvantage of implying the theoretical possibility of negative prices, although generally volatilities will be such that the probability assigned to such anomalous values will be vanishingly small. This is one reason some practitioners prefer to assume a lognormal distribution.

Practically, the two give results well within the typical bid-ask spread of $\frac{2}{32}$nds. Table 5.1 illustrates normal and lognormal price (Black-Scholes) model prices for options with various strikes and expiration dates. The underlying security is assumed to be priced at par (100.00), with a risk-free rate of 8%.

Care should be taken in comparing (or converting) volatilities between normal and lognormal price models. While volatilities quoted in relative terms (percentage daily price change) can easily be converted to absolute terms (multiplying by the forward price and a time-scaling term), it must be remembered that the underlying distributions assumed by the two models are different. This can be particularly important in comparing implied volatilities generated by two such models. In general, within price and volatility regimes for which the two models' assumptions are both valid, consistency is often a more important consideration than the choice of a particular model.

Short-Dated American Options: Use Simple Lattice-Based Price Models, Barone-Adesi and Whaley's Analytical Approximation, or Bounded European Option Prices

Rough adjustments can be made to guard against the most obvious undervaluation of American options computed from standard European

Table 5.1 Normal Price Versus Black-Scholes

Option Terms		Normal Price				Black-Scholes			
		Call		Put		Call		Put	
Term	Strike	Price	Hedge	Price	Hedge	Price	Hedge	Price	Hedge
1 mo.	98.00	2.20	0.705	0.20+	0.287	2.19	0.724	0.19	0.276
	100.00	1.13+	0.496	1.13+	0.496	1.12+	0.507	1.12+	0.493
	102.00	0.20+	0.287	2.20	0.705	0.20	0.292	2.19+	0.708
3 mo.	98.00	3.15	0.617	1.16+	0.363	3.13+	0.644	1.14+	0.356
	100.00	2.11+	0.490	2.11+	0.490	2.10+	0.512	2.10+	0.488
	102.00	1.16+	0.363	3.15	0.617	1.16	0.381	3.15	0.619
6 mo.	98.00	4.10+	0.569	2.13	0.392	4.08+	0.611	2.11	0.389
	100.00	3.09	0.480	3.09	0.480	3.08	0.517	3.08	0.483
	102.00	2.13	0.392	4.10+	0.569	2.13	0.474	4.10+	0.576

Option prices are in thirty-seconds; a plus indicates an additional sixty-fourth.

option pricing models. For example, a lower bound on the American call price is given by taking the *maximum* of the European call price and its intrinsic value. The analytical approximation derived by Barone-Adesi and Whaley (1987) can also be used as an alternative. Such approximations are generally good enough for most practical purposes for short-dated options. For example, for three- to six-month options close to the money, about 80% of the premium for early exercise is corrected for by such approximations. As noted above, however, the accuracy of analytical approximations for option *sensitivities* is often not as good as for the option prices themselves.

The simple lattice-based models of Chapter 3 can, of course, also be used to provide accurate pricing of American options. In practice, the difference in accuracy achieved between these models and the less computation-intensive analytical approximations is usually insignificant.

Remarks. Our suggestions concerning models for options on bond future contracts all use the contract's *price* as the driving stochastic variable. A bond future contract is, however, an interest rate instrument, and its price varies with the yield of its cheapest-to-deliver issue. Because the cheapest-to-deliver bond may change as interest rates change, the contract's dependence on interest rate movements is very complicated. Practitioners who need to know a future contract's detailed price dependence on interest rate movements should consult Tang (1988) for a treatment of this effect, and how it can be modeled using option pricing techniques.

Long-Dated Options

There is currently no market for truly long-dated options on bond futures contracts; quotes on near-the-money options are available only for the next three contracts at any one time. In general, lattice-based term structure models of the sort described in Chapter 4 are widely accepted as the only appropriate choices for pricing long-dated American options.

Options on Cash Bonds

Short-Dated European Options: Use Lognormal Yield Model, or Adjusted Lognormal or Normal Price Models

Price- or yield-based closed-form analytical models, such as Black-Scholes, or a lognormal yield model such as was described in Chapter

Table 5.2　Black-Scholes Versus Lognormal Yield

Option Terms		Black-Scholes		Lognormal Yield	
Term	Strike	Price	Hedge	Price	Hedge
3 mo.	98.00	3.06+	0.620	3.08	0.609
	100.00	2.05	0.487	2.06	0.478
	102.00	1.12	0.357	1.12+	0.349
6 mo.	98.00	3.28	0.576	3.29+	0.562
	100.00	2.29	0.481	2.30	0.468
	102.00	2.04	0.389	2.04+	0.377

Option prices are in thirty-seconds; a plus indicates an additional sixty-fourth.

3, are generally adequate for short-dated options on cash bonds. Price-based models must, however, be adjusted to use the forward price (spot-carry) as the center of the distribution at expiration.

For instruments traded on a yield basis, a yield-driven model makes most sense. As previously noted, a yield-based model also automatically addresses some of the issues of time-dependent variance and amortization to par in cash bond prices that can complicate and distort models with price-based dynamics. While price- and yield-based models generally give very similar option prices and hedge ratios for the ranges of price/yield levels and volatilities commonly encountered in the market, the trader should remain alert to the fact that the two kinds of models do have some underlying differences that can matter, for example, in computing implied volatilities.

Table 5.2 shows comparisons of option prices and hedge ratios calculated for options on cash bonds using price- and yield-based models. While the results are comparable, identical values cannot be expected from models driven by two such different dynamics.

Short-Dated American Options: Use Simple Lattice-Based Yield Models or Barone-Adesi and Whaley's Approximation

Analytical approximations such as that of Barone-Adesi and Whaley can again be used to price these American options, and will usually capture enough of the effect of early exercise for most practical purposes for short-dated options. The yield-driven lattice-based models described in

Chapter 3, however, will provide the most reliable and accurate pricing of such American options on cash bonds.

Long-Dated Options

This market has been developing very rapidly, and is an area of active research. The lattice-based, rate movement models described in Chapter 4 (AR models and others) have proven their value in practice. Any trader active in this market should have such a model at his or her disposal, but should be aware that calculated prices and hedge ratios (or implied volatilities) may be highly sensitive to the parameters of the model, which must themselves be estimated from available empirical data for a range of bonds and options or optionlike instruments. When pricing new and unfamiliar options, or any instrument depending in subtle ways on the evolution of the term structure of interest rates over the course of its term, it is also recommended that market participants should have full simulation capabilities, and should compare the results of several pricing models or variants with simulation calculations, whenever possible for a range of potential contract terms and market conditions, as a confirmation of model accuracy and robustness.

VOLATILITY TRACKING AND ESTIMATION

A number of input variables go into the bond option pricing formulas of Chapter 3:

- Current price of the underlying bond or futures
- The strike price of the option
- The time to option expiration
- Coupon and term financing rates (for cash bonds)
- Risk-free interest rate to expiration
- Volatility of underlying bond or futures between current date and expiration

The strike price, expiration, and coupon rate are known, and the current price, term financing rate, and risk-free interest rates are generally readily observable from the market. The critical, but most illusive, input to the option pricing model is the actual volatility of the underlying bond price between the current and expiration dates. Significant rewards await those traders or investors who can consistently estimate future volatility accurately.

What is Volatility?

The price **volatility** of a bond is the standard deviation of its daily relative price change, expressed as an annual percentage. A bond trading at 12% volatility suggests that there is an approximately 68% chance (assuming that daily relative price change follows the normal distribution) that its price will remain within plus and minus 12% of the current value during the next year. Its daily volatility, 0.7442%, is computed by dividing 12% by the square root of 260 (trading days in a year), and the price of this bond on the next trading day is expected to fall within its current price plus or minus 0.7422%, with a 68% probability.

Volatility estimates therefore reflect the expected price variability of the underlying security over the option life. A bond whose price goes up (or down) at a steady rate has a low volatility because the standard deviation of its relative price change will be small, whereas a bond with wildly fluctuating price moves is extremely volatile. In other words, volatility is not a market-direction measure. Rather, it is a measure of the price variability risk premium built into option prices.

How to Measure Historical Volatility

Suppose that the closing prices of a bond in the last 21 trading days are as shown in Table 5.3. The actual volatility of the bond during this 21-trading-day period can be computed as follows (see Table 5.4).

Table 5.3 Bond Price Variability Data

Day	Price	Day	Price	Day	Price
1	88.219	8	89.969	15	88.281
2	88.250	9	89.438	16	88.688
3	88.375	10	89.031	17	88.781
4	88.531	11	89.031	18	88.813
5	89.406	12	89.125	19	88.813
6	89.469	13	88.281	20	89.594
7	89.594	14	88.406	21	90.406

Table 5.4 Bond Price Volatility Calculations

Day i to Day $(i + 1)$	Relative Price Change (%)	$\ln\left(\dfrac{Price\ (i + 1)}{Price\ i}\right)$ %
1 to 2	0.035	0.035
2 to 3	0.142	0.142
3 to 4	0.177	0.176
4 to 5	0.988	0.984
5 to 6	0.071	0.070
6 to 7	0.140	0.140
7 to 8	0.419	0.418
8 to 9	−0.590	−0.592
9 to 10	−0.455	−0.456
10 to 11	0.000	0.000
11 to 12	0.106	0.106
12 to 13	−0.947	−0.952
13 to 14	0.142	0.142
14 to 15	−0.141	−0.142
15 to 16	0.461	0.460
16 to 17	0.105	0.105
17 to 18	0.036	0.036
18 to 19	0.000	0.000
19 to 20	0.879	0.876
20 to 21	0.906	0.902
	Std. Dev. = 0.472	Std. Dev. = 0.472

Step 1

Compute the relative price change from day i to day $i + 1$. For example,

a. from day 1 to day 2, the relative price change is:

$(88.250 - 88.219)/88.219 = +0.0351\%$

b. From day 12 to day 13, the relative price change is:

$(88.281 - 89.125)/89.125 = -0.9470\%$

Step 2

The standard deviation of the 20 (not 21) relative price changes, 0.472%, is the daily price volatility. The corresponding annualized price volatility is 7.417% (0.472% × $\sqrt{260}$).

The daily price volatility can also be computed by first finding the continuously compounded daily price returns, each of which is equal to the natural logarithm of the price ratio from day $(i + 1)$ to day i. The logged price ratios of our bond data are also shown in Table 5.4, and it is clear that they are almost the same as the daily relative price changes. (This is because, for small r, we have $\ln(1 + r)$ approximately equal to r. For very volatile prices, there would be some difference in the two measures.)

The same methodology can be used to compute the actual volatility of any set of historical price data. Historical volatilities are descriptive measures of past price movements. They normally do not provide good estimates of future (now to option expiration) volatility because volatility changes erratically over time, and past figures cannot be expected to reflect future price variability. Traders and dealers should keep track of actual volatility so that they can have a clear historical perspective of the wide variability of volatility itself. But, how many past data points should be used in measuring historical volatility?

For those who insist on using historical volatilities as their estimates of the current and future volatilities, thereby making the implicit assumption that volatilities stay relatively constant over time, a statistically better estimate is obtained when more past data recorded at smaller time intervals (daily rather than weekly, for example) are used. Unfortunately, if volatility has been trending upward or downward, the estimate based on a long history will not reflect current volatility as well as one based on only recent past data. Since bond volatility has been varying widely in the past eight years, price data from the last 20, 40, and 60 trading days are suggested for use in tracking historical volatility; at least, these are likely to be closer to the current volatility. This method of measuring actual volatility can be generalized by allowing weights to be put on the various relative price changes when computing their standard deviation. For example, more recent data can be given higher weights if the user believes that volatility is indeed trending.

Using Daily High and Low Prices

Suppose that the historical high and low prices for each of the trading days are also known. Then another measure of actual volatility can also be computed. Instead of finding the natural log of the ratio of consecutive closing prices, the natural log of the daily high-to-low price ratio, adjusted for statistical efficiency by a factor of 0.601 (see Parkinson, 1980), is first computed. For example, if the high and low bond prices on a given day are 91.000 and 89.250, respectively, then the daily volatility estimate based on these data is 1.17%, which is the product of ln(91.000/89.250) and 0.601. If high and low data from 20 trading days are used, then the volatility estimate is the arithmetic average of the 20 daily estimates. High and low prices are extreme statistics indicating the day's trading range; they therefore provide a much better volatility measure than the arbitrarily timed closing prices. Moreover, it frequently happens that two consecutive closing prices are the same but the price fluctuates wildly between the closes. A good historical measure, however, may not be a close estimate of the current or future volatility; these measures are best used for providing a historical perspective and as a benchmark to judge the attractiveness of the volatility implied by the trading option price.

Implied Volatility

As pointed out earlier in this section, the key unobservable input to an option pricing model is the bond's volatility between the current and expiration dates. But options are being traded throughout the day, and the market participants' expectation of the bond's current volatility can be obtained by inverting the usual use of an option pricing model; since the option *price* is known, the *volatility* may be solved for. Volatilities computed from prices of options on the underlying bond are called **implied volatilities**. Note that such implied volatilities, which are backed out of a pricing formula, depend to some extent on the pricing model as well as on market data. While most models in common use will give reasonably close values, traders should be wary of comparing implied volatilities based on different pricing models too freely, especially when the models are based on significantly different dynamics (such as price-versus yield-based models). Table 5.5 shows implied volatilities calculated from the same market data for three-month options on a cash bond using the Black-Scholes (price-driven) and lognormal yield (yield-driven) models. While similar, the numbers do exhibit some systematic variation.

Implied volatilities computed for different options trading on the same underlying bond are usually different. Taking the arithmetic average of these as an aggregate estimate of volatility will not take into account the fact that options at different strikes have very different sensitivities to volatility level. For example, in-the-money options have low sensitivity to volatility change, especially when they are close to expiration, whereas at-the-money options are the most sensitive to volatility changes (see

Table 5.5 Implied Volatilities: Black-Scholes Versus Lognormal Yield

Strike	Option Price	Black-Scholes Volatility	Lognormal Yield Volatility
99.00	0.16	5.212	5.008
	1.00	7.152	6.848
	1.16	9.008	8.672
100.00	0.16	6.960	6.704
	1.00	8.832	8.560
	1.16	10.688	10.384
101.00	0.16	8.400	8.192
	1.00	10.304	10.080
	1.16	12.192	11.952

Figure 5.1). To get a better estimate of the market's sentiments, implied volatilities obtained from different options should therefore be weighted according to their relative price sensitivity to volatility. A simpler approach is to find the average implied volatilities of only those options that are near or at the money, since their values are the most sensitive to volatility specification, while the other options offer little additional information because the effects of volatility on their prices are relatively

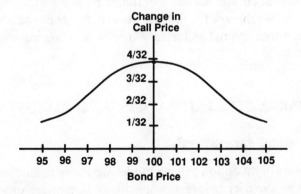

FIGURE 5.1 Change in option price for 0.05% change in volatility as a function of bond price.

obscured by the "noise" of other factors. Another reason for using the specified options is that they are also the most frequently traded, and therefore their implied figures are more trustworthy. Dealers enjoy a significant advantage over nondealers, because they have much better access to options pricing data, and hence to implied volatility information.

Using Historical and Implied Volatilities

Most dealers keep daily records of historical volatilities (for the past 20, 40, and 60 trading days, for example) and implied volatilities of the most active bonds and figures. This information is stored in a data base and is readily available to traders, who can thus track the actual and traded volatilities movements. Profit opportunities arise when:

1. Implied volatility is trading at a much lower (higher) level than the bond's actual historical variability; options on the bond are then considered to be cheap (rich) relative to the historical volatility experience.
2. Implied volatilities of different options on the same bond are trading at drastically different levels; traders will buy the relatively underpriced option and simultaneously sell the overpriced one against it, with all the other, non-volatility-related risks appropriately hedged.

Specific investment and relative-value examples illustrating how to take advantage of these opportunities will be given in the following chapters. Historical and implied volatilities are useful not because they necessarily provide accurate estimates of future bond volatility, but because they provide a benchmark for judging the relative cheapness or richness of an option, either against historical experience or against other options on the same bond.

MODEL PARAMETER ESTIMATION AND ROBUSTNESS

What Are Model Parameters?

The **parameters** of an option pricing model are those quantities that must be specified by the user before any specific option prices or sensitivities can be calculated. Strictly speaking, even the terms of the option contract, such as the strike price and term to expiration, or the current price of the underlying security can be viewed as parameters, but these quantities are generally well defined, and there is usually no difficulty determining their values in any given application of a model. Of greater importance in evaluating the overall usefulness of a model or class of models is their dependence on those parameters that are *not* easily and unambiguously determinable from the contract terms or from empirical market data. Chief among these is the **volatility** of the underlying security. Volatility estimation is so important that we have devoted an entire section of this chapter to the theme. Our general comments in this section on parameter estimation and model robustness also apply to volatility estimation, however. Another important model parameter is the **short-term interest rate,** which is assumed to be known, and constant over the term of the option, by many widely used models, such as the Black-Scholes pricing model.

Volatility- and interest rate-related parameters can sometimes appear in many guises. The sizes of up and down steps in a lattice-based model are a measure of volatility. The transition probabilities in a lattice-based model are related to assumptions about market trends. The δ and π parameters in Ho and Lee's arbitrage-free rate movement model described in Chapter 4 involve both volatility and assumed investor attitudes toward risk. Other model parameters are sometimes hidden away in assumptions about the functional form of the yield curve and its associated discount function. While some of these model parameters may not be accessible to the user (they may be "hard coded" into the model), the sophisticated user should be aware of such modeling assumptions and of any potential impact they could have on the reliability of the model should the prevailing regime of interest rates happen to alter radically.

Parameter Estimation and Forecasting

Most model parameters, such as volatility and short-term interest rate, have the property that their future values can be predicted using historical information. There is always an implicit assumption in such forecasting: either that the future will resemble the (recent) past, or that it will differ in some known, predictable fashion. (For example, the user might project a certain trend in interest rates, or market levels.) Of course, there is always some uncertainty associated with any such forecasting. It is therefore important to be especially aware of the sensitivity of model values to changes in parameter values.

Because the future may not replicate the past, and because expectations about market trends won't always be borne out, it is valuable to supplement standard tests and measures of model sensitivities with **scenario analysis** capabilities (see Chapter 7 for more discussion of scenario analysis). By comparing model values for current parameter settings with values resulting from significant shifts in some of these parameters—for example, a doubling of volatilities, or a full percentage point move in interest rates—one gains perspective on the potential variability of option prices and sensitivities under best case and worst case scenarios.

Not even a full knowledge of the instantaneous sensitivities of all model parameters can provide the insight given by scenario analysis. Imagine the true price of an option as a complex function of all the input variables and parameters—strike price, term to expiration, price of the underlying security, interest rates, volatility, and the like. A model provides an approximation to this true pricing function. Each possible set of values of the model variables and parameters represents a possible state of the market, to which the model associates an option price. If we could visualize it, this function would give us an n-dimensional picture of the *simultaneous* dependence of the option price on *all* these variables and parameters. The *sensitivity* of the model, for a given state of the market, is just a measure of the *slope* of the resulting function at that point; it gives a one-dimensional (linear approximation) snapshot of the dependence of the option price on one of the model variables or parameters in that particular state of the market. But these sensitivities are increasingly misleading as guides to the behavior of the option price as the values of these variables and parameters shift away from that one precise state. This is because most model pricing functions are *curved* in every direction. This is the problem of what options traders refer to as **convexity**. Scenario analysis is one important tool for handling this problem.

Model Robustness

Simple model parameters are typically estimated through established statistical procedures from current or historical market data. Some of the procedures followed in estimating volatilities, for example, are outlined and discussed in the previous section. The direct economic significance of other model parameters, such as Ho and Lee's δ and π, or Cox et al.'s κ, θ, σ, and λ, may be less obvious, however, and it may be difficult to estimate such parameters directly from available market or econometric data. Instead, such parameters are estimated by a kind of bootstrap process. A set of traded securities are chosen for which the model should give accurate prices (i.e., a set of securities for which all the modeling assumptions are met). These should ideally be securities for which the market is as liquid and efficient as possible—that is, the trader should be as confident as possible that the observed market prices of these securities are fair, and that there are few if any significant price distortions among them. Theoretical prices for these securities are then calculated using the model in question, starting with arbitrary guesstimated values for the model parameters one seeks to estimate. In general, the resulting theoretical prices will *not* match the observed market prices. By modifying the parameter values in a stepwise manner, repeatedly recalculating the theoretical prices, eventually parameter values generating theoretical prices very close to the observed prices are obtained. This process is similar to the calculation of an *implied volatility* from traded option prices (see above).

Of course, we are sloughing over a lot of technical detail here. What do we mean by "very close"? How do we decide *which* parameters to modify, and in which direction? These aren't frivolous questions, and to understand the issue of **model robustness** the practitioner should have at least a general idea of how they are answered.

The issue of what is meant by "very close" can be dealt with by adopting a common (although by no means the only) measure of closeness: the sum of the squares of the differences between the observed and theoretical prices. Since squares are always positive, this measure *has* a minimum. Minimizing this "sum squared error" is thus a well-defined task. How we approach *finding* that minimum is much less straightforward. What we face here is a process of *nonlinear estimation*. The model pricing function will in general be nonlinear in all its parameters. This means that while for some combinations of parameter values increasing one parameter may *reduce* the sum squared error, for other combinations it may *increase* the sum squared error. About all we can say without knowing the specific functional form of the model in question is that general techniques do exist to attack this kind of problem, and that for the functional forms generally taken by option pricing models (which aren't *too* irregular in their nonlinearity) these techniques give good results.

So, let us suppose we have found values for the model parameters that lead to theoretical prices closely approximating the observed market prices of our chosen set. In theory, the parameters we have just estimated aren't tied to the specific securities we used to estimate them—they are *structural* parameters, having to do with the projected volatility of some underlying security or class of securities, or with term interest rates, or possibly with the functional form of the yield curve. It should therefore be possible to proceed to price *any other securities* meeting the model constraints, using our newly estimated model parameters, and have confidence that the resulting option prices are fair.

In general, this is precisely what is done. As the reader may suspect, however, there are a number of potential pitfalls here. While such considerations are frequently overlooked (technically sophisticated pricing models tend to inspire an awe, which leads to sometimes unjustified passivity in accepting model assumptions!), we strongly recommend paying them some attention. Among the possible concerns are the following.

Residual Error in Parameter Estimation

As implied above, the model prices for the chosen benchmark securities used to estimate the model parameters may never *exactly* match the market prices of these securities. In part, this may be due to market inefficiencies and mispricings—that is, the theoretical prices may in fact be *more* fair than the observed prices! But a large residual error after the estimation process has been completed may also signal distortions in the modeling assumptions and/or shortcomings in the parameter estimation process. (In nonlinear estimation it is possible to come up with a local minimum that is optimal with respect to small perturbations of the parameter values, but may not be the best possible overall solution.) Users should always be aware of the residual error in the parameter estimation process.

Robustness of Parameter Estimation

It is also wise to test just how much the parameter values change if the original set of benchmark securities is replaced by another set, and whether the estimation process is strongly affected by adding or removing individual securities from the benchmark set. A benchmark set used for parameter estimation should not contain *outliers*, the inclusion or exclusion of which strongly biases the results of the estimation process. But neither should it be so homogeneous as to consist essentially of copies of a single security (in technical terms, the members of the benchmark set should not be too highly autocorrelated). For major applications, when model parameters will be used to price a wide range of securities, it is wise to compare parameter values estimated based on several independent benchmark sets. The variance in the resulting parameter values is one measure of model robustness.

Stability of Model Parameters over Time

In a volatile market environment, it is also prudent to have a good sense of just how sensitive model parameters are to changes in market levels. Of course, model parameters can be reestimated as frequently as it is necessary; volatility and short-term interest rate parameters to the simpler pricing models are usually reset at least daily. But with some of the more complex models, because parameter estimation can be more cumbersome there is sometimes a tendency not to reset often enough. By estimating hypothetical model parameters for a few different market scenarios, the practitioner can gain a sense of just how sensitive they are to changes in market levels and volatilities, and thus how frequently they should be recalculated.

As noted in Chapter 4, simulation methods can provide a useful test of the accuracy and robustness of general option pricing models. Bookstaber (1989) outlined an approach to testing even proprietary pricing models using simulation techniques. Such techniques can be adapted to take into account the periodic recalibration of model parameters. Note that it is enough for present purposes to test the accuracy and stability of pricing of *European* options. The logic of a lattice-based model guarantees that if it accurately prices European options, it will closely approximate the premium associated with early exercise, since this is tested explicitly at each lattice step.

Relative Pricing

The bootstrapping process of parameter estimation described above means that some pricing models are always tuned in relation to some chosen benchmark securities. As we have noted, the accuracy of the resulting model will in general be contingent on the accuracy or fairness of the prices of these benchmark securities. Where there is reason to emphasize this dependence, such models are sometimes referred to as **relative pricing models**. Ho (1988) emphasized this relative aspect of his arbitrage-free rate movement model, noting that the AR model "provides an integrative framework to value one bond sector in relation against another and a particular bond against other bonds." Ho also noted that in some sense most option pricing models are "relative," even if only to the price of the underlying security. For some applications, it makes sense to emphasize this relationship because what may be of primary importance to the user is the *relative* richness or cheapness of one sector or security in relation to another. This reduces the potential importance of any systematic price distortions in the benchmark sector. It does not, however, reduce the importance of considerations of model robustness and sensitivity to time change in model parameters.

REFERENCES

Little attention is given to issues of parameter estimation in most surveys of options pricing techniques. Press et al. (1988) provides a good, practical discussion of nonlinear models, including a section on confidence limits for estimated model parameters. Most of the standard surveys of option pricing technique cited here provide some insight into the appropriateness of particular models for particular problems, but they generally concentrate on options in an equities context, and deal with bond options and/or long-dated options only in passing, if at all. [Ritchken (1987) and Hull (1989) are two exceptions.] Unknown to us, Dyer and Jacob (1989) also wrote a guide to fixed-income option pricing models. While their recommendations and conclusions are similar to ours in this chapter, the two treatments are quite different.

Barone-Adesi, G., and R. E. Whaley, "Efficient Analytic Approximation of American Option Values," *The Journal of Finance*, June:301–320, 1987.

Bookstaber, R., *Simulation Methods for the Evaluation of Option Models*, Morgan Stanley, New York, October 1989.

Brown, S., "Estimating Volatility," in *Financial Options: From Theory to Practice*, Proceedings of a conference at the Salomon Brothers Center, New York University, December 1988.

Cox, J., and M. Rubinstein, *Options Markets*, Prentice-Hall, Englewood Cliffs, N.J., 1985.

Dyer, L., and D. P. Jacob, "Guide to Fixed Income Option Pricing Models," in Fabozzi, F., ed., *Handbook of Fixed-Income Options: Pricing, Strategies & Applications*, Probus Publishing Company, Chicago, 1989, pp. 63–109.

Ho, T. S. Y., *Valuing Option Embedded Bonds Using Relative Pricing Models*, Global Advanced Technology Corporation, New York, 1988.

Hull, J., *Options, Futures, and Other Derivative Securities*, Prentice-Hall, Englewood Cliffs, N.J., 1989.

Jarrow, R. A., and A. Rudd, *Option Pricing*, Dow Jones–Irwin, Homewood, Ill., 1983.

Parkinson, M., "The Extreme Value Method for Estimating the Variance of the Rate of Return," *Journal of Business*, January:61–65, 1980.

Press, W. H., B. P. Flannery, S. A. Teukolsky, and W. T. Vetterling, *Numerical Recipes in C: The Art of Scientific Computing*, Cambridge University Press, Cambridge, England, 1988.

Ritchken, P., *Options: Theory, Strategy and Applications*, Scott Foresman and Company, Glenview, Ill., 1987.

Tang, E. M., *The Effect of Delivery Options on Interest Rate Futures and Option Contracts*, Portfolio Management Technology, San Francisco, 1988.

6
Dealing in Bond Options

Marketmakers play a major role in options trading because they provide liquidity in the market by continuously quoting bids and offers. For strategic options traders and investors, it is useful to know how marketmakers behave because their quotations define a major part of transaction costs. This chapter focuses on how options dealers come up with their quotes, hedge away unwanted risks, and profit from their marketmaking activities. The first section describes, in general, what marketmakers are expected to do and how they can become successful. Since individual bond options have relatively low order and transaction volumes, options marketmakers must exploit the price relationships among options on the same underlying bond and the bond itself to make competitive quotes and, in turn, reasonable profits. Specific examples will be used in the next four sections to illustrate the various quoting and hedging methods used by options marketmakers. Most successful dealers focus their efforts on "volatility dealing"; this strategy and its associated risks will be highlighted.

MAKING MARKETS IN BOND OPTIONS

Roles and Expectations

Marketmakers play a central role in both over-the-counter (OTC) and exchange-listed options trading because they provide liquidity in the bond option markets. The trading mechanism for listed options is the same as that of the underlying futures contracts: an open outcry auction with competing marketmakers ("scalpers") freely quoting bids and offers. [See Silber (1988) for an excellent description of dealing in options on futures.] A broker with a market order from a customer to buy (sell) options with standardized strike prices and expiration dates can therefore go into the futures pit and "lift the offer" ("hit the bid") of a market-maker. A number of U.S. government bonds primary dealers make markets in OTC options on cash bonds, quoting bids and offers on options with strike prices and expiration dates specified by the customers.

Marketmakers are expected to make money by selling at offer what was bought at the bid, and not by speculating on market direction. Their profit opportunities are not risk free, however, because as market prices change continuously, dealers are often caught long (short) in the market after a bid has just been hit (an offer lifted). This market risk is significant when the price gaps up or down and the order flows are one sided. Dealers therefore have more profitable opportunities when the market prices fluctuate wildly as a large volume of both buy and sell orders come in. Successful marketmakers are good at distinguishing order flows that will quickly reverse from more permanent market trends. Many of them base their judgments on price movements in related markets; for example, cash bond quotes are based on bond futures prices; options quotes are based on the underlying bond prices; and so forth. Dealers are also very quick in adjusting their quotes as their market intuitions change. Experience does count a lot in marketmaking and it is certainly more art than science.

Order Flow Problem for Options Dealers

A major problem confronting options dealers is the relatively sparse order flow for any given option; this problem is especially severe for OTC marketmakers because these bond options do not have standardized strike prices and expiration dates and every option is a unique security. Under such circumstances, it is difficult to make quotes based on order flows. Options marketmakers therefore make a very wide bid-offer spread to compensate for the uncertainty and the associated price risk. [In the U.S. bond option market, the bid-offer spread for at-the-money options is about $5/32$nds for cash (30-year) bonds, while it is less than $2/32$nds for listed options on Treasury bond (T-bond) futures.] This significant transaction cost has driven some potential options users to employ the more liquid bond futures to create synthetic options by dynamic hedging techniques (see Chapter 11).

In the options market for Japanese Government Bonds (JGBs), which started trading in 1989, options on issues other than the most liquid benchmark issue have traded very thinly, and with wide bid-ask spreads. Difficulty in financing short positions in cash bonds has also complicated hedging strategies and led to wider bid-ask margins, and to the use of JGB futures for dynamic hedging (see Chapter 2).

How Options Marketmakers Respond to the Challenge

Options on the same underlying bond and the bond itself have well-established price relationships defined by pricing models. Marketmakers can take advantage of these dependencies to quote prices, hedge risks, and make profits. The following trading and hedging methods and their risks are discussed in this chapter:

1. Since cash bonds and futures are very liquid and their quotes are readily available, options dealers can use pricing models to determine options quotes from the trading bond prices. Examples are given below to show how dealers use the put-call parity relationship (see Equation 3.2 in Chapter 3) to make markets in thinly traded options.
2. Because the use of put-call parity is limited in its effectiveness, dealers make extensive use of *option price sensitivities*, including the option's **delta**, or hedge ratio, **gamma, theta,** and **kappa,** to establish profitable positions with minimal risk exposure. These measures are defined later in the chapter, as is the widely used strategy of **delta hedging**, whose applications to marketmaking are demonstrated with worked examples.
3. Bond dealers often offset some of their risks by using the trading relationships among different cash bonds and futures. Similarly, options on bond futures or on benchmark bonds are sometimes used as hedges against options on a given cash bond. The resulting cross-market spread risk and the effectiveness of this hedge are discussed later.

The bid-offer spread for bond options would be much wider if marketmakers did not know how to use these trading relationships and hedging tools to reduce their inventory risks. Competition among marketmakers also contributes to reducing the spread quoted for individual options.

USING PUT-CALL PARITY FOR BOND FUTURES

What is Put-Call Parity?

Options marketmakers often make use of the **put-call parity** relationship in determining what bid-ask spread they will quote for a given option. Specific examples are provided below to illustrate how marketmakers quote prices of options on bond futures using put-call parity. These illustrations also show how arbitrageurs can take advantage of temporarily mispriced options. The major reasons for using listed options in the examples include easy trade execution and low transactions costs, because both futures and options on them are very liquid and they both trade on the Chicago Board of Trade (CBT). The other consideration is that, as later examples will demonstrate clearly, leveraged trades involving cash bonds must take carrying costs into account, and such treatments would make these simple examples more tedious than necessary.

Recall from Chapter 3 that the put-call parity principle (Equation 3.2) asserts that there is a *necessary relationship* between the prices of put and call options struck at the same price K, and the price S of the underlying bond future:

$$P = C - DF(S - K) \tag{6.1}$$

where P is the price of a put option

           C is the price of a call option

           S is the price of the underlying bond future

           K is the strike price

       $DF(.)$ is the discounting function giving the net present value of the variable (in parentheses) at expiration

Put-call parity, as demonstrated in Chapter 3, is *independent of any particular pricing model*. It is a general consequence of the payoff behavior at expiration of puts and calls with the same strike price.

Put-call parity can be expressed in many different forms; the two ap-

Table 6.1 Price Information for
Examples 6.1 and 6.2

Strike Price	Call Price	Put Price
80	[4-40]	[0-54]
82	[3-18]	[1-25]
84	[2-08]	[2-13]
86	[1-18]	[3-20]
88	[0-46]	[4-46]
90	[0-25]	[6-24]

proximate forms that are most often used by marketmakers to help make market quotes are:

1. "Buying a call on a bond future" is almost equivalent to "buying a put (same strike and expiry as call)" and "buying long the future at the strike price."
2. "Buying a put on a bond future" is almost equivalent to "buying a call (same strike and expiry as put)" and "selling short the future at the strike price."

For example, on August 15, 1988, the December 1988 T-bond future had a closing price of 83 and $^{30}/_{32}$nds. The closing prices of options on this contract were as shown in Table 6.1. The three-month risk-free rate on this date was 7.225%. Note that the price quote [4-40] stands for a price of 4 and $^{40}/_{64}$ths.

EXAMPLE 6.1: MAKING QUOTES ON A THINLY TRADED OPTION

THE PROBLEM

Minutes before the close of trading, when the December T-bond contract is trading at 83 and $^{30}/_{32}$nds, an options marketmaker is asked to make a market for a December 1982 call. Since the calls have not traded all day, the marketmaker is not able to give quotes based on order flow information. The December 1982 puts, however, have been very active and are trading at [1-23] bid and [1-27] offer. Based on this market information, how can the marketmaker make a market for the December 1982 call?

USING PUT-CALL PARITY

From the given information, the marketmaker is willing to do the following trades:

December 1982 put: Buy at [1-23]   Sell at [1-27]

December T-bond: Buy at 83 $^{30}/_{32}$nds   Sell at 83 $^{30}/_{32}$nds

Using put-call parity as stated in form 1 above, the marketmaker is therefore willing to buy a synthetic December 1982 call by:

a. buying a December 1982 put at [1-23], and
b. going long the T-bond contract at 83 and $^{30}/_{32}$nds.

This synthetic call has a payoff diagram almost equivalent to that of a December 1982 call purchased at [3-19], which is obtained by taking $\{[1\text{-}23] + (83\ ^{30}/_{32} - 82)\}$. This does not mean that the marketmaker is willing to bid [3-19] for the December 1982 call, because the synthetic call he or she is willing to buy has an initial cash payment of [1-23], which is [1-60] less than [3-19]. Since the three-month risk-free interest rate on August 15, 1988, is 7.225%, the interest cost from this day to option expiry (November 18, 1988) for the [1-60] difference is approximately [0-02]. The marketmaker will therefore make a bid of only [3-17], which is [3-19] − [0-02], for the December 1982 call. This bid of [3-17] can be obtained directly by using Equation 6.1, which states that:

$$C = P + DF(S - K)$$
$$= [1\text{-}23] + DF(83\ ^{30}/_{32} - 82)$$
$$= [1\text{-}23] + \left\{ [1\text{-}60] \times \left(1 - \frac{0.07225}{4} \right) \right\} = [3\text{-}17]$$

Similarly, the marketmaker is willing to sell a synthetic December, 1982, call by:

a. selling a December 1982 put at [1-27], and
b. shorting the T-bond contract at 83 and $^{30}/_{32}$nds,

which has a payoff diagram almost equivalent to that of a December 1982 call sold at [3-23] ([3-23] = $\{[1\text{-}27] + (83\ ^{30}/_{32} - 82)\}$). Taking into effect the [0-02] three-month interest on the difference between [3-23] and [1-27], and since the marketmaker takes in more cash up front from the actual call, he or she should be willing to offer the December 1982 call at [3-21]. Again, this offer of [3-21] can be obtained directly by applying Equation 6.1. (Note that the financing cost for the futures margin is assumed to be negligible.)

THE QUOTES

The marketmaker has to take into account the fact that the December T-bond contract may trade at a price different from 83 and $^{30}/_{32}$nds. The expected quote for this December 1982 call is [3-16] bid and [3-22] offer. The $^{6}/_{64}$ths bid-ask spread is really not that wide, given that the call has not traded all day.

The previous example shows how marketmakers can use put-call price relationships to help them make markets. As demonstrated in the following example, the actual profit they can expect to make in such trades is far less than the bid-ask spread.

EXAMPLE 6.2: PROFIT MARGIN IF QUOTE IS HIT/LIFTED

THE FOLLOW-UP TRADE

Suppose that the [3-16] bid made on the December 1982 call by the marketmaker in Example 6.1 was hit by a customer. To make a [0-02] profit, the marketmaker can reduce the offer from [3-22] and [3-18], hoping for a quick sale to completely offset his or her position. Suppose that there is no buyer of the December 1982 call even at [3-18]. This marketmaker will have missed a profit-making opportunity in spite of the superior offer, which is a direct result of his or her transaction flow. Based on the information given in the previous example, what follow-up trades should the marketmaker do to hedge his or her risk or to lock up profits?

USING PUT-CALL PARITY

The marketmaker just bought a December 1982 call at a price of [3-16]. From the given information, the current price quotes are:

December 1982 put: [1-23] bid: [1-27] offer
December T-bond: trading at 83 and $^{30}/_{32}$nds

To offset his or her position, the marketmaker has to sell a synthetic December 1982 call. From the put-call relationship from 1 above, this can be done by:

a. selling a December 1982 put at the current bid of [1-23], and
b. selling short the T-bond contract at 83 and $^{30}/_{32}$nds.

(Note that the put is sold on the *bid*, and not on the offer, side.)

The combined position, including the bought call, is served a **reverse conversion**. This position has a riskless profit of about [0-01], calculated as follows. The three-month interest cost of the initial cash payout of [1-57], based on the 7.225% risk-free rate, is about [0-02]. The combined position, excluding the interest cost, gives a payout of [0-03] no matter what the December T-bond price is at the close of trading on November 18, 1988. For example, if the December T-bond closes at 82,

  a. the T-bond contract will bring in a [1-60] gain;
  b. the December 1982 call will expire worthless and bring a [3-16] loss; and
  c. the December 1982 put will expire worthless and bring a [1-23] gain.

The net gain is [0-03]. The result of this analysis stays the same no matter what the closing December T-bond price is.

REMARK

If the marketmaker has instead sold a December 1982 call at [3-22], and follows that up by

  a. buying a December 1982 put at [1-27], and
  b. buying long the T-bond contract at 83 and $^{30}/_{32}$nds,

the combined conversion position has a riskless profit of about [0-01], which is made up of a [0-02] interest gain and a [0-01] net loss for this position on November 18, 1988.

Riskless Arbitrage

Riskless arbitrage opportunities occur when an option and its synthetic equivalent are trading at different prices, after adjusting for any difference in interest costs. Arbitrage traders, with the help of advanced computer technology, continuously monitor, identify, and profit from such opportunities. Consequently, quoted option prices for customers of the broker-dealers are almost always closely in line with the put-call parity relationships; as with the August 15th closing data in Table 6.1, any discrepancy is within the usual bid-ask spread.

The $\frac{1}{64}$th "riskless" profit in this example is much smaller than the marketmaker's $\frac{9}{64}$ths bid-ask spread; if the financing cost of the futures margin is not neglected, there may not be any profit at all. Instead of hitting the bid or lifting the offer, marketmakers often go after bigger profits by trying to put the offsetting synthetic option position on at a better level, knowing full well that they are taking market risk on the inventory.

Need for a Better Strategy

As pointed out earlier, dealers want to make quick, riskless profit by buying at the bid price and selling at the offer. Good order and transaction flows are absolutely essential, however, because they generate better quotes and quicker profits. Without good order flows—and most OTC bond options have this problem—marketmakers may not be able to offset their inventory risks even if they can use the put-call relationship to give reasonable quotes. They must therefore resort to more sophisticated strategies to try to lock in profits while keeping their risk exposure to a minimum.

The trading and hedging techniques most widely used by options dealers are illustrated in the examples given later in this chapter. They all make use of the fact that options prices vary with the underlying bond prices and their expected volatilities according to some pricing model, and therefore obey certain definite relationships. The keys to both a *qualitative* and a *quantitative* understanding of these relationships are the *option's price sensitivities* to changes in fundamental parameters, including the underlying bond price and its expected volatility. These sensitivities are introduced below.

OPTION SENSITIVITIES

Delta—Sensitivity to Underlying Bond Price Change

The variable of most fundamental importance to the option trader is the price of the underlying security. Option prices are directly affected by changes in the price of the underlying security—call prices go up, and put prices down, when the underlying security price rises. However, option prices do not vary dollar for dollar with the price of the underlying bond. At any given price level, there is a *ratio*, called the option's **delta**, measuring how much the option price changes for a given (small) change in the price of the underlying security. Figure 6.1 shows the price of a call option on a bond struck at par, as a function of the price of the

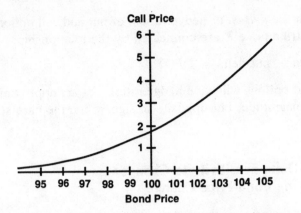

FIGURE 6.1 Call price as a function of bond price (60-day call option struck at 100).

underlying bond. It also shows how the option's time value varies with the bond price.

Delta is just the *slope* of the call value curve at any given point. (In mathematical terms, it is the *derivative* of the option price as a function of the bond price.) The delta of this call option is shown in Figure 6.2. Note that the option's delta is close to zero for way-out-of-the-money options, and close to one for deep-in-the-money options. Since the price of a deep-in-the-money option is mostly intrinsic value (little time value), it will clearly move almost dollar for dollar with the bond price.

The put-call parity relationship (Equation 6.1) also has the conse-

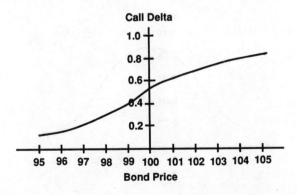

FIGURE 6.2 Call delta as a function of bond price (60-day call option struck at 100).

quence that the *deltas*, or hedge ratios, of put and call options struck at the same strike price K are connected by the relationship:

Call-delta − put-delta = $DF(1)$

Call and put options will have hedge ratios that are approximately equal to 0.50 in magnitude, but opposite in sign, when they are struck at the money.

Gamma—Delta Sensitivity to Change in Underlying Bond Price Change

Note that as the price of the underlying bond changes, *the option's delta will also change.* That is because the graph of the option price in Figure 6.1 is *curved*—it doesn't have a constant slope. As we will see, the option's delta is used to determine how to *hedge* an option position. The fact that the delta itself changes with the underlying bond price means that a hedged position can become unbalanced—imperfectly hedged—as the market moves. The measure of susceptibility to such hedging slippage is the option's **gamma**, which is just the sensitivity of the option delta to changes in the price of the underlying security. In other words, gamma is the *slope* of the graph of *delta* at a given price. (It is mathematically the *second derivative* of the option price as a function of the underlying bond price.) Geometrically, gamma is a measure of the *curvature* of the graph of option price as a function of the underlying security price. Figure 6.3 shows the gamma of the call option from Figures 6.1

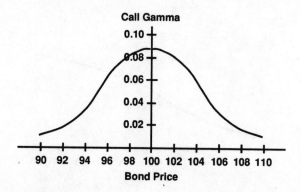

FIGURE 6.3. Call gamma as a function of bond price (60-day call struck at 100).

and 6.2. Note that the option gamma is *greatest* when the option is *at the money*, and falls toward zero as the option moves farther into or out of the money. The practical implications of this qualitative behavior are explored in Examples 6.3–6.5

Theta—Time Decay

Another important measure of an option's sensitivity is its **theta**, the option's *time decay*. Every option loses value as its term to expiration dwindles. The time value of an option will decrease over time even if there is no change in the underlying bond price, because more days to expiration means a greater likelihood that the option will end up (further) in the money, hence having greater time value. Figure 6.4 shows the price of an at-the-money call option as a function of time to expiration. Figure 6.5 shows the theta of this option as a function of time to expiration. Note that the option theta rapidly becomes more negative as the option approaches expiration. This is because the value of an at-the-

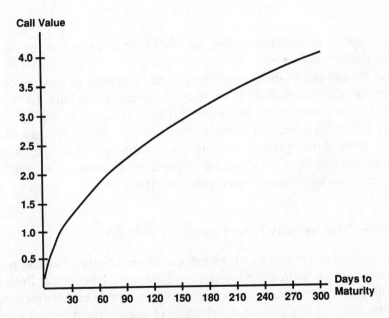

FIGURE 6.4   Call price as a function of time to expiration (at-the-money call option struck at 100).

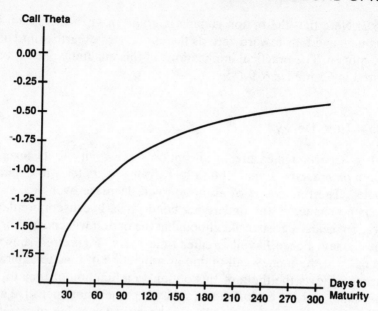

FIGURE 6.5 Call theta as a function of time to expiration (at-the-money call option struck at 100).

money option is pure time value, and this time value decreases rapidly as expiration approaches.

For in- and out-of-the-money options, the behavior of theta as option expiration approaches is different from at-the-money options. The option theta first becomes more negative, but at a certain point it begins to become less negative. For in-the-money options, this is because the intrinsic value of the option eventually overshadows its time value; for out-of-the-money options, it is because the option has already lost almost all its time value when it gets very close to expiration.

Kappa—Price Sensitivity to Change in Volatility

Finally, there is **kappa**, which measures the sensitivity of option prices to changes in the *anticipated volatility* of the underlying bond. Both call and put option prices increase as the bond's expected volatility increases, because this implies a wider distribution of underlying prices at expiration, and hence a greater likelihood of ending (further) in the money. Figure 6.6 shows the price of an at-the-money call as a function of vol-

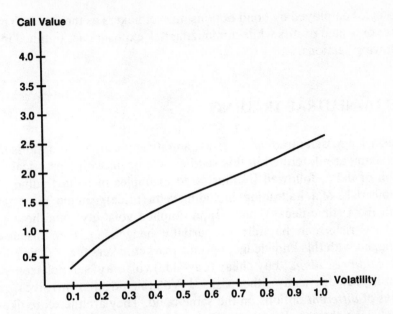

FIGURE 6.6   Call price as a function of volatility (30-day-at-the-money call option struck at 100).

atility. Like an option's gamma, kappa is greatest for at-the-money options. This is to be expected, because such options have the greatest time value.

Remarks

In practice, these various sensitivities interact in a complex fashion. Price changes are not instantaneous; they occur over time, accompanied by time decay. Volatilities usually do not change significantly unless the underlying bond price itself fluctuates—any expectations of future changes in the underlying price detected in the options market are likely to be detectable in the market for the underlying security as well. Other factors, such as liquidity squeezes, can temporarily distort the qualitative behavior of some options.

Every options marketmaker must have an intuition for the qualitative behavior of option prices and their sensitivies. Pricing models, and computerized analytics, allow the marketmaker to *quantify* these intuitions, and turn them into trading strategies. Some of the most important trading strategies employed by bond options marketmakers as they seek to maximize expected profits while minimizing risk exposure are outlined in the following sections.

DELTA-NEUTRAL TRADING

The basics of delta trading, its risks, and its applications to options marketmaking are described in this section. We begin with a practical definition of delta, followed by illustrated examples of delta trading. The various risks of delta trading, including **delta** (price), **gamma** (price variation), **theta** (time decay), and **kappa** (implied volatility), and how each of these risks can be fully or partially hedged are then discussed. Equipped with this knowledge, options marketmakers focus their efforts on *volatility dealing*: "buy cheap (buy-side) volatility; sell rich (sell-side) volatility; hedge away other risks." Volatility dealing involves delta trades of *different* options on the same bond. They are therefore likelier to get done than trades where the marketmaker tries to make the bid-ask spread on a given option; while the transaction volume of an individual option may be low, the order flow for *all* options on a particular bond is much larger.

What is Delta?

The delta of an option is the price change that results from a one-unit change in the price of the underlying bond or future:

$$\text{Delta} = \frac{\text{price change in option (in points)}}{\text{price change in underlying bond (in points)}}$$

It can be easily computed from this basic definition once a pricing model or formula is selected. Its value ranges from zero to one for calls and zero to negative one for puts.

Suppose a call option on a bond future has a delta of 0.52. This call will have a price increase of *approximately* 0.52 points, or about $^{16.6}/_{32}$nds, if the bond future price goes up by a point; the approximation gets worse as the underlying price change gets bigger. Delta is sometimes known as the **hedge ratio** because the price risk of an option, for small changes in the market, can be hedged by holding its **delta equivalent** in the underlying bond. For example, the call option above can be hedged by selling short

Table 6.2 Cash and Options Positions on UST 7.25% Bond
of May 15, 2016

Long or Short	Type	Strike	Days To Expiry	Price	Amount in $MM	Delta	Amount-Weighted Delta
Short	Call	86 05/32	28	8/32	−20	0.18	−3.60
Long	Call	86 06/32	7	1/32	1	0.03	0.03
Long	Put	84 26/32	27	1 19/32	15	−0.65	−9.75
Short	Put	81 20/32	42	14/32	−10	−0.23	2.30
Long	Cash			83 26/32	14	1.00	14.00
					Position	Delta	2.98

0.52 future contracts; if the contracts go down by half a point, the call will go down by 0.26 points but at the same time the short position will have gained 0.26 points to completely offset the loss.

The deltas of different options on the same underlying bond can be added together to give the delta of the set of options. For example, an OTC options dealer currently has the cash and options positions on the U.S. Treasury (UST) 7.25% bond of May 15, 2016, shown in Table 6.2. The four OTC bond options in the dealer's position have different strikes and days to expiry. Since the dealer is short in $20 million in calls struck at 86 and $\frac{5}{32}$nds, the amount shown for this option is −20. The prices and deltas are computed using a lognormal yield pricing model. The delta of the set of options, including the $14 million cash position, is 2.98; this is actually (amount-) weighted average of the five deltas and it states that the dealer has an exposure equivalent to being long in $2.98 million of the bond.

The prices and deltas of a 30-day call and a 30-day put on the March T-bond contract struck at 92, for different T-bond prices, are shown in Table 6.3 and are plotted in Figures 6.7 and 6.8. Both option price and delta vary with the underlying bond price. (Note that [3-14] represents a price of 3 and $\frac{14}{64}$ths.) For example, if the T-bond contract increases in value from 91 to 92, the March 92 call delta changes from 0.361 to 0.497 while the put delta changes from −0.632 to −0.497. As a call (put) moves more and more into the money, its delta approaches one (negative one) and the call (put) moves almost one to one (−negative one) with the bond. This behavior reflects the limited price risk of a call (put) option because its delta decreases in absolute value as the bond goes down (up) in price. This also explains why deltas are only approximate hedge ratios

Table 6.3   Prices and Deltas of 30-Day Call and 30-Day Put

	March 1992 Call		March 1992 Put	
March T-bond	Price	Delta	Price	Delta
85.00	0-00	0.004	7-00	−1.000
86.00	0-01	0.013	6-00	−1.000
87.00	0-02	0.033	5-00	−0.960
88.00	0-06	0.074	4-04	−0.920
89.00	0-13	0.141	3-12	−0.853
90.00	0-25	0.238	2-25	−0.755
91.00	0-45	0.361	1-45	−0.632
92.00	1-09	0.497	1-09	−0.497
93.00	1-46	0.630	0-47	−0.364
94.00	2-27	0.746	0-28	−0.248
95.00	3-14	0.837	0-16	−0.156
96.00	4-07	0.901	0-08	−0.092
97.00	5-02	0.943	0-04	−0.050
98.00	6-00	1.000	0-02	−0.026
99.00	7-00	1.000	0-01	−0.012

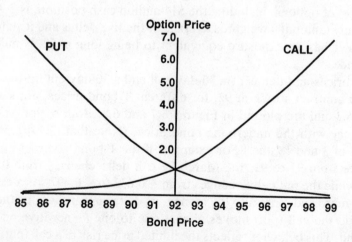

FIGURE 6.7   Prices of 30-day options on UST 7.25% issue of May 15, 2016.

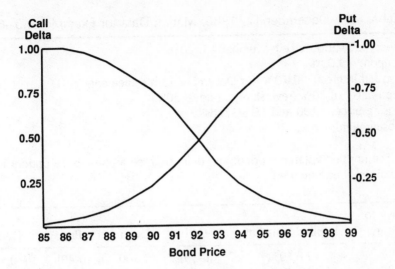

FIGURE 6.8   Deltas of 30-day options on UST 7.25% issue of May 15, 2016.

when bond prices change drastically. Finally, as the market level varies, the delta of a set of options changes and readjustment of cash and/or options positions is often needed to keep the set appropriately hedged.

Two examples of delta-neutral trades will be presented next to illustrate the basics of delta trading. The market data for these examples are shown in Table 6.4.

EXAMPLE 6.3: A DELTA-NEUTRAL TRADE WITH POSITIVE GAMMA AND NEGATIVE THETA

USING IMPLIED VOLATILITY TO MAKE MARKETS ON OTC OPTIONS

Suppose that in the afternoon of December 12, 1988, the UST 9% issue of November 15, 2018, is trading at 100 and $^{15.5}$⁄₃₂nds (^{14}⁄₃₂nds bid; ^{17}⁄₃₂nds offer). An OTC options dealer is asked to make a market for a $1 million 30-day at-the-money call on this bond. It has been an hour since the last trade on this option, but the dealer knows that the last traded implied volatility on this option was 10.40%. Using this volatility and the 100 and ^{14}⁄₃₂nds bid on the bond, the call price is computed to be [1-06]. Since options marketmaking is more risky than simple bond dealing, there should be, say., an additional ³⁄₃₂nds on the option's bid-ask spread. The OTC options dealer should therefore give a [1-03] bid, which has an

Table 6.4 December 12, 1988, Market Data for Examples 6.3–6.6

Issue: UST 9.00% of November 15, 2018
Coupon: 9.00%
Accrued interest: 0.70% (for December 13th settlement)
Repo rate: 8.30% (reverse repo rate: 8.20%)
Closing price: 100 and 15.5/32nds
Closing yield: 8.952%

The implied volatility, price, and delta of three at-the-money options near the close of trading were:

Days to Expiry	Implied Volatility	Call	Delta	Put	Delta
7	11.10%	[0-39]	0.500	[0-40]	−0.500
30	10.40%	[1-08]	0.500	[1-11]	−0.500
90	10.30%	[1-56]	0.500	[2-01]	−0.500

The March 1989 T-bond future contract has a closing price of 89 and 11/32nds.

implied volatility of 9.92% (based on the bond bid price). Similarly, using 10.40% volatility and the bond offer price of 100 and 17/32nds, the option is valued at [1-10]; adding another 3/64ths (not 3/32nds) for the "volatility spread" gives an offer of [1-13], which has an implied volatility of 10.88%.

The quote on this 30-day at-the-money call is likely to be [1-03] bid and [1-13] offer. Equivalently, the dealer is willing to "bid 9.92% and offer 10.88% volatility" on this 30-day option.

DELTA HEDGING AFTER BID IS HIT

Suppose that the [1-03] bid was hit by an institutional investor. To make a quick, riskless profit, the dealer can reduce the offer dramatically from [1-13] to [1-07] and hope for an offsetting sale. This is, however, very unlikely to happen in the OTC options market because each option has its own strike and expiration date. (For example, the most popular OTC options are the at-the-money and one-point-out ones; these options vary with time because as bond price changes, the strike prices change as well.) To avoid inventory risk on the $1 million in call options, the dealer should use the delta hedging method. His or her ultimate objective, however, is to buy options at the bid volatility and sell them at the offer, by using combinations of delta trades.

Since the dealer bought the 30-day call struck at 100 and $^{15.5}$⁄₃₂nds for [1-03], the implied volatility is 9.92% and the option's delta is found to be 0.493. With this knowledge, the dealer can hedge his or her $1 million option position by selling short $0.493 million in bonds at the bid price of 100 and ^{14}⁄₃₂nds; this bond will be borrowed and financed at the prevailing reverse repo rate of 8.20% (see Table 6.4). If the bond price subsequently drops ^{8}⁄₃₂nds in that afternoon, the dealer knows that his or her call will drop about ^{4}⁄₃₂nds ($= ^{8}$⁄₃₂ × 0.493) in value, and the loss in the call position is offset by the gain in the cash bond position. Since the risk of small price change in the option is completely hedged using a delta equivalent of underlying bonds, this option position is said to be **delta neutral**.

RISKS IN DELTA-NEUTRAL TRADES

Delta-neutral trades are not riskless. The three main risk factors that must be taken into consideration are:

gamma—the risk of major price movements
theta—the inevitable time decay in option premium
kappa—the risk of adverse changes in implied volatility

Since the carrying cost of the cash portion of a delta trade is dependent on prevailing repo rates, rapid changes in special reverse repo rates (perhaps due to a short squeeze) can at times also become a critical risk factor.

The dealer's delta-neutral trade can be summarized as follows:

Long: Bought $1 million in 30-day calls on UST 9.00% issue of November 15, 2018, struck at 100 and $^{15.5}$⁄₃₂nds at a price of [1-03]. The total purchase price of $10,468.75. This amount is assumed to be borrowed at a rate of 7% per annum.

Short: Short sell $0.493 million in UST 9.00% issue of November 15, 2018, at a price of 100 and ^{14}⁄₃₂nds. Since the accrued interest is equivalent to $^{22.4}$⁄₃₂nds, the invoice price is 101 and $^{4.4}$⁄₃₂nds and the total selling price of these bonds is $498,607.88. These bonds are borrowed at the prevailing reverse repo rate of 8.20%.

1. WHAT IS THE GAMMA OF THIS TRADE?

The best way to answer this question is by asking how well this trade will do if the bond price goes up or down by one point later that same afternoon. If the bond price *goes up* by one point,

a. The call price, conservatively assuming implied volatility to stay the same in spite of the sudden price jump, will increase by [0-37] to a new bid of [1-40], resulting in a gain of $5,781.25 ($= $1,000,000 \times {}^{37}\!/_{64}\%$) on the long side of the trade.

b. On the short side, assuming a bid-ask spread of ${}^{3}\!/_{32}$nds in the cash bond market, the total loss is 1 and ${}^{3}\!/_{32}$nds of a point, which amounts to $5,392.19 ($= $493,000 \times [1 + {}^{3}\!/_{32}]\%$).

Net result: The total gain is $389.06 or $851.25 without the ${}^{3}\!/_{32}$nds bond transaction cost. The new delta of the call is 0.632; the position's new delta is 0.14.

If the bond price *falls* by one point,

a. The call price, again assuming same volatility, will decrease by [0-27] to a new bid of [0-40], resulting in a loss of $4,218.75 on the long side of the trade.

b. On the short side, again assuming a ${}^{3}\!/_{32}$nds bid-ask spread, there is a gain of $4,467.81.

Net result: The total gain is $249.06 or $711.25 without the ${}^{3}\!/_{32}$nds bond transaction cost. The new delta of the call is 0.3551; the position's new delta is -0.14.

This delta-neutral trade therefore makes a profit, after taking into effect all transaction costs, if the bond price either moves up or down a point. Similar analysis can be used to show that this profit increases with the magnitude of the price change; the worst case occurs if the bond price stays the same and the resulting loss is due only to the transaction costs. This apparent risk-free day trade is a direct consequence of the fact that an option's delta changes with the underlying bond price. Call delta increases with the underlying bond price; in this case, from an original value of 0.493, delta increases (decreases) by about 0.14 to 0.632 (0.355) if the price goes up (down) by a point. Consequently, as the bond price moves up (down), the original delta-neutral position becomes desirably delta positive (negative), since delta has changed but the position has not been readjusted to neutrality. Such a delta-neutral trade is often said to be "long gamma" because it benefits from price variations.

This desirable feature of an option position is best summarized by gamma, which measures the change in delta of the position as the underlying bond price changes:

$$\text{Gamma} = \frac{\text{change in delta}}{\text{change in underlying bond price (in points)}}$$

For this delta-neutral trade, the gamma is about 0.14 or 14% [=0.632 − 0.493)/(1) or (0.355 − 0.493)/−1], and is therefore said to have *positive gamma*. Such a delta-neutral, positive-gamma position will make substantial profits if prices vary significantly. [Note that a call option by itself also has positive gamma, but because of its positive (not neutral) delta, it will only make profits when the underlying bond price goes up.]

2. WHAT IS THE THETA OF THIS TRADE?

There is no free lunch, and this trade is no exception. The time decay problem of this delta-neutral, positive-gamma position will now be examined. Suppose that the bond price stays exactly the same as the rest of that afternoon and the entire following day. How much will the dealer lose if the position is closed out near the close of trading on the following day?

On the long side,

a. The call price, optimistically assuming implied volatility to stay the same in spite of no price movement, will decrease by [0-01] to a bid of [1-02], resulting in a loss of $156.25.

b. The 7.00% interest to be paid on the $10,468.75 loan borrowed to buy the call is $2.01 ($=\$10,468.75 \times {}^{7\%}\!/_{365}$).

On the short side,

c. Assuming a bid-ask spread of $\frac{3}{32}$nds in the cash bond market, there is a trading loss of $462.19 ($493,000 × $\frac{3}{32}$%).

d. The accrued interest, based on the bond's 9% coupon, to be paid to the bond lender, is $121.56 ($=\$493,000 \times {}^{9\%}\!/_{365}$).

e. The 8.20% reverse repo interest, to be received from the bond lender, is $113.57 ($=\$498,607.88 \times {}^{8.2\%}\!/_{360}$).

[Note that from (*d*) and (*e*), the daily cost of carrying the short $0.493 million bond position is $7.99.] The total net loss is therefore $628.44, which is the sum of the following components:

Time-decay of option premium in (*a*):	$156.25
Interest costs on option premium in (*b*):	$ 2.01
Transaction costs on cash bond in (*c*):	$462.19
Carrying costs of cash bond position in (*d*) and (*e*):	$ 7.99
Total loss:	$628.44

The major part of the loss is due to the transaction costs on the cash bond. Most OTC options dealers are also primary dealers in cash bonds, and hence they very often can keep this transaction cost much lower than the assumed $\frac{3}{32}$nds spread here. Transaction costs are overhead investments made by the dealers; they will not be considered as an options-dealing risk factor in all subsequent discussions in this chapter. However, the option premium always decays over time for stable market prices, and it represents the price the dealer is paying to have a delta-neutral, positive-gamma options position.

Time decay of an option is measured by its theta, its change in price per unit change in time to expiration:

$$\text{Theta} = \frac{\text{change in option price (in points)}}{\text{decrease in time to expiration (in years)}}$$

For the dealer's 30-day call option, theta is -5.70 $[=(-\frac{1}{64})/(\frac{1}{365}) = {}^{-365}\!/_{64}]$, because its price will go down by $\frac{1}{64}$th of a point in a day. A negative theta therefore implies time decay in option premium. Because of interest costs on the option premium and carrying costs on the cash bonds, the dealer's options *position* actually has a slightly more negative theta than the call itself. (As was noted, an option's theta gets more negative as expiration date approaches. We will examine the consequences of this fact below, where we review the various risk factors in option positions. The inverse relationship between theta and gamma will also be discussed there.)

3. ARE THERE OTHER RISKS?

The dealer currently has a delta-neutral, positive-gamma, and negative-theta position. Ignoring transaction costs, this position will lose $166.25 a day, but the profit potential is significant if the bond price changes drastically; for example, a one-point gain in bond price will bring a profit of $851.25. To complicate matters further, there are other nontrivial risks.

The above analysis assumed that the traded implied volatility stays the same no matter what happens to the bond price. This is not realistic because (*a*) if the price moves up or down by more than a point in an afternoon, the implied volatilities generally tend to trade upward as well; and (*b*) if the price does not change for a day or two, these volatilities may actually trade at a lower lever. There may also be times when some news or events may trigger a change in the market's perception of future volatility. To measure this implied volatility risk, the kappa of an option is used:

$$\text{Kappa} = \frac{\text{change in option price (in points)}}{\text{change in implied volatility (in percent)}}$$

If the implied volatility of the 30-day call is increased from 10.4% to 11.4%, the call's value will change from [1-08] to [1-15]. Its kappa is therefore equal to $\frac{7}{64}$ths or 0.11 points. The dealer's option position also has this kappa risk; it will go down in value by $1,093.75 (= $1,000,000 × $\frac{7}{64}$%) if the call's implied volatility drops to 9.4%.

Another risk factor to be considered is hidden in the options pricing models and the carrying costs of the cash bonds. The repo market is very liquid for overnight transactions but becomes thinner as the time period of the repo agreement is increased. Dealers often finance their bond positions using up to seven-day repos. They usually have to roll and refinance their positions when the repo term is up, thereby facing a repo (or financing) rate risk. The repo rate also has a direct impact on the calculation of the forward price of a bond, which is the difference between the spot bond price and the bond's carrying cost from settlement to expiration.

WHAT ACTUALLY HAS THE DEALER DONE?

The dealer starts off by making a market on a $1 million 30-day at-the-money OTC option, [1-03] bid and [1-13] offer, using the volatility information from the last trade on that option. His or her market is equivalent to bidding to buy 9.92% and offering to sell 10.88% volatility on the given option.

When the [1-03] bid is hit, the dealer's obvious objective is to sell the bought options at a higher price for a quick profit. This is unlikely to happen immediately because each OTC option is different and there may not be any party interested in the given option. To offset inventory risk, the dealer uses delta hedging and sells short a delta-equivalent $0.493 million of the underlying bond at 100 and $\frac{14}{32}$nds. He or she ends up with a position with the following characteristics:

1. *Delta neutral (delta = 0).* There is no price risk for small changes in the underlying bond price.
2. *Positive gamma (gamma = 0.14).* The position will profit from price variations; for example, if the bond price moves up (down) by one point, the delta of the position will change from zero to

about 0.14 (−0.14), which brings with it a profit of $851.25 ($711.25).

3. *Negative theta (theta = −5.70).* Since the call will decrease in value by 5.7 points per year or ⅟₆₄th per day, the $1 million call in the position will have a time decay of $156.25 per day; there is also a daily interest cost of $2.01 on the option premium and a daily bond-carrying cost of $7.99 on the $0.493 million in bonds.

4. *Positive kappa (kappa = 0.11).* The option will increase in value by ⁷⁄₆₄ths points for every 1% change in the implied volatility; the position value will therefore decrease by $1,093.75 if the implied volatility of the 30-day bond drops by 1% to 9.40%.

The dealer is therefore taking on theta, kappa, and repo rate risks instead of inventory price (or delta) risk. As a temporary dealer's position, a delta-neutral trade with positive gamma is superior to an unhedged option position because the combined theta, kappa, and repo risks are less than the delta or price risk. The option dealer's ultimate objective is to make profits without incurring any risk. Delta trading is an essential tool for these dealers because they can make low-risk profits by combining delta-neutral trades with offsetting gamma, theta, kappa, and repo rate risks. The following example shows a delta-neutral options position with negative gamma, positive theta, and negative kappa. It will be shown that the dealer will make riskless profits by adding this new position to his or her existing one.

EXAMPLE 6.4: A DELTA-NEUTRAL TRADE WITH NEGATIVE GAMMA AND POSITIVE THETA

Our intention here is to give an example of a delta-neutral trade with negative gamma and positive theta. We show that the dealer in Example 6.3 will have exactly such a position if the offer is lifted and the dealer delta hedges his or her option position. Using this as the benchmark example, we argue that the dealer can profit from buying bid-side and selling offer-side volatility by combining delta-neutral trades executed at different bond price levels.

WHAT IF THE OFFER IS LIFTED INSTEAD?

In Example 6.3, the dealer's quote for the 30-day at-the-money call on the UST 9.00% issue of November 15, 2018, is [1-03] bid and [1-13] offer. Suppose that an investor bought $1 million in such calls, struck at

100 and $^{15.5}\!/_{32}$nds, at [1-13]. The dealer has therefore sold the calls at 10.88% implied volatility and the delta of the sold option is 0.507; this value is different from the 0.493 delta given in Example 6.3 because it is computed using the **offering** (not bidding) bond price of 100 and $^{17}\!/_{32}$nds. With this computer-fed knowledge, the dealer delta hedges his or her $1 million short option position by buying long $0.507 million in bonds at the offer price of 100 and $^{17}\!/_{32}$nds; this bond purchase is financed at the prevailing repo rate of 8.30%.

The dealer's position can be summarized as follows:

Short: Sold $1 million in 30-day calls on UST 9.00% issue of November 15, 2018, struck at 100 and $^{15.5}\!/_{32}$nds at a price of [1-13]. The total sale price is $12,031.25. This amount will be earning interest for the dealer at an assumed annual rate of 7.00%.

Long: Bought $0.507 million of UST 9.00% issue of November 15, 2018, at a price of 100 and $^{17}\!/_{32}$nds. Since the accrued interest is equivalent to $^{22.4}\!/_{32}$nds, the invoice price is 101 and $^{7.4}\!/_{32}$nds and the total purchase price of these bonds is $513,242.44. This amount is borrowed at the 8.30% repo rate to finance the bond purchase.

RISKS OF THE DELTA-NEUTRAL SHORT-OPTION POSITION

The risk characteristics of the dealer's position are:

1. *Delta neutral (delta = 0)*. The delta of this option position is zero because the $1 million short call position is delta hedged with $0.507 million in cash bonds; there is no price risk for small changes in the underlying bond price.

2. *Negative gamma (gamma = −0.14)*. The gamma is −0.14 because if the bond price moves up (down) by one point, the delta of this position will change from zero to about −0.14 (0.14), which brings a loss of $711.25 ($851.25).

3. *Positive theta (theta = 5.70)*. The call will decrease in value by 5.7 points per year or $\frac{1}{64}$th per day. Since this position is short $1 million in such calls, it will increase in value by $156.25 per day; there is also a daily gain of $2.31 interest from the option premium and a daily bond-carrying gain of $6.68.

4. *Negative kappa (kappa = −0.11)*. The option will increase in value by $\frac{7}{64}$ths points for every 1% change in the implied volatility. The position value will decrease by $1,093.75 if the implied volatility of the 30-day bond trades up by 1% to 10.40%.

IMPORTANT NOTE: The above characteristics apply to *all* 30-day at-the-money calls on the same bond, *as long as they have the same implied volatility* (10.40%). Consequently, when the bond is trading at 100, the 30-day call struck at 100 will have very similar risk exposures to those of the 30-day call struck at 102 when the bond price has moved to 102.

The dealer is therefore taking on gamma, kappa, and repo risks in this delta-neutral position. Contrary to Example 6.3, this position makes small amounts of money from the option's time decay and the bond's positive carry; however, there can be significant losses if the bond price either gets or is expected to get much more volatile. As expected, by combining this position with the one in Example 6.3, the resulting delta-neutral position will have zero gamma, theta, and kappa. The dealer's ultimate goal is to execute these two offsetting delta-neutral trades simultaneously because this is exactly the same as selling, on the offer side, the options that were just bought on the bid side. Again, because of the lack of order flows in a given option, such quick-profit opportunities occur infrequently.

Low-Risk Options Dealing

Steps to Follow in Options Dealing

Delta-hedging reduces the options dealer's risk while he or she tries to profit from the bid-ask spread. The following steps are essential in options dealing:

Step 1. Make a market on calls, for example, using "last trade" volatility.

Step 2. If the bid is hit, delta hedge the long call position by selling short delta-equivalent cash bonds; the resulting position is delta neutral.

Step 3. Aggressively try to sell the call position by giving a slightly lower offer than the competitors. While waiting for the offer to be lifted, no significant risk is experienced because the position has zero delta and positive gamma.

Remark:

It is important to note that the dealer does not have to sell the exact call that was just bought, since, as noted earlier, all 30-day at-the-money calls with the same implied volatility on the same bond have very similar risk characteristics. For example, if the dealer bought a 30-day at-the-money call when the bond price was at 100 and $^{15\cdot4}\!/_{32}$nds, he or she does not have to sell this call (strike = 100 and $^{15\cdot5}\!/_{32}$nds) if the bond price is now at 101. The dealer will do equally well by selling the new 30-day at-the-money call (strike = 101) as far as offsetting his or her current long volatility position is concerned.

Step 4. When the offer is eventually lifted, delta hedge the short call position by buying long delta-equivalent cash bonds. (This is often equivalent to buying back the cash bond sold in step 2.)

The bottom line for the dealer is that he or she manages to buy at the bid and sell at the offer without incurring inventory risk. The dealer's risks here are limited to time decay (theta) and to lower implied volatility (kappa). If the dealer sells the call first, however, his or her position is exposed to gamma and kappa risks, which can be significant in times of sudden extreme volatility. Risk-averse dealers, therefore, generally like to be long in gamma or volatility; they will be very aggressive in buying options if their current position has negative gamma.

Profit-Taking by Adjusting to Delta Neutrality

Suppose that a dealer, at the end of step 2, has a delta-neutral position with positive gamma. The bond price suddenly goes up by a point. As shown in Example 6.3, the dealer's option position now has a delta of 0.139:

Long: $1 million in 30-day calls on the UST 9.00% issue of November 15, 2018, struck at 100 and $^{15\cdot5}\!/_{32}$nds, valued at [1-40] when the bond price is 101 and $^{15\cdot5}\!/_{32}$nds. These calls were bought at a price of [1-03]. The delta of this option position is 0.632.

Short: $0.493 million of the same bonds. These bonds were sold short at a price of 100 and $^{15\cdot5}\!/_{32}$nds.

This originally delta-neutral position has gained $851.23 in value, and its new delta, 0.139, is the sum of (1×0.632) and (-1×0.493).

The dealer wants to take the $851.25 profit that has been gained, but the OTC call seller may not want to buy it back at this point in time. To lock in this profit, the dealer should adjust his or her position to delta neutrality by selling short another $0.139 million in bonds at the new price of 101 and $^{15\cdot5}\!/_{32}$nds. If the bond price goes back down one point, and the dealer readjusts his or her position to delta neutral again by buying $0.139 million in bonds back at 100 and $^{15\cdot5}\!/_{32}$nds, he or she will have the same delta-neutral position as the initial one, but will also have made a profit of $1,390 (= $139,000 × 1%). Notice that the dealer would have missed this profit opportunity if he or she did not readjust his or her position to delta neutrality; in this case, the final position would also be the same as the starting one. It can be shown, using the same analysis, that a similar profit opportunity exists if the bond price goes down one point first.

Risks of Option Positions

The gamma, theta, and kappa risks of an option position were introduced and defined in Example 6.3. Important notes concerning these risk factors are presented here.

Positive or Negative Gamma

Gamma measures the change in delta of a position as the underlying bond price changes:

$$\text{Gamma} = \frac{\text{change in delta}}{\text{change in underlying bond price (in points)}}$$

1. The delta of a positive gamma position increases (decreases) if the underlying bond price increases (decreases).
2. A delta-neutral position with positive gamma will benefit from major up or down price movements. Its profit potential is enormous.
3. Such a position loses money slowly over time because of its negative theta. It is also susceptible to gradual decline in implied volatility.
4. Risk-averse dealers and traders should not be exposed to negative gamma, especially for a prolonged period.
5. A long call or put option position has positive gamma. A long call *and* put position has a more positive gamma than either one of its components. Buying both a call and a put at the same strike price is called a **long straddle**; if these options are equally out of the money instead, the position is a **long strangle**.
6. At-the-money options have the highest gamma value. As an option gets farther in or out of the money, its gamma value decreases toward zero. In other words, as an example, the difference between the deltas of an at-the-money and a one-point-out option is greater

than the difference between those of a two-point-out and a three-point-out option.

Effects of Time Decay

Time decay of an option is measured by its theta, its change in price per unit change in time to expiration:

$$\text{Theta} = \frac{\text{change in option price (in points)}}{\text{decrease in time to expiration (in years)}}$$

1. Time decay is not a risk—it is a certainty. (Since for each extra day to expiration the option owner has another opportunity for favorable price movement, option premium will decrease over time as expiration approaches if all other factors remain the same.)
2. A positive gamma position has time decay or a negative theta.
3. Theta is a function of the time to expiration. The daily time decay of an option increases rapidly as the expiration date approaches. A position with a long three-month call and a short three-week call, both at the money, will therefore have a positive theta (and negative gamma).
4. At-the-money options have the highest gamma value and the most negative theta. Theta gets closer to zero as an option gets farther in or out of the money.
5. Positive-gamma, negative-theta positions are attractive when options are trading at very low implied volatilities or when options are believed to be very underpriced relative to normal bond price variabilities.

Up or Down Implied Volatilities

The risk associated with possible changes in implied volatility is:

$$\text{Kappa} = \frac{\text{change in option price (in points)}}{\text{change in implied volatility (in percent)}}$$

1. Options holders (sellers) have kappa risk because the value of their holdings may drop if the marketplace decides that the future volatility of the underlying bond will be getting lower (higher).
2. Kappa and gamma risks are both volatility driven. A high-gamma position will benefit from wild swings in the underlying bond price,

whereas a high-kappa position will enjoy such benefits only if the actual price variability induces a rise in the bond's implied volatility. If implied volatility changes even when the price has been stable, there will be kappa risk and no gamma risk.

3. At-the-money options are the most sensitive to volatility changes and they have the highest kappa values.

EXAMPLE 6.5: RISKS OF A SPREAD TRADE

Suppose, on that same December 12th afternoon when the UST 9.00% issue of November 15, 2018, is trading at 100 and $^{15.5}\!/_{32}$nds (see Table 6.4), that the dealer buys a 90-day at-the-money straddle for a price of [3-47] (implied volatility = 9.90%), and sells a seven-day at-the-money straddle for a price of [1-25] (implied volatility = 12.55%) (see Table 6.5). What are the risks of the dealer's overall position?

1. *Delta = 0.009.* The delta of this position is the (amount-) weighted average of the options deltas. With a slightly positive delta, this position will have a small gains (losses) in value if the bond price moves up (down).

2. *Gamma = −0.262.* The gamma of this position is the (amount-) weighted average of the option gammas. With a negative gamma, this position stands to lose about $^{10}\!/_{64}$ths (computed from actual option price changes, not directly from the gamma value) if the market moves up or down by a point.

3. *Theta = 34.22.* The theta of this position is the (amount-) weighted average of the option thetas. With a positive theta, this position will have a daily increase of 34.22/365, or $^{6}\!/_{64}$ths, points in value if other factors stay the same. It should be noted that the theta for the 7-day options is four times as high as that for the 90-day ones, while the gamma is only two and one half times that of the latter.

Table 6.5 A Spread Trade

Long or Short	Type	Strike Price	Days to Expiry	Option Price	Amt. ($MM)	Delta	Gamma	Theta	Kappa
Long	Call	100 15.5/32	90	[1-51]	1	0.504	0.086	−5.70	0.1875
Long	Put	100 15.5/32	90	[1-60]	1	−0.497	0.087	−5.70	0.1875
Short	Call	100 15.5/32	7	[0-44]	−1	0.501	0.217	−22.81	0.0625
Short	Put	100 15.5/32	7	[0-45]	−1	−0.499	0.218	−22.81	0.0625

4. *Kappa = 0.25.* The kappa of this position is the (amount-) weighted average of the option kappas. This position will decrease in value by 0.25 point if each of the implied volatilities drops by 1%. The implied volatility of the 90-day options will, however, decrease by less than that of the 7-day ones, because the latter's volatility is at a much higher current level.

In summary, the dealer has an almost delta-neutral position with a very attractive, positive theta, while facing a moderately negative gamma. This position is also susceptible to big drops in implied volatilites. Dealers often take such positions when they expect little price movement in the near term, especially when the short-dated options have much higher implied volatility.

CROSS-MARKET HEDGING

When Is It Necessary?

In the earlier examples, it was assumed that the dealer can easily finance his or her bond borrowing and lending activities by using the repo market. This will not always be the case. In the JGB options market, for example, delta hedging of an option using the underlying bond is difficult, since the repo market is not yet well developed in Japan. Participants in the Japanese repo market have to pay a transfer tax; this extra transaction cost also makes delta hedging prohibitively expensive. In early trading, therefore, the bid-ask spread in options on JGB cash bonds has been fairly wide.

The Japanese bond repo market will undoubtedly mature very quickly. Meanwhile, it is still necessary to look for alternative ways to hedge a cash bond option position, perhaps by using the highly liquid bond futures contracts or the benchmark bond issue. In Example 6.6 below, using the data shown in Table 6.4 for the U.S. cash bond and futures markets, we show how the bond futures contract can be used to hedge a cash option position. The additional **basis risk** involved in such cross-market hedging is also explained. This example has obvious applicability to the peculiarities of the JGB options market. Finally, we point out the advantages and disadvantages of using the more liquid benchmark issue to hedge an option position on a side issue.

EXAMPLE 6.6: CASH BOND OPTIONS HEDGED WITH FUTURES

The March 1989 T-bond contract is trading at 89 and $^{11}/_{32}$nds when the UST 9.00% bond of November 15, 2018, is trading at 100 and $^{15.5}/_{32}$nds, just before the close of futures trading on December 12, 1988 (see Table 6.4). As in Example 6.3, suppose that the dealer just bought a $1 million 30-day call on the bond struck at 100 and $^{15.5}/_{32}$nds for a price of [1-03]. Assume that, unlike Example 6.3, the bond's repo rate is trading at 2.00% (instead of the real 8.25%), perhaps because of a short squeeze in the bond. Since the cost of carrying a short position in the underlying bond is very high in such a case (similar to the high costs in borrowing JGB bonds), the dealer does not want to delta hedge his or her long option position with the underlying bond.

WHAT IS THE ALTERNATIVE?

The dealer knows that the correct delta hedge is to short $0.493 million of the cash bond against his or her long option position. Let us assume for now that the dealer also knows the relationship between the cash bond price P and the March T-bond futures price F:

$$P = (r \times F) + b \tag{6.2}$$

The dealer knows, then, that if the cash bond price P goes down by one point, the March T-bond futures price will drop by $(1/r)$ points. Given such knowledge, shorting $0.493 million in cash bonds is equivalent to shorting $(0.493 \times r)$ million in the futures contract, and the dealer can therefore short sell $(0.493 \times r)$ million in March T-bond to delta hedge his or her long option position.

USING THE BOND'S FUTURES CONTRACT CONVERSION FACTOR AS r

In both the U.S. and Japanese bond markets, there is a conversion factor for each of the cash bonds that is deliverable against the given futures contract. On the futures contract's settlement date, short sellers of the contract will have to sell one of the deliverable bonds to the buyers at a price equal to the product of the bond's conversion factor and the contract's settlement price. Therefore, on that date, the so-called cheapest-to-deliver issue, j, must have a price P_j exactly equal to $f_j \times F$, where f_j is its conversion factor and F is the contract's settlement price. That is, on the contract's settlement date:

$$P_j = (f_j \times F) + b_j$$

where $b_j = 0$. Note that for any other deliverable bond i, i not equal to j:

$$P_i = (f_i \times F) + b_i$$

where $b_i > 0$.

Most dealers therefore use the bond's conversion factor as r in Equation 6.2. For example, the conversion factor of the UST 9.00% issue of November 15, 2018, for the March 1989 T-bond futures contract is 1.1126. The dealer in our example would accordingly short $0.5485 million ($= \$493{,}000 \times 1.1126$) in March T-bond contracts to hedge his or her long $1 million call on the cash bond.

Unfortunately, a bond's basis, b_i, which is equal to $P_i - (f_i \times F)$, does not remain constant over time. Dealers using a bond's conversion factor as r will therefore incur the risk of adverse changes in the bond's basis. When the dealer shorts $0.5485 million in March T-bond contracts in our example, the basis of the UST 9.00% bond is trading at $^{34.5}\!/_{32}$nds $[100\ ^{15.5}\!/_{32} - (1.1126 \times 89\ ^{11}\!/_{32})]$. If the bond price stays the same but the March contract goes up in price by $^{4}\!/_{32}$nds, the bond's basis will have (adversely) decreased by $^{4.5}\!/_{32}$nds, and this basis change also represents the loss in the dealer's cross-market, delta-hedged option position. The dealer in this case, however, will have additional profits if the bond's basis increases. In summary, dealers using a futures contract to hedge a long option position in the cash bond will take on the bond's basis risk. They should use such a cross-market hedge only when they believe this basis is not about to decrease; they therefore should avoid using futures to hedge against the most deliverable bonds because these bases generally decrease to zero as the contract settlement date approaches. Of course, if such deliverable bonds currently have a negative basis, then such a cross-market hedge will be very desirable.

Another close estimate of r is the ratio:

$$r = \frac{\text{value of a basis point of the bond}}{\text{value of a basis point of the future contract}}$$

The user of this estimate must first determine the value of a basis point of the futures contract, however. Tang (1988) provides an excellent description of the specific approach needed for such valuation for a futures contract (see also Schwarz et al., 1986).

USING HISTORICAL INFORMATION TO ESTIMATE r

Historical price movements provide precious information on how bond prices behave and how they relate to one another. Specifically, historical data can be used to check if a given bond's cash price indeed varies with the futures contract's price in the linear fashion described in Equation 6.2. The same set of data can also be used to provide a statistically sound estimate of r.

Statistical regression analysis, described in most standard statistics texts, can be used to analyze these historical price data. Using the historical cash bond price as the dependent variable and the corresponding futures price as the independent variable in a regression run, residual analysis of the results will indicate whether the linear model assumed in Equation 6.2 is valid. Moreover, the slope coefficient obtained in the same regression run will provide a reasonable estimate of r.

Some dealers use this estimate, r_i, of r to calculate the appropriate amount of futures contracts needed to hedge their option position on bond i. The basis risk they face in this instance is given by the difference $P_i - (r_i \times F)$.

What About Hedging a Side Issue with the Benchmark Bond?

The bond basis movements in the Japanese market are very different from those in the U.S. market. Since the JGB future contract is the most liquid instrument, it tends to move up (down) first, followed in turn by the benchmark bond and then the side issues. Consequently, a bull (bear) market, the basis of a side issue tends to narrow (widen) first and then reverses its trend. Therefore, even if a side issue's basis may eventually go up, it may go down substantially first when there is a rally in the bond market.

In the Japanese bond market, the usually very liquid benchmark issue can also be used to hedge against options on a side issue. The major points of consideration are:

1. Even benchmark issues are sometimes difficult to borrow.
2. There is no additional risk if a bond's price P is exactly related to the benchmark's price B as follows:

$$P = (r \times B) + c$$

   where r and c are constants.
3. A close estimate of r is the ratio:

$$r = \frac{\text{value of a basis point of the bond}}{\text{value of a basis point of the benchmark}}$$

The newly introduced risk here is the risk of adverse change in the yield spread between the bond and the benchmark issue. Again, because the benchmark issue is more liquid, it has a tendency to move up (down) before a side issue does in a bull (bear) market; consequently, the yield spread between the bond and a side issue may vary with the market direction, at least temporarily.

4. An alternative approach is to estimate r from historical price data using regression analysis. The new spread risk, for the i-th bond, will be a function of $P_i - (r_i \times B)$.

REFERENCES

Most options books focus on pricing and investment strategies, and very little has been written on the actual marketmaking process, especially for OTC bond options. Schwarz et al. (1986) discusses the bond futures market in some depth, but has scant coverage of options. The papers by Silber (1984, 1988) are excellent references for dealing in options on futures. Cox and Rubinstein (1985) gives additional details on the qualitative behavior of option prices and sensitivities, based on the Black-Scholes option pricing model.

Cox, J., and M. Rubinstein, *Options Markets*, Prentice-Hall, Englewood Cliffs, N.J., 1985.

Schwarz, E. W., J. M. Hill, and T. Schneeweis, *Financial Futures: Fundamentals, Strategies, and Applications*, Dow Jones–Irwin, Homewood, Ill., 1986.

Silber, W., "Marketmaker Behavior in an Auction Market: An Analysis of Scalpers in Futures Markets," *Journal of Finance*, September 1984.

Silber, W., "Marketmaking in Options: Principles and Implications," in *Financial Options: From Theory To Practice*, Proceedings of a conference at the Salomon Brothers Center, New York University, December 1988.

Tang, E. M., *The Effect of Delivery Options on Interest Rate Futures and Option Contracts*, Portfolio Management Technology, San Francisco, 1988.

7

A Computerized Options Trading and Risk Management System for Dealers

To be competitive in bond options dealing, a financial institution must have in place a computerized trading system with pricing, position tracking, risk management, and accounting capabilities. Certain questions about the specification of these capabilities, as well as about hardware and software design issues, have to be answered before such a system can be built. This chapter addresses these questions. The emergence of advanced trader workstations and their role in cash bonds and bond options dealership activities are summarized in the first section. The risk management tools most useful for trading systems are then discussed.

The most important functional capabilities of a dealer-oriented options trading and risk management system using such advanced workstations are specified in some detail. Such a system, in summary, must provide fast and powerful tools to implement the dealer's intuitions about the market, and to meet the most common needs of active traders: ready availability of pricing and sensitivity information, and analysis of short-term exposure to important risk parameters. It must also produce all necessary accounting data, including position exposure and profit-and-loss statements by dealer account, and allow the risk manager to reduce a portfolio of highly complex trades to easily understandable measures of risk. Whether a trading firm decides to build or buy such a system, its in-house staff will have to go through this functional specification process.

Finally, some indications are given of possible future developments in computerized trading and risk management systems.

COMPUTERIZED TRADING SYSTEMS

Role of Computer Technology

In today's volatile, competitive, and interdependent global financial marketplace, dealers and strategic traders frequently have to make intelligent and profitable decisions, based on massive amounts of market information, within a matter of seconds. To stay competitive in the trading arena, dealers must have information as good as or better than the information their competitors and institutional clients are getting. Decision support tools must also be in place to help traders analyze market information and implement their decisions quickly and accurately. Meanwhile, trading desk managers must monitor and control the risk capital committed by traders. With these competitive and internal pressures growing as the world financial markets witness the effects of an extraordinary electronics revolution, dealership management has begun to invest in many of the technological advances that are directly applicable to the trading desk.

As pointed out in a recent *Wall Street Computer Review* article by Pavan Sahgal (1989) on automation at the big four Japanese securities firms, it is not unusual for large Japanese securities firms to allocate as much as $1 billion or more in technology expenditures spread over five- or ten-year plan periods. In the same *Review* issue, Ivy Schmerken (1989) reported on how various U.S. securities firms respond to the question of *building or buying* a trading system. Desktop multi-tasking super-microcomputers that have sophisticated windowing systems, graphics support, mathematics coprocessors, and the like, functioning as **trader workstations,** represnt a technology that is being used by more and more trading firms. For example, in a 1988 conference on "Advanced Trader Workstations" in New York, Ian Hobson of San Francisco's Hambrecht & Quist made a presentation on the real-time over-the-counter (OTC) stock trading system he has installed on a Stratus computer (with networked workstations for traders). The author presented the architecture of the next generation's bond trading room in the same conference

(Wong, 1988); a major component of this architecture is again the **advanced trader workstation,** which runs a variety of applications simultaneously, including broker and exchange information display, trading analytics, and decision execution. In the following discussion, it is assumed that the options dealing system described will be built to run on such a trader workstation.

Trader Workstations—The Technological Infrastructure

The notion of an advanced trader workstation entails certain *hardware* and *software* requirements. We do not intend to go into the details of computer hardware requirements in this book, but for the benefit of professionals evaluating alternatives for the purchase or development of a trading support system, we briefly outline some of the functional requirements of such a system.

Multi-tasking

A trader workstation must be capable of true multi-tasking, to a degree still beyond the capability of even most advanced personal computers. Market data feeds, access to historical pricing and volatility data, trader analytics, decision support programs, and trade entry must all be active simultaneously and in close to real-time performance. The addition of extra tasks and rapid switching between windows and programs must not cause unacceptable delays while programs are activated and/or "swapped" in and out of memory. This means that useful trader workstations must have plenty of random access memory (RAM) installed—typically up to 32 megabytes as of this writing, and undoubtedly even more in the near future.

Bit-Mapped Graphics

To be useful to the working professional, a trader workstation must support a clear, user-friendly visual interface. Key to the use of multiple application programs is a powerful *windowing* system. High-quality, bit-mapped graphics support is the technological *sine qua non* for such an interface. Also extremely desirable are oversized monitors, which allow for display of more, and more legible, windowed applications, and even dual-monitor workstations, which can allow the segregation of "pages" from market data feeds and even the possibility of integration of video data feeds into a single workstation environment.

Mathematics Coprocessor Support

In order to support acceptable performance by the kinds of sophisticated analytics required by today's traders, mathematics coprocessors (also known as floating point accelerators, or "fpa" boards) are a must. Some proprietary analytics packages available today already require customized hardware—*vector processors*—to speed execution of highly computation-intensive applications.

Networking

Today's trader does not act in a vacuum. As important as the advanced technological capabilities of his or her own workstation is a trader's connectivity with other traders, brokers, market data feeds, and the electronics world in general. An advanced trader workstation must be part of a fast, reliable electronic *network*, including access to more powerful computer resources than can presently be installed in any stand-alone workstation. Such networking is also very important from the *risk management* point of view, because it allows management a firm-wide view of aggregate position and exposure information.

Data Base Access

To the trader, information is money. Rapid, convenient access to current and historical price, yield, and volatility data is essential to the process of making accurate, timely trading decisions. No trader in today's market can be without access to a comprehensive relational data base management system (RDBMS).

Compute Server Access

For the most high-powered analytics, especially some models involving mortgages and the complex derivative instruments, computing power beyond the capability of a stand-alone workstation is required. Network access to a powerful *compute server*, perhaps a mini-supercomputer, can provide convenient access to such analytics. The ability to distribute computational tasks throughout a network of workstations also provides the opportunity to take advantage of slack capacity in some machines while avoiding overloading of others.

While by no means covering all the technological considerations involved in planning or evaluating a trader workstation environment, these are some of the most important areas for consideration, and none of them should be overlooked by the serious professional.

Sources of Competitive Advantage

Sophisticated trading systems built to operate on these advanced workstations provide traders with computational tools for information assimilation and analysis, and with quick and accurate decision implementation facilities. Such systems will lead to reduced risks in marketmaking activities. In addition, arbitrage opportunities can be spotted more quickly, which will increase the likelihood of profitable trades being executed. Since "what if . . ." analysis can also be performed more readily and in a timely manner, trading efficiency will be significantly improved. Finally, risk managers can monitor their market exposure closely without disrupting the traders.

As the author pointed out in a study on technology investment strategy (see Wong, 1987), trading firms must actively monitor and adopt new technologies to avoid losing ground competitively, but this advanced equipment by itself will generally not create competitive advantages. It is possible, however, to build sustainable competitive advantage if the acquired technology can be used to exploit or further leverage a firm's existing nontechnology-based sources of competitive strength and uniqueness.

Proprietary Analytics

One important source of such a competitive edge lies in the firm's **proprietary analytics**. By this we mean that set of models, methods, and techniques developed or acquired by the firm that are not in common currency among other firms, and that serve to distinguish the firm in its approach to the analysis of market data and trading decision support. Proprietary analytics can include new or modified quantitative models, which may offer more precise prices and sensitivities, or new quantitative measures giving a new angle on certain market phenomena. They can also include innovative *qualitative* approaches to the analysis of market data and/or trading decision support. For example, a firm might have a particular slant on scenario analysis, or an approach to yield curve arbitrage, that sets it apart from its competitors.

The ability of a firm to effectively exploit the competitive edge offered by its proprietary analytics will depend to a considerable extent on its ability to *leverage* that potential advantage through appropriate technological implementation. To be effective, proprietary analytics must reach the traders' desktops, and be put into active, daily use by the firm as a whole.

Risk Management

Another potential area of competitive advantage lies in a firm's choice of a particular set of *risk management* policies and safeguards. Sloppy, poorly understood, or imperfectly implemented risk management systems are an obvious source of loss to a firm (and to its clients). Overly conservative, inflexible, or clumsily implemented risk management systems can also tie traders hands, constraining available capital and allowable trading strategies, and represent a potential source of *opportunity loss*.

A properly designed and implemented computerized trading support system can help ensure responsiveness and appropriate use of firm resources in risk management by providing timely position and exposure information by an individual trader, trading group, or market sector, or on a firm-wide basis. It can also provide essential information on a wide range of possible hedging strategies and scenario analysis capabilities, giving the risk managers more flexibility in their task. Whether a firm decides to build or buy its trading system, its in-house staff must make sure that its own proprietary trading analytics and risk controls are readily available on the resulting system. In the next section, the various kinds of risk management tools essential for bond trading systems are presented.

Human Potential

A third source of competitive advantage, of course, lies in the human factor: the market insight, skill, and productivity of traders and support staff. Marketmaking is an art as well as a science, but both artists and scientists depend on their tools, and, more than in many media, the availability of appropriate tools will condition the performance of any financial professional. A fast, flexible, and user-friendly computerized trading and risk management system will surely enhance any inherent competitive advantage provided by top-quality personnel. This is what we mean by using appropriate technology to *leverage* nontechnological sources of competitive strength and uniqueness.

Protected Customer Base

Other factors may contribute to competitive advantage. For example, a protected customer base is a potential source of competitive uniqueness. Japan's Nomura Securities Company quickly became a leading primary dealer in U.S. government securities because they had privileged access to Japanese institutional investors. The challenge to Nomura and to other Japanese securities firms, as to any possessor of competitive advantage, is to find ways to use advanced technology to protect and exploit their uniqueness.

In Chapters 3 and 4 we have presented some of the state-of-the-art quantitative analytics required to make the bond options trader competitive in today's markets. In this chapter, we present a framework for the functional specification of a computerized bond options trading risk management and decision support system.

RISK MANAGEMENT TOOLS FOR TRADERS

Risk management is a major aspect of a trader's daily routine, but it is only one aspect. To design an exposure management system without consideration of the trader's other activities is like designing the top floor of a house without knowing what is to occupy the lower floors. To help the reader envision what a computerized trading system must do, and to help prevent prematurely obsolete systems from being built, the broad scope of a trader's activities are outlined in this section. The system developer must always consider risk management issues in the context of a comprehensive trading system.

What Does a Trader Do?

A trader's job is to continuously monitor the state of world financial markets, searching for opportunities to put on trades with attractive risk/return characteristics. Successful traders consistently find and execute profitable trades, while simultaneously keeping track of how their complicated portfolios of related trades are performing. Since good trades can often become bad ones as market environments change, traders must constantly reevaluate the desirability of their positions. A decision support system to help traders do their jobs more effectively should therefore have the following functional capabilities:

- On-line global news and information
- Current price information from all brokers and exchanges
- Quick access to historical security price and economics data in graphic or table format
- Real-time analytical tools for pricing derivative products, determining hedge ratios, and spotting cross-market arbitrage opportunities
- On-line trade entry
- Scenario-driven performance analysis for actual and hypothetical trading portfolios
- Net position summary with profit-and-loss (P&L) exposure to various risk parameters
- Accounting capabilities

Remark:

Many traders would also like to have some tools for spotting technical trends, thresholds, and the like. Since many market participants religiously use technical analysis, traders ought to keep an eye on the *technicals*, whether they believe in such analysis or not.

An ideal computerized trading system would provide support for all these functions in an *integrated* format. This would provide the user with the capability of interfacing between these different facets of the system, using historical data as inputs to scenario analysis, for example, to track the hypothetical performance of "paper trades" under historical market conditions, or feeding current market data into the analytics to display, for example, current implied volatilities for a range of options.

Such a system would give the traders all the tools they need in performing their daily functions. Financial market data would be summarized in a convenient format. Traders could perform analytics and display graphics using current and historical data to help them form their market opinions and identify attractive trades with appropriate hedges. They could simulate the performance of their trades under various market scenarios, to better understand their risks and potential returns. They could easily execute and enter trades into their accounts. Periodic updates of their net positions would help them keep track of their trades and show them their P&L exposures to various risk parameters, including interest rate and volatility levels. Daily accounting routines, including measures of trader performance, would also be executed automatically by the system. Such a system would also provide a consolidated position summary and risk exposure analysis for the trader or desk or floor manager.

Scenario-Driven Performance Analysis

The key risk management tools for traders and dealers are **net position summary** and **scenario-driven performance analysis**. The latter is a sophisticated calculator that the individual trader, or the desk or floor manager, can use to examine specific scenario outcomes, at a specified horizon, for actual (or hypothetical) trade portfolios. Such a scenario calculator requires as input:

1. Initial (settlement) trade portfolio positions and prevailing market conditions, including yields, prices, and volatilities.
2. A list of intermediate actions, including trades to be taken off between settlement and horizon, options to be exercised, and bonds to be delivered against futures, so that the makeup of the horizon portfolio, including any cash position, can be determined (this input is not necessary if the specified horizon is either today or the next trading day).
3. The horizon market conditions.

Given the specified horizon market scenario, the calculator uses financial pricing models to evaluate the portfolio and, in turn, to compute the portfolio's performance (taking into account the financing costs for carrying the portfolio from settlement to horizon and reinvestment of any intermediate cash flows).

The scenario performance calculator is a sophisticated computational system that presupposes the existence of accurate pricing models for a broad range of financial instruments, and assumes that traders and risk managers can reasonably specify the settlement-to-horizon market conditions. It provides marketmakers and strategic traders with a powerful tool to perform "what if . . ." analysis on their trading positions, but it is limited in its forecasting accuracy by its pricing models and its *settlement-to-horizon* market movement assumptions. (It is often unclear, for example, at what interest rate intermediate cash flows, such as coupon income, should be reinvested if the yield curve is assumed to have moved significantly between settlement and the horizon date. This problem is compounded by the possibility of early exercise of option positions, in that written call options may be exercised against a trader during the scenario period, leading to additional, and more substantial, cash flows to be reinvested.) For more distant horizon dates, scenario anaysis is much better suited to strategic traders who frequently reevaluate the desirability of a small number of conceptually similar relative-value trades than to marketmakers whose trading positions regularly change drastically from day to day.

Net Position Summary and Exposure Report for Dealers

The net position summary report is the single most useful risk management tool for dealers. It provides them with answers to questions like:

"What is my position?"
"Am I long or short in the ten-year benchmark issue?"
"Am I long or short in volatility? How about gamma and theta?"
"What is my cash-to-futures basis risk?"

This report does *not* provide a forecast; instead, it summarizes actual and hypothetical trade portfolios into net positions in terms of a user-specified reference bond issue (e.g., the current ten-year benchmark issue) and displays the portfolio's short-term exposure to various risk variables, including price (delta), actual volatility (gamma), implied volatility (kappa), and time decay (theta). A net position summary report of a hypothetical dealer's option account is shown in Example 7.1 to illustrate the basic calculations involved.

EXAMPLE 7.1: NET POSITION SUMMARY

A bond option dealer often has many different securities in his or her trading position. Suppose that a dealer is (*a*) short $5 million in 7-day at-the-money calls, (*b*) long $3 million in 90-day at-the-money puts, and (*c*) long $4 million in cash bonds, all on the U.S. Treasury (UST) 9.00% bond of November 15, 2018. The net position summary on this simple account is shown in Table 7.1. Suppose that this dealer is also (*d*) short $5 million in 7-day at-the-money puts, (*e*) long $3 million in 90-day at-the-money puts, and (*f*) short $4 million in cash bonds, on the UST 7.25% bond of May 15, 2016. The net position summary of these securities is shown in Table 7.2. The dealer's total net position in terms of the UST

Table 7.1 UST 9.00% Issue of November 15, 2018, Holdings

Bond Issue	Type	Strike	Days to Expiry	Option Price	Amt. ($MM)	Delta	Gamma	Theta	Kappa
9.00 11/18	Call	101 30/32	7	[0-34]	−5	0.502	0.274	−17.1	0.063
9.00 11/18	Put	101 30/32	90	[1-56]	3	−0.495	0.080	−5.7	0.203
9.00 11/18	Cash				4	1.000	0.000	0.0	0.000
9.00 11/18	Net					0.005	−1.130	68.4	0.294

9.00% issue of November 15, 2018, the reference security, is obtained by combining the net position in Tables 7.1 and 7.2; it has a delta of 0.002, a gamma of −2.15, a theta of 125.3, and a kappa of 0.489.

Note that to net out a position consisting of several different Treasury issues (and options on them), we must convert the position in a given issue into an equivalent amount in the reference security. This is done by calculating a **hedge ratio** between the two securities. The hedge ratio (HR) between security A and security B (the reference security) is just the ratio of the **dollar value of a basis point (DVBP)** for the two securities:

$$HR_{AB} = \frac{DVBP_A}{DVBP_B}$$

where the DVBP is just the price change for a one-basis-point change in the yield (Y):

$$DVBP = \frac{\Delta P}{\Delta Y}$$

The hedge ratio HR_{AB} thus tells us, for a change of one basis point in

Table 7.2 UST 7.25% Issue of May 15, 2016, Holdings

Bond Issue	Type	Strike	Days to Expiry	Option Price	Amt. ($MM)	Delta	Gamma	Theta	Kappa
7.25 5/16	Call	83 27/32	7	[0-29]	−5	−0.495	0.306	−17.1	0.047
7.25 5/16	Put	83 27/32	90	[1-38]	3	0.507	0.100	−5.7	0.156
7.25 5/16	Cash				−4	1.000	0.000	0.0	0.000
7.25 5/16	Net					−0.004	−1.230	68.4	0.234
9.00 11/18	Net[a]					−0.003	−1.023	56.9	0.195

[a] The values of a basis point of the UST 7.25% issue of May 15, 2016, and the UST 9.00% issue of November 15, 2018, are, respectively 2.841 and 3.413; therefore, $1 million of the UST 7.25% issue has a risk exposure similar to $0.832 million (=2.831/3.413 × $1,000,000 of the UST 9.00% issue.

the yield of each security, how much the price of security A changes in proportion to the change in the price of security B. Multiplying the amount of security A by the hedge ratio will give an amount of security B with the same price sensitivity. (Options on nonreference issues must have their deltas—and other sensitivities—multiplied by this same hedge ratio, $(HR_{AB}.)$

The *DVBP* is related to the *duration* (D_{mod}) introduced in Chapter 2, since:

$$\frac{\Delta P}{\Delta Y} = \frac{P}{100} \times D_{mod}$$

Netting out a position in terms of a reference security is just a way of obtaining an equivalent position *in terms of a single, fixed duration.* But note that this procedure implicitly assumes that *yield curve shifts will be parallel*; that is, it is assumed that when the yield of security A moves by one basis point, so will the yield of security B. This is generally adequate for securities of similar durations, but for securities with very different durations it can be misleading. For this reason, more sophisticated net position summary systems will allow for *multiple* reference securities, one for each *sector* of the yield curve.

Remark:

Since position reports should be updated frequently during the trading day, a complete dealing system should have an on-line trade-entry component, and should have a direct digital price feed from the brokers.

It is also important for a dealer to know exactly how his or her net position and P&L will change with various market factors, including yield, implied volatility, financing rate, and time. **Yield** is a key risk factor since it drives the bond prices. **Volatility,** which drives options values and the cash-futures basis, and **financing rate,** which affects carrying costs and in turn futures, forward, and option prices, are other important factors. **Time** is a unique risk parameter because it is certain to change; it captures time decay in options and futures positions and carrying cost effects in financed cash bond positions. Analysis of actual performance exposure to each of these risk variables enables dealers to get a snapshot of their trading positions in a manageable form. They may not always have a specific scenario in mind for what may happen tomorrow, but when tomorrow comes, traders are always going to want to have a very good idea of the impact any changes have had on their P&L performance.

As shown in Example 7.1, if the prices of various financial instruments and their derivatives were perfectly related by pricing models, a dealer's position and risk exposures could be easily summarized by choosing a single benchmark issue and expressing all other issues and instruments in terms of the benchmark. Unfortunately, such exact models generally do not exist, and bottom-line net position summaries and exposures must be viewed as only good approximations. For instance, as we have noted, in Example 7.1 the yield spread between the two bonds, UST 7.25% and UST 9.00%, is assumed to be constant when the ratio of their values of a basis point is used to find the amount of UST 7.25% that is risk equivalent to $1 million in UST 9.00%. But these bonds will often actually trade at changing yield spreads. The cash bond-to-futures basis movement also frequently deviates from that described by any model. These spreads among instruments and issues, even within the same market segment, must therefore be considered as additional risk parameters in the exposure report.

The major components of a dealer-oriented option-trading system built on an advanced trader workstation are outlined in the next section. Such a system is especially important for participants in the OTC bond option market because this market allows buyers and sellers to customize transactions, and each OTC option is a unique security. Consequently, this business brings with it many interesting management problems, which can only be solved by using advanced technology wisely. First, keeping track of a large number of individual securities represents an accounting and processing nightmare: strike price, underlying issue, counter-party, and exercise date all have to be accurately maintained or exercises can be missed. The large number of different options have to be converted into common risk units for ease of management. With a number of risk factors, including cash bond price, volatility, and financing rate, affecting evaluation, controlling the risk of options portfolios can be extremely difficult. Finally, aggregating the large number of individual trades to calculate overall P&L is not trivial. Dealers in the OTC option market, therefore, must have an excellent grasp of these risk management issues, and generally require a full-scale computerized trading system to support them.

COMPONENTS OF AN OPTIONS DEALING SYSTEM

The aim of this section is to specify the major functional capabilities of a dealer-oriented trading system. Such a system is intended to provide tools to supplement the dealer's market intuitions and decision making, and to meet his or her most common needs: (a) ready availability of pricing and hedging information, (b) rapid, straightforward summary of current net position in terms of a current (benchmark) issue that is of greatest interest, and (c) short-term exposure analysis for key risk variables. There are six major components (or screens on a workstation) in such a system:

- Options pricing
- Trade entry
- Net position summary
- Exposure analysis
- Accounting
- Volatility tracking

Option Pricing

As pointed out in Chapter 6, the dealer's job is to make a market on a bond option based on the bond's trading price and implied volatility. The dealer also needs to know the option's delta and gamma in order to delta hedge his or her option position using the underlying bond. A dealing system therefore must have a pricing screen that will display, for a given option contract on a specified bond, the option price, delta, and gamma for each value of a **vary-by variable** (most often the underlying bond price or its volatility). The display of pricing information for a range of possible values of a specified vary-by variable is crucial in providing the dealer with a quantitative measure of the sensitivity of price information to key market parameters.

Such a pricing screen (see Exhibit 7.1) should have three groups of information:

GROUP 1: CHARACTERISTICS OF UNDERLYING SECURITY

maturity
coupon
price (or yield)
volatility
repo rate

GROUP 2: OPTION CONTRACT INFORMATION

trade and its settlement date
underlying bond or future contract

Exhibit 7.1 Option Pricing Screen

Screen	Pricing
As of	07/11/88Mo
Model	
Vary	Price
By	0-01
Security	912810EA2
Type	T-Bond
Maturity	05/15/18Tu
Coupon	9.125%
Price	100-09
Yield	9.095%
Price Vol	0.800
Repo	6.000%
Carry	0-03+
Option	Call
Amer/Euro	American
Expires	07/25/88Mo
Days	14
Trd. Days	10
Strike	100-09

		Option Pricing Screen			
Price	Yield	Call	CHedge	Put	PHedge
99-31	9.126%	0=52	0.43870	1=15	−0.5610
100-00	9.123%	0=53	0.44362	1=14	−0.5560
100-01	9.120%	0=54	0.44855	1=13	−0.5511
100-02	9.117%	0=55	0.45348	1=12	−0.5462
100-03	9.114%	0=56	0.45842	1=11	−0.5412
100-04	9.111%	0=57	0.46336	1=10	−0.5363
100-05	9.108%	0=58	0.46831	1=09	−0.5313
100-06	9.104%	0=58	0.47326	1=07	−0.5264
100-07	9.101%	0=59	0.47822	1=06	−0.5214
100-08	9.098%	0=60	0.48317	1=05	−0.5165
100-09	9.095%	0=61	0.48812	1=04	−0.5115
100-10	9.092%	0=62	0.49308	1=03	−0.5066
100-11	9.089%	0=63	0.49803	1=02	−0.5016
100-12	9.086%	1=00	0.50298	1=01	−0.4967
100-13	9.083%	1=01	0.50793	1=00	−0.4917
100-14	9.080%	1=02	0.51288	0=63	−0.4868
100-15	9.077%	1=03	0.51782	0=62	−0.4818
100-16	9.074%	1=04	0.52276	0=61	−0.4769
100-17	9.071%	1=06	0.52769	0=61	−0.4720
100-18	9.068%	1=07	0.53261	0=60	−0.4670

Note that 100-09 denotes a price of 100 and 9/32, and 1 = 04 represents a price of 1 and 4/64. Also, the price volatility shown is the daily relative price volatility.

option type
expiration and its settlement date
strike price or yield

GROUP 3: DISPLAY FORMAT

pricing model
vary-by variable
center and step size of vary-by variable

Suppose that a dealer has to make a market on a 14-day at-the-money call on the UST 9.125% issue of May 15, 2018. The cash bond is trading at 100 and $\frac{9}{32}$nds, with a volatility of 12.9% and a repo rate of 6.00%. Since the bond price is moving rapidly, the dealer wants the trading system to generate a display of the option's price and delta for a range of cash bond prices, similar to the one shown in Exhibit 7.1. The system should provide such a display once the dealer performs the following procedure.

Step 1. Select pricing from a master screen menu to obtain the relevant application window or page.

Step 2. Identify or menu-select the underlying security.

Remark:

All actively traded bonds and future contracts should be easily specifiable using unique names, identifiers, or system-specific aliases; for example, the current ten-year note could be specified by using a nickname, "10-year." Commonly referenced issues should also be selectable from a "pop-up" menu, to save keystrokes. When a bond is identified as an option's underlying security, its characteristics, including coupon, maturity date, repo rate, and volatility, should automatically appear on the screen for easy reference.

Step 3. Input option contract information, including type, strike price, and expiration date.

Step 4. To obtain a display of option price (and delta) as a function of the underlying bond price in steps of $\frac{1}{32}$nd, set the "vary" field to [Price] and the "by" field to [$\frac{1}{32}$].

Remark:

The system should also allow the user (*a*) to select such other vary-by variables as volatility, repo rate, or days to expiration; and (*b*) to have the option's gamma, theta, or kappa displayed on the screen in addition to its price and delta.

Trade Entry

Active dealers do many options transactions during the course of a trading day. They need facilities that will allow them to enter actual or hypothetical trades into new or existing accounts, to cancel or correct trades already in their trading positions, and to have records of what they have actually done. With these facilities, they can get quick updates on their net trading positions and on their positions' exposures to various risk factors. They can also use hypothetical trades to figure out what the best hedges are for their current positions. Such facilities should be made available on a trade-entry screen by allowing the following operations.

Step 1: Account Selection

All trading accounts should be easily specifiable on this screen. It should also allow the opening of new accounts. For a new account, the user would specify the amount name, creator's name, date of creation, and other account characteristics (e.g., actual or hypothetical).

Step 2: Trade-Entry Operation Selection

The three essential operations that must be supported are:

 a. adding a new trade to an existing account
 b. deleting a trade from an existing account, and
 c. editing or correcting a trade in an existing account.

Step 3: Transaction Information Specification

There are three kinds of information:

 1. Characteristics of the underlying security, including coupon and maturity
 2. details of the option contract, including type, strike, and expiry
 3. transaction particulars, including date, price, quantity, buy/sell, financing rate, and counter-party. The system should also automatically time and date stamp each actual trade and provide a "ticket output."

Net Position Summary

As pointed out above, the net position summary is the most useful risk management tool for dealers. It provides them with answers to questions like: (*a*) "What is my position in terms of the current ten-year bench-mark?" (*b*) "Am I long or short in delta, gamma, theta, and kappa?" and (*c*) "Do I have any basis risk?" This summary report also keeps the trading desk (floor) managers informed about their desk's (floor's) exposure to short-term changes in various risk variables.

On the *net position summary* screen, the user should be able to specify a trading account and obtain a summary report of that account's position. Such a display, for example, might be broken out by underlying bond (in order of maturity date), by strike price, and by expiration date. For each option entry, the user should see the following two groups of fields:

GROUP 1: ORIGINAL TRANSACTION AND OPTION CONTRACT

transaction ID
counter-party
trade date
buy/sell
amount
put/call
traded price
underlying security
expiration date
current value

GROUP 2: RISK PARAMETERS

delta, gamma, theta, and kappa
net position (in terms of underlying bond)
conversion factor (to a selected reference security)
net position (in terms of the selected reference security)

(Methods for determining conversion factors are given in Chapter 5.)

Remarks

1. With a digital price feed, current option prices and their sensitivity parameter values should be based on the last traded prices and volatilities for all the underlying securities. Without such a digital feed, dealers typically use the last trading day's closing data, which would normally be updated in a batch run overnight and made available to the system when the current trading session was begun.
2. This screen should also display net position subtotals and totals

according to the classes by which the summary report is broken out. For example, for all the options in a given account that are based on the same underlying bond, their net position in terms of the selected reference security should be displayed.

3. The system should give the user the ability to vary the reporting format flexibly. The user should be able to specify the categories by which the report is to be broken out, the sorting order for each category, the fields to be displayed, where subtotals are desired, and so forth.
4. Every OTC option trade should be tracked separately, even where the underlying bonds, strikes, and expiration dates are identical, because different counter-parties have different credit risks. The system therefore should net out a trade and remove it from the active file only when the trade is reversed.

Risk Exposure Analysis

It is very important for a dealer or risk manager to be able to find out exactly how his or her account's performance would change with changes in various market factors, including yield, volatility, financing rate, and time. Specifically, the dealer wants to know how his or her net position and P&L would vary with these risk factors, both on the given and on the following trading day (so that any time decay effects would be apparent). A dealing system therefore must have a *risk exposure* screen that will display, for a given trading account, its net position and P&L for each value of a selected vary-by risk variable (most often the underlying bond price or its volatility).

On the risk exposure screen, the user should be able to specify a trading account and the particular risk variable to be analyzed. All information concerning the specified account should also be accessible to the user. As in the pricing screen, all the user should have to do is to specify the "center" and "step size" for the risk variable. The exposure screen should then display, for each value of the risk factor, two sets of numbers; one for those levels of the risk variable *today*, and the other for those levels *tomorrow* (the next trading day). The figures included in each display set should be the account's P&L and its net position (delta) and gamma in terms of a selected reference security.

Remarks

1. The exposure screen gives exact results on changes in P&L and in net position delta and gamma as market parameters change. Unlike

net position summary, all financing costs are taken into consideration in exposure analysis.

2. Conversion factors among bonds must be readily available to compute net position delta and gamma; methods for determining such factors are given in Chapter 5.
3. The system should allow a risk manager to examine the risk exposure of different combinations of trading accounts.

Accounting

There is clearly a need for some accounting mechanism in a dealing system. Since accounting rules and conventions vary, some of the relevant issues that need to be resolved when designing an accounting function are listed here, but no specific format is proposed.

P&L STATEMENTS

On what basis should P&L figures be calculated?
Should the position be marked to market every day?
For Japanese government bonds (JGBs), for example, should the position be marked only on the settlement dates, or according to some other convention?

TRANSACTION HISTORY

When and how can offsetting positions within a single account be netted out?
What kind of longer term transaction log (or history) should be kept?
Should users be allowed to cancel/correct trades?

Many of these issues will appear trivial to the financial accounting professional. The important point here is to make sure that the trading system is integrated with the back-office system so that inconsistency and redundancy will be avoided.

As a final note, an options dealing system must be supported by an appropriate data base maintenance system. This data base must keep track of various information, including:

1. Dealer accounts—including all their individual trades.
2. Records of the bond issues—with all their characteristics, including maturity date, coupon, and callable features.
3. Historical price, volatility, and carry information for active issues.

4. Customer (or counter-party) information—including trading history, current holdings and exposure, and credit updates.

For the new JGB options market, for example, while the initial volume of data required to support a JGB options trading system may not be large, because of the small number of underlying issues that are of interest, the eventual diversity of data and the variety of ways in which users will be accessing that data strongly suggest the use of a data base, instead of flat data files, to drive such an options trading system.

Volatility Tracking

As demonstrated in Chapter 6, options dealers are marketmakers of the underlying bond's implied volatility. They should have access to (a) real-time implied volatilities and (b) historical data on actual and traded volatilities on all regularly traded bonds and futures. An options dealing system therefore must have a *volatility tracking* screen that will display, for a specified security group, current and historical volatilities.

Options dealers keep daily records of historical volatilities (typically for the past 20, 40, and 60 trading days) and implied volatilities of all regularly traded bonds and futures. This information is stored in a data base, and should be made available on the *volatility tracking* screen. Such a screen should allow the user to:

1. Quickly spot big discrepancies in implied volatilities of options on the same underlying security.
2. Calculate and compare different historical volatilities for a given security.
3. Examine the historical volatility relationships among a set of securities.

FUTURE DIRECTIONS

We have so far emphasized the importance of up-to-date technology in providing essential trader support and risk management tools and in leveraging a firm's competitive advantage. In today's fast-moving markets, however, the serious professional must constantly be forward looking, and just as traders must constantly adapt to new financial instruments, so too must they be prepared to adapt to technological innovations. In this final section, we provide a peek at some possible technological innovations that are looming on the horizon.

Digital and Video Feeds

Already a reality on some trading floors, integrated digital feeds from multiple market data vendors and/or brokers offer an opportunity for the marketmaker to automate the process of searching for the best quote and/or detecting fleeting price mismatches (for which read: arbitrage opportunities). Integration of video feeds with traditional workstation graphic displays would allow for an important consolidation of hardware and a reduction in the number of separate windows and devices a trader must manage. Such integration of market data feeds is a necessary precondition to the kind of *market-minding functions* described below.

New Graphic and Analytic Tools

The advent of ever-faster and higher resolution workstations allows us to envision the wide availability of increasingly sophisticated analytical models and graphics presentation interfaces, including three-dimensional, color, and animated graphics displays. For those with the quantitative skills to use them, user-friendly statistical analysis packages will put sophisticated time-series analysis tools in the hands of traders and traders' assistants for the analysis of historical data and technical trends.

Alternative Models

Faster workstations and network access to mini-supercomputers as compute server resources will allow the user of increasingly sophisticated and customized mathematical models. Traders will have the ability to tune model parameters on the fly, and/or compare results from alternative models in tabular or graphic form. It will be feasible to perform real-time, on-line simulations to evaluate complex, path-dependent contingent claims.

Market-Minding Functions

New programming techniques, and the availability of real-time digitized market data feeds, make it possible to implement *market-minding function*, application programs that can be "trained" by the user to detect certain market conditions and alert the user to potentially profitable opportunities—or to automatically take some predetermined action. Such programs will never replace the global intuitions and savvy of top traders, but can provide important decision support tools in an environment where there are literally hundreds and even thousands of key numbers changing second by second. Such functions can also be used to monitor intra-day risk exposure, and similar techniques are already in use on some exchanges for regulatory monitoring purposes.

ACKNOWLEDGMENTS

Mr. Frank Duquette, who is responsible for system planning at Greenwich Capital Markets, Inc., made significant contributions to this chapter. I would like to thank the option traders at GCM, and especially Tim Dann, for sharing insights on the risk management problem for traders and dealers.

REFERENCES

Dann, T., "Risk Management System," Greenwich Capital Market Inc. Internal Working Paper, Greenwich, Conn., 1988.
Duquette, F., "Graphic Workstation in the Trading Room," presented at the *IBM Symposium on Computers in Finance: Bridging the Gaps between Theory and Practice,"* IBM Corporate Education Center, Thornwood, N.Y., October 27, 1987.
High, Robert, "The Workstation Revolution: A Case Study," presented at the *"SUN Microsystems Seminar on Workstations in the Financial Community,"* Hong Kong and Singapore, May 1989.
Hobson, I., "Advanced Trader Workstations," keynote address presented at the *"Advanced Trader Workstation"* conference sponsored by Waters Information Services of Binghamton, N.Y., New York City, May 17, 1988.
Sahgal, P., "Automation at the Big Four Japanese Securities Firms," *Wall Street Computer Review*, January:22–67, 1989.
Schmerken, I., "Trading Systems: To Build or To Buy?," *Wall Street Computer Review*, January:31–44, 1989.
Wong, M. A., "Role of Computer Technology in Finance," keynote address presented at the *"IBM Symposium on Computers in Finance: Bridging the Gaps between Theory and Practice,"* IBM Corporate Education Center, Thornwood, N.Y., October 28, 1987.
Wong, M. A., "Third Generation Fixed-Income Trading Room," presented at the *"Advanced Trader Workstation"* conference sponsored by Waters Information Services of Binghamton, N.Y., New York City, May 17, 1988.

8

Relative-Value Trading in Bond Options

Central to the success of trading establishments is an adherence to the principles of relative-value analysis. Rather than speculating on the direction of interest rates, relative-value traders identify price disparities among groups of essentially similar securities, profiting as market forces eventually bring the prices back to an equilibrium. The basics of relative-value trading in bonds are presented in the first section. Following is a description of the various methods for relative-value analysis in bond options. The critical steps to be taken by traders are then illustrated by a specific example using listed options.

RELATIVE-VALUE TRADING IN BONDS

Relative-value trading often involves the simultaneous buying of a *relatively cheap* security and selling short a *relatively rich* security. For example, two U.S. Treasury notes with very similar maturities and coupons are expected to have very similar prices; if not, there would be profit opportunities in doing a **relative-value trade** because the two prices are likely to become very similar eventually. Such trading activities are often referred to as **fixed-income arbitrage** even though they are not risk free. To be successful in this type of trading, a trader has to (*a*) know how to perform relative-value analysis, (*b*) be consistently hardworking and vigilant, and (c) use his or her experience and intelligence to exercise risk control and to train and improve his or her professional judgment. A trader must constantly perform a balancing act: aggressive but risk conscious; realistic but enterprising.

Applying Relative-Value Analysis to Bond Dealing

Consider a marketmaker in U.S. Treasury bonds. When his or her bid on bond X is hit (or offer is lifted), the marketmaker's job is to sell (buy) this bond at a higher (lower) price as soon as possible at a better price so that there will be quick profits and no inventory risk. If bond X is very liquid and the dealer has a large share of the bond trading market, it may not be difficult for the marketmaker to profit from the bid-ask spread on this bond. But if bond X is an off-the-run (side) issue, the marketmaker may have a tough time completing the second leg of his or her trade because there may not be any buyer (seller) of the bond.

Suppose that the marketmaker knows relative-value analysis, and his or her hard work has suggested that within his or her trading sector of the bond market, bond C is relatively cheap and bond R is relatively rich. Equipped with this knowledge, when his or her bid on bond X is hit (or offer is lifted), in addition to simply turning around and selling (buying) X at a better price, the marketmaker also has the option to sell (buy) a risk-equivalent amount of bond R (bond C). With the additional choices, the marketmaker is in a much better position to hedge his or her position, and is therefore able to reduce inventory risk. Moreover, if the marketmaker's analysis is correct, he or she can expect to earn some extra money when bond R (bond C) eventually becomes relatively cheaper (richer); of course, if the analysis is wrong and the marketmaker actually thinks bond R is cheap instead, then he or she may end up losing money.

Remark:

In the above discussion, bond C and bond R can easily be replaced by future or forward contracts.

Using Relative-Value Analysis in Portfolio Management

The responsibility of a fixed-income portfolio manager is to get the best return possible under his or her risk constraints. To achieve this goal, the manager may actively trade or passively manage his or her portfolio to match a selected bond index. In either case, the portfolio is often made up of many different bonds. At various points in time, some of the bonds in the portfolio may be relatively rich to other bonds in the same sector. The portfolio's performance can therefore be enhanced if the manager sells the *relatively rich* bonds and replaces them with the *relatively cheap* ones. Relative-value analysis has been used by portfolio managers as a tool to enhance the return of index funds (see, e.g., Fong and Fabozzi, 1985).

Remark:

One important consequence of relative-value trading is that securities within the same sector will tend to become fairly priced and hence the financial markets will be more efficient.

The methods for relative-value analysis in bond options will be given to illustrate how *arbitrageurs* take advantage of deviations from **implied volatilities** relationships.

RELATIVE-VALUE ANALYSIS IN BOND OPTIONS

RELATIVE-VALUE ANALYSIS IN BOND OPTIONS

Role of Implied Volatilities

As pointed out in Chapter 3, the only unobservable input to an option pricing model is the bond's volatility between the current and expiration dates. For a selected model, and with the values of all other input parameters completely specified, the price of an option can be computed given the underlying bond's volatility; inversely, the bond's implied volatility can be found given the option's price. The future volatility of a bond, and hence the fair value of its option, is unknown and can only be estimated. Options traders often track a bond's past volatilities, but historical volatility is normally not a good estimate of future volatility because a bond's volatility varies erratically over time. Options dealers and relative-value traders focus their attention on implied volatilities, not because these volatilities necessarily provide accurate estimates of future bond volatilities, but because they can be used to judge the *relative* cheapness or richness of an option, either against other options on the same underlying bond or against options on other related bond instruments.

Remark:

Implied volatilities computed from different options pricing models are generally different. While the most commonly used models will give reasonably close values, traders should be wary of comparing implied volatilities based on different models too freely, especially if the models are based on significantly different assumptions.

Table 8.1   December 12, 1988, Data on March 1989, T-Bond Contract

Strike Price	Call	Implied Vol. (%)	Delta	Put	Implied Vol. (%)	Delta
86	[3-56]	12.018	0.759	[0-39]	12.255	−0.228
88	[2-26]	11.449	0.614	[1-09]	11.771	−0.373
90	[1-21]	11.126	0.430	[2-01]	11.449	−0.552
92	[0-42]	11.288	0.259	[3-20]	11.610	−0.719
94	[0-20]	11.771	0.141	[4-60]	12.255	−0.833

Relationships Between Implied Volatilities

Relative-value options traders pay special attention to significant deviations from the following *implied volatilities* relationships.

1. Consider put and call options with the same strike, expiration date, and underlying bond. Their implied volatilities should be the same.

This is a direct consequence of the put-call parity described in Chapters 3 and 4. For example, the December 12, 1988, closing prices and the corresponding implied volatilities of options on the March 1989 U.S. Treasury bond (T-bond) contract are shown in Table 8.1. Although the implied volatilities of puts and calls with the same strike are different, these differences are very small. The biggest discrepancy occurs at the 94 strike; the 94 put (call) has an implied volatility of 12.255% (11.771%). As pointed out in Chapter 4, relative-value traders, with the help of advanced computer technology, continuously monitor, identify, and profit from the riskless arbitrage opportunities that occur when option prices deviate from put-call parity. Consequently, as with the December 12, 1988, data, quoted prices always have implied volatilities that are in line with the put-call relationships.

The closing price of the March 1989, T-bond contract was 89 and $^{11}/_{32}$nds. The implied volatility, price, and delta of the five nearest-to-the-money options are given in Table 8.1. Note that these options have 66 days to expiration, and [2-01] represents a price of 2 and $\frac{1}{64}$ths.

2. Consider put (or call) options with the same expiration date and underlying security. Their implied volatilities should have a structured pattern across strike prices.

Another interesting characteristic of the implied volatilities shown in Table 8.1 is that the volatilities differ across strike prices for both calls and puts. Specifically, implied volatilities increase as strike prices get farther and farther away from the current March 1989, T-bond contract price of 89 and $^{11}\!/_{32}$nds. Out-of-the-money options are much more actively traded than deep-in-the-money ones. The observed pattern indicates that out-of-the-money options have higher implied volatilities than near-the-money ones; however, because of put-call parity, the thinly traded deep-in-the-money options also have higher implied volatilities than near-the-money ones. From a dealer's perspective, as long as the *structure* of implied volatilities across strike prices (relative to the current price of the underlying security) is stable from day to day, he should continue to use that pattern as a guideline for making market quotes. From a relative-value trader's perspective, any deviation from such a structure reflects a profit opportunity. In such situations, options with implied volatilities higher (lower) than that of a known structure are considered to be relatively rich (cheap). The relative-value trader would then simultaneously buy a relatively cheap option and sell a relatively rich one, hedge away all other risk exposures, and wait for the implied volatilities to get back in line with the known structure. A specific example will be given later in this chapter to show how relative-value traders use this approach to make money.

From a conceptual perspective, all market participants would question why such a pattern for implied volatilities persists. Since all the options in Table 8.1 are on the same underlying bond future contract and have the same expiration date, their implied volatilities reflect different estimates of the same actual volatility of the T-bond contract during the life of these options. How can the estimates be so different? And why do near-the-money options have lower implied volatilities?

The option pricing models described in Chapter 3 make the simplifying assumption that the bond market is continuous and prices evolve smoothly over time. These models are not appropriate if prices are expected to make sudden drastic changes, and the bond market has sometimes exhibited such discontinuous movements in the past. (The bond market was extremely volatile during the first week of April in 1987 and also during the week of October 19, 1987.) Buyers of way-out-of-the-money options are speculators who clearly expect the market to be discontinuous during the life of the option; otherwise, their investments would be wasted because their options would expire worthless with high probability. At the same time, knowledgeable sellers are reluctant to price these out-of-the-money options using models that assume a continuous market. Moreover, even with delta-neutral hedging (see Chapter 4), these sellers still face significant gamma and kappa risks in such *short-volatility* option positions. To compensate for their risks, sellers will push up the prices of these options.

In summary, there are two major reasons for way-out-of-the-money options to have higher implied volatilities than near-the-money ones. First, buyers of way-out-of-the-money options are speculators who expect the market to be discontinuous and are therefore willing to pay a slightly higher price consistent with such expectations. (This price will give a higher implied volatility if this volatility is computed from a model using a continuous market assumption.) Second, even after hedging away their delta risks, sellers of these options still have gamma and kappa risks that can be especially significant if the market is discontinuous. Consequently, they will only sell such options if the corresponding implied volatilities are high enough to compensate for their risks.

3. Consider put (or call) options with the same strike and underlying security. Their implied volatilities across expiration dates should not be significantly different.

Options with different times to expiration *can* have very different volatilities. For example, a 7-day option can be expected to have a significantly higher volatility than a 30-day one if important political and economic events are scheduled to happen within the next 7 days and no such major events are to occur in the subsequent 23 days. Conversely, if no significant events are expected in the next 7 days, and this period is expected to be followed by 23 eventful days, then the 7-day option should have a much lower implied volatility than the 30-day one. Some traders, however, argue that the 7-day volatility is a subset of the 30-day one, and that therefore these two volatilities should not be significantly different. As already shown in Example 4.5 in Chapter 4, traders and investors like to put on time spreads when at-the-money options with different expiration dates have drastically different implied volatilities; however, the risks involved in such a trade cannot be ignored.

4. Consider at-the-money options, with the same expiration date, on two different underlying securities. The ratio of their implied volatilities should be close to the ratio of their values of a basis point.

A bond's value of a basis point, value(bp), is its price change if its yield is changed by one basis point. Assuming that the yields of the two underlying bonds move in parallel, the ratio of their value(bp)s reflects the relative volatility of the two bonds. Bond yields, of course, do not always move in parallel; however, for any two bonds, the ratio of their at-the-money implied volatilities is generally very close to the ratio of their value(bp)s. The relationship between implied volatilities of a cash bond and a bond future contract can be similarly established. Since a future contract does not have a value(bp), approximations have to be used. One suggestion is to identify a few bond issues that are most likely to be delivered against the contract, and use the average value(bp)s of these issues as the contract's own value(bp). A more precise approach is given in Tang (1988), where the contract's value(bp) is explicitly evaluated. Alternatively, the relative volatility of the two instruments can be estimated from historical price data using regression analysis (see Chapter 6).

A RELATIVE-VALUE TRADE USING LISTED OPTIONS

Identifying Relatively Mispriced Options

A relative-value trader, whose job is to consistently make money trading listed options on T-bond future contracts, has available a trader workstation that will show continuously, in real time, the last traded prices and the corresponding implied volatilities of all these options. He or she has been trading these options and knows that, most of the time, the implied volatilities of the five nearest-to-the-money options of the March T-bond have followed the December 12, 1988, closing pattern shown in Table 8.1 above. Specifically, implied volatilities increase as strike prices get farther away from the current contract price. These relationships among the put implied volatilities are quantified and summarized in Table 8.2.

Suppose that in the morning of December 13, 1988, the March 1989 T-bond contract was trading at 89 and $^{11}/_{32}$nds, the previous day's closing price. The trader noticed that the 88 put was trading at an implied volatility of 12.578% while the 90 put was still trading at 11.449%. From Table 8.3, it is clear that the 88 put option was relatively overpriced. This window of opportunity might last only a few moments. Either the implied volatility of this 88 put would decrease and get back in line with the other puts, or the other implied volatilities would increase as well. In either case, the relative-value trader must take action quickly.

Table 8.2 Structure of Puts' Implied Volatilities across Strike Prices

Strike Price	Strike Minus 89 11/32	Put Price	Implied Vol. (%)	Relative (to 90 put) Impl. Vol.
86	−3 11/32	[0-93]	12.255	1.070
88	−1 11/32	[1-09]	11.771	1.028
90	21/32	[2-01]	11.449	1.000
92	2 21/32	[3-20]	11.610	1.014
94	4 21/32	[4-60]	12.255	1.070

STEP 1: Sell ten 88 puts on the March 1989 T-bond contract.

Hedging Away Unwanted Risks

The trader found that the 88 put was a *relatively overpriced* option and quickly sold ten such puts. (Note that each contract has a $100,000 face value.) If the trader did not hedge his or her *short option* position, which had a delta (in millions of dollars) of 0.381 ($= -1 \times -0.381$), he or she would lose a lot of money should the price of the March T-bond contract take a large fall. The option was only *relatively* overpriced; a short position in it would still have significant market risk.

Delta-Neutral Hedging Using the Underlying Bond Contract

The 88 put has a delta of −0.381. Since the trader was short ten such puts, his or her unhedged position delta (in millions of dollars) was 0.381.

Table 8.3 A Snapshot of March 1989, T-Bond Options Prices on December 13, 1988

Strike Price	Put Price	Implied Vol. (%)	"Expected" Implied Vol. (%)	Put Delta
86	[0-39]	12.255	12.255	−0.228
88	[1-16]	12.578	11.771	−0.381
90	[2-01]	11.449	11.449	−0.552
92	[3-20]	11.610	11.610	−0.719
94	[4-60]	12.255	12.255	−0.833

As discussed in Chapter 6, theoretically the trader could delta hedge this option position by selling short 3.81 March T-bond contracts. Since he or she cannot sell fractions of a contract, the trader probably would hedge by selling short four contracts; the resulting hedged position has the following risk parameters:

1. *Delta* = -0.019. With a slightly negative delta, this position would have a small loss (gain) in value if the contract price moved up (down).

2. *Gamma* = -0.079. With a negative gamma, this position would lose money if the T-bond contract moved up or down significantly. Specifically, this position would lose about $^{4.6}\!/_{64}$ths (computed from actual option price changes, not directly from the gamma value) if the contract price went up by one point.

3. *Theta* = 5.70. With a positive theta, this position would have a daily increase of 5.7/365, or $\frac{1}{64}$th, point in value should other factors stay the same.

4. *Kappa* = -0.14. Suppose that the implied volatility dropped from the traded 12.578% to the *expected* volatility of 11.771% (see Table 8.3), a decrease of 0.807%; this position should then make a $^{7}\!/_{64}$ths ($= \frac{9}{64} \times 0.807$) profit.

This hedged position would therefore make the *expected* $^{7}\!/_{64}$ths profit should the 88 put's implied volatility return to 11.771%. Unfortunately, there would not be any profit if, instead, the other implied volatilities eventually moved up to its level. Worse still, this position would lose money, if the March contract's actual or implied volatility jumped up significantly.

Hedging with Other Put Options

From Table 8.3, the trader would decide that all other puts on the March, 1989, T-bond contract were relatively well priced. As a relative-value trader, he or she would like to hedge away as many risks as possible and could do this by hedging his or her 88 put position with the most similar options. In this case, the best hedge would be to buy five 86 puts and five 90 puts.

STEP 2: Buy five 86 puts and five 90 puts to hedge.

The risk characteristics of the individual options in this hedged position are summarized in Table 8.4, and the position's risk parameters were:

Table 8.4　Hedged Position in March T-Bond Puts

Long or Short	Type	Strike Price	Option Price	Amt. ($MM)	Delta	Gamma	Theta	Kappa
Long	Put	86	[0-39]	0.5	−0.228	0.063	−5.70	0.1094
Short	Put	88	[1-16]	−1.0	−0.381	0.079	−5.70	0.1406
Long	Put	90	[2-01]	0.5	−0.552	0.091	−5.70	0.1406

1. delta = −0.009
2. gamma = −0.002
3. theta = 0.000
4. kappa = −0.0156

This hedged position has negligible delta, gamma, and theta risks. It would decrease in value by 0.0156 point or ¹⁄₆₄ths, if all three implied volatilities increase by 1%, and therefore its kappa risk is also very small. Moreover, profits would be made should the implied volatilities eventually get back to the *expected* relative pattern. This will now be demonstrated using the three scenarios.

Scenario 1: If T-Bond Price Stayed the Same at 89 and 11/32nds

a. *If the 88 Puts Implied Volatility Dropped Back to 11.771%.* In this case, as the prices shown in Table 8.3 would indicate, the price of the 88 put would drop from [1-16] back to [1-09]. Since the trader was short ten (or $1 million) 88 puts, he or she would make a profit of ⁷⁄₆₄ths or $1,093.75.

b. *If the Implied Volatilities of the 86 and 90 Puts Increased to Levels That Would Be Consistent with the Expected Pattern.* The implied volatility of the 88 put was trading at 12.578%. If the relative implied volatilities shown in Table 8.2 were to hold true, then the 86 put's implied volatility would be 13.092% (= 12.578% × $^{1.070}/_{1.028}$), and the 90 put's implied volatility would be 12.235% (= 12.578% × $^{1.0}/_{1.028}$). Using these implied volatilities, the 86 and 90 puts, respectively, would be worth [0-45] and [2-08]. Since the trader was long five (or $0.5 million) 86 and 90 puts, he or she would make a profit of $^{6.5}/_{64}$ths, the sum of ([0-45] − [0-39])/2 and ([2-08] − [2-01])/2, or $1,015.63.

The only risk in this scenario was that the 88 put would get relatively more expensive, in spite of the *expected* pattern.

Scenario 2: If T-Bond Price Decreased by Two Points to 87 and 11/32nds

a. If All the Implied Volatilities Stayed the Same. In this scenario, all three puts would go up in value because the T-bond contract price went down by two points. If all the implied volatilities stayed the same, then (a) the 86 put, with a 12.255% volatility, would increase in value from [0-39] to [1-11] for a $^{36}/_{64}$ths gain, (b) the 88 put, with a 12.578% volatility, would increase in value from [1-16] to [2-09] for a $^{57}/_{64}$ths gain, and (c) the 90 put, with a 11.449% volatility, would increase in value from [2-01] to [3-17] for an $^{80}/_{64}$ths gain. The trader would therefore make a profit of $^{1}/_{64}$th, which is the sum of $0.5 \times {}^{36}/_{64}$, $-1.0 \times {}^{57}/_{64}$, and $0.5 \times {}^{80}/_{64}$. This result is not unexpected because the position had a very small negative delta. If the 88 put volatility eventually dropped back to 11.771%, its price would be [2-01] (instead of [2-09]) and there would be an additional profit of $^{8}/_{64}$ths. This case, however, would be unlikely to occur because it would imply that the 86 and 88 puts, closest to the money after the price of the T-bond contract had moved to 87 and $^{11}/_{32}$nds, would end up having higher implied volatilities than the 90 and 92 puts. The following case would be a more likely event.

b. If All the Implied Volatilities, Relative to the Contract Price, Remained the Same. In this case, after the contract price had moved by exactly two points, the 86, 88, and 90 puts would, respectively, take on the old volatilities of the 88, 90, and 92 puts. Consequently, (a) the 86 put, with the new 12.578% volatility, would increase in value from [0-39] and [1-13] for a $^{38}/_{64}$ths gain, (b) the 88 put, with the new 11.449% volatility, would increase in value from [1-16] to [1-62] for a $^{46}/_{64}$ths gain, and (c) the 90 put, with the new 11.610% volatility, would increase in value from [2-01] to [3-18] for an $^{81}/_{64}$ths gain. The trader would therefore make a profit of $^{13.5}/_{64}$ths, which is the sum of $0.5 \times {}^{38}/_{64}$, $-1.0 \times {}^{46}/_{64}$, and $0.5 \times {}^{81}/_{64}$. Even if the 86 put's (not 88 put's) volatility dropped back to 11.771%, its price would be [1-06] (instead of [1-13]) and there would still be a profit of $^{10}/_{64}$ths!

Scenario 3: If T-Bond Price Increased by Two Points to 91 and 11/32nds

a. If All the Implied Volatilities Stayed the Same. In this scenario, all three puts would go down in value because the T-bond contract price went up by two points. If all the implied volatilities stayed the same, then (a) the 86 put, with a 12.255% volatility, would decrease in value from [0-39] to [0-18] for a $^{21}\!/_{64}$ths loss, (b) the 88 put, with a 12.578% volatility, would decrease in value from [1-16] to [0-43] for a $^{37}\!/_{64}$ths loss, and (c) the 90 put, with a 11.449% volatilty, would decrease in value from [2-01] to [1-08] for a $^{57}\!/_{64}$ths loss. The trader would therefore have a loss of $^2\!/_{64}$ths, which is the sum of $0.5 \times -^{21}\!/_{64}$, $-1.0 \times -^{37}\!/_{64}$, and $0.5 \times -^{57}\!/_{64}$. This result is not unexpected because the position had a very small negative delta. If the 88 put volatility eventually dropped back to 11.771%, its price would be [0-37] (instead of [0-43]), and the trader would end up making a profit of $^4\!/_{64}$ths!

   b. If All the Implied Volatilities, Relative to the Contract Price, Remained the Same. In this case, after the contract price had moved by exactly two points, the 86, 88, and 90 puts would, respectively, take on the old volatilities of the 84, 86, and 88 puts. (The 84 put's old volatility is assumed to be 12.255% in the following analysis.) Consequently, (a) the 86 put, with the new 12.255% volatility, would decrease in value from [0-39] to [0-18] for a $^{21}\!/_{64}$ths loss, (b) the 88 put, with the new 12.255% volatility, would decrease in value from [1-16] to [0-41] for a $^{39}\!/_{64}$ths loss, and (c) the 90 put, with the new 12.578% volatility, would decrease in value from [2-01] to [1-18] for a $^{47}\!/_{64}$ths loss. The trader would therefore make a profit of $^5\!/_{64}$ths, which is the sum of $0.5 \times -^{21}\!/_{64}$, $-1.0 \times -^{39}\!/_{64}$, and $0.5 \times -^{47}\!/_{64}$. Even if the 90 put's (not 88 put's) volatility dropped back to 11.771%, its price would be [1-11] (instead of [1-18]) and there would still be a profit of $^{1.5}\!/_{64}$ths!

Summary

In summary, if the trader hedged his or her short ten 88 puts position with five 86 puts and five 90 puts, his or her overall position would have very small exposure to the various risk factors. The delta risk would be small (delta $= -0.009$) and gamma and theta risks would be almost zero. Meanwhile, the trader would make significant profits if the implied volatilities eventually return to a *normal* pattern. However, he or she would end up losing $^4\!/_{64}$ths (the initial cost of the trade) should the 88 put remain relatively overpriced throughout the duration of the option contract.

REVIEW

The above example illustrates the approach taken by relative-value traders to make steady profits in the options markets. Such profit opportunities tend to occur with some regularity, although the figures used in the example are exaggerated; a listed option (like the 88 put) mispriced by $\frac{7}{64}$ths is difficult to find in real-life trading. As long as their analyses are correct, relative-value traders will make money while incurring very limited risks. However, they can be expected to lose some money when fundamental shifts occur, albeit infrequently, in the options markets. For example, if relative implied volatilities were to make a permanent structural change, all traders would think a profit opportunity existed; they would end up losing money when the relative volatilities never reversed back to their old structure. Unlike outright speculators, relative-value traders have to work hard to get consistent, moderate profits, but they lose infrequently and their down-side risks are limited.

Remarks

1. Advanced computer technology also plays an important role in relative-value trading. Trader workstations with digital price feeds can be used to identify mispriced options in a timely fashion, which will increase the likelihood of profitable trades being executed. A scenario-driven performance sytsem for evaluating actual and hypothetical trades is an essential tool for relative-value traders because they will be able to perform sophisticated "what if . . ." analysis.

2. Relative-value traders want to take advantage of relatively mispriced options. They do not want any unnecessary market risk in their trade positions. As demonstrated in the above example, to hedge a position on an option, the best strategy is to use other options that are most similar to it. This way, the trader can eliminate most, if not all, of the other risks, and can wait to make some profits when the relatively mispriced options eventually become fairly priced. Moreover, if the identified option is relatively overpriced, the trader should hedge with options that are relatively underpriced; if no underpriced options can be found he or she should use fairly priced ones.

3. Relative-value traders always take profit immediately after the relatively mispriced option returns to a fair price. There is no reason for them to stay with the trade because it is not expected to make any more profit.

REFERENCES

Relatively little has been written on relative-value trading. A collection of articles on *arbitrage* can be found in Weisweiller (1986). Some basic strategies in U.S. yield curve arbitrage can be found in Breaks (1987). The chapter on "Option Trading Strategy" in Bookstaber (1987) provides an excellent description of relative trading in stock options.

Bookstaber, R. M., *Options Pricing and Investment Strategies*, Probus Publishing Company, Chicago, 1987.

Breaks, J. D., "Yield Curve Arbitrage and Trading," in *Handbook of Treasury Securities: Trading and Portfolio Strategies*, Probus Publishing Company, Chicago, 1987, pp. 184–214.

Fong, H. G., and F. J. Fabozzi, *Fixed Income Portfolio Management*, Dow Jones–Irwin, Homewood, Ill., 1985.

Tang, E. M., *The Effect of Delivery Options on Interest Rate Futures and Option Contracts*, Portfolio Management Technology, San Francisco, 1988.

Weisweiller, R., *Arbitrage*, John Wiley & Sons, New York, 1986.

9

Strategies Driven by Estimated Forthcoming Volatility

As explained in Chapter 6, every naked option position has exposure to delta, gamma, theta, and kappa risks. Any such option position can be turned into a delta-neutral position by using a hedge involving either the underlying security or some other option on the security. However, the resulting delta-neutral position will still have exposure to gamma, theta, and kappa risks. This chapter describes the various delta-neutral trading strategies, using examples to illustrate the risk/return characteristics of these trades.

OPTIONS TRADING IS VOLATILITY TRADING

If an options trader knew exactly what the actual forthcoming volatility of the underlying security would be between the option's trade and expiration dates, he or she could make handsome profits, as long as the option's implied volatility was significantly different from the forthcoming volatility, even though the trader might have no idea whether the security's price would end up going higher or lower. Indeed, the trader would not even have to know exactly what the actual forthcoming volatility would be. It would be enough to know, with some certainty, that an option's implied volatility was too high or too low relative to the forthcoming volatility. The trader might not make money on every option trade, but in the long run, with this kind of knowledge, he or she would inevitably be very successful. Most experienced option traders prefer volatility bets because they believe that they have a proper framework for assessing a given security's forthcoming volatility relative to the volatilities implied by the market prices of the options on that security.

Every naked option position has exposure to delta, gamma, theta, and kappa risks. A trader sees an option as mispriced if it is trading at an implied volatility significantly higher or lower than the expected forthcoming volatility of the underlying security. To take advantage of such mispricing, the trader must somehow hedge away his or her option position's *delta risk*. As noted in Chapter 6, any option position can be hedged using either the underlying security or other options on the security to create a *delta-neutral position*. The resulting delta-neutral position only has exposure to gamma (actual volatility), theta (time decay), and kappa (implied volatility) risks. Such strategies are driven by comparisons between an option's implied volatility and the trader's expectation of the underlying security's forthcoming volatility, but are indifferent to the actual direction of the market.

DELTA-HEDGING USING THE UNDERLYING SECURITY

EXAMPLE 9.1: A DELTA-NEUTRAL CALL POSITION WITH NEGATIVE GAMMA

Suppose that in the afternoon of December 12, 1988, the U.S. Treasury (UST) 9% issue of November 15, 2018, was trading at a price of [100.15+] (yield = 8.952%), and its seven-day, at-the-money calls were quoted at 12.55% implied volatility. A trader believing that the bond's actual forthcoming volatility over the next seven days would be much lower than the calls' 12.55% implied volatility could sell $2 million in seven-day at-the-money calls on the bond. If the calls were sold at a price of $^{44}/_{64}$ths, the trader would receive a total premium of $13,750.00. To eliminate the option position's negative delta risk (delta = −0.501), the trader could hedge his or her position by buying $1 million in the UST 9% issue of November 15, 2018, the underlying bond, at a price of [100.15+]. Since the bond would have an accrued interest of $^{22.4}/_{32}$nds for December 13th settlement, the bond's total invoice price would be 101 and $^{5.9}/_{32}$nds, and the trader would pay a total purchase price of $1,011,843.75.

If this delta-neutral position were held to expiration, the long cash bond position would gain seven days of accrued interest. Moreover, if *P* is the price of the UST 9% issue of November 15, 2018, on December 19, 1988, the position's additional risk/return characteristics can be expressed as follows. Let *IPP* be the position's investment profit in points. Then:

$$IPP = (100\ ^{15.5}\!/_{32} - P) + (2 \times\ ^{44}\!/_{64}), \quad \text{if } P \geq 100\ ^{15.5}\!/_{32}$$
$$IPP = (P - 100\ ^{15.5}\!/_{32}) + (2 \times\ ^{44}\!/_{64}), \quad \text{if } P < 100\ ^{15.5}\!/_{32}$$

This option position would make a profit, in addition to the interest income, as long as the bond's price on December 19, 1988, was between [99.03 +] and [101.27 +]. The investment profit in dollars would be equal to $1 million times 1% times the profit in points. The short-term risk exposures of this strategy would be:

1. *Delta* = $(-2 \times 0.501) + (1 \times 1.000) = -0.002$. Using an appropriate long position in the underlying bond to hedge the short calls, the resulting delta-hedged position has a delta of nearly zero.
2. *Gamma* = $(-2 \times 0.217) + (1 \times 0.000) = -0.434$. This delta-neutral position still has a negative gamma, and would lose money if the price of the underlying bond made a significant up or down move.
3. *Theta* = $(-2 \times -22.81) + (1 \times 0.000) = 45.62$. This delta-neutral, negative-gamma position, however, would benefit from time decay. With a positive theta, this position would have a daily increase in value of $^{45.62}\!/_{365}$, or $^{8}\!/_{64}$ths, points if all other factors stayed the same.
4. *Kappa* = $(-2 \times 0.0625) + (1 \times 0.000) = -0.125$. The trader is assumed to have sold the options when their implied volatility was trading at 12.55%. Should this volatility increase by 1%, this option position would decrease in value by 0.125, or $^{8}\!/_{64}$ths, points.

In summary, this delta-hedge short option position would have a negative gamma, positive theta, and negative kappa. A long option position similarly delta hedged by the underlying security would have a positive gamma, negative theta, and positive kappa.

STRADDLES AND STRANGLES

Instead of using the underlying security to delta hedge an option position, a delta-neutral position can also be obtained by using combinations of different options on the same underlying security. A long 30-day at-the-money call position with delta = +0.50 can be combined with a long 30-day at-the-money put position with delta = −0.49 to form an option position with delta = +0.01. This is an example of a **long straddle position,** consisting of a long call and a long put where both options have the same strike price and expiration date. A **long strangle position** also consists of a long call and a long put, both having the same expiration date; however, in a strangle, the call and the put have different strike prices.

EXAMPLE 9.2: BUYING A STRADDLE

Suppose that in the afternoon of December 12, 1988, the UST 9% issue of November 15, 2018, was trading at a price of [100.15+] (yield = 8.952%), and its 90-day at-the-money options were quoted at 9.90% implied volatility. A trader who believed that the bond's actual forthcoming volatility over the next 90 days was likely to be higher than the 9.90% implied by the options' market price might decide to buy a $1 million 90-day at-the-money straddle on this bond. Buying the 90-day call and put, respectively, at prices of 1 and ^{5}¹⁄₆₄ths and 1 and ^{60}⁄₆₄ths, the trader would pay a total premium of 3 and ^{47}⁄₆₄ths, or $37,343.75.

If the options were held to expiration, and P were the price of the UST 9% issue of November 15, 2018, on March 12, 1989, the risk/return characteristics of this speculative position could be expressed as follows, where, as before, IPP is the investment profit in points:

$$IPP = (P - 100\ ^{15.5}\!/_{32}) - 3\ ^{47}\!/_{64}, \quad \text{if } P \geq 100\ ^{15.5}\!/_{32}$$
$$IPP = (100\ ^{15.5}\!/_{32} - P) - 3\ ^{47}\!/_{64}, \quad \text{if } P < 100\ ^{15.5}\!/_{32}$$

This option position would make a profit as long as the bond's price on March 12, 1989, was higher than [104.07] or lower than [96.24]. The investment profit in dollars would be equal to $1 million times 1% times the profit in points. The short-term risk exposures of this strategy would be:

1. *Delta = (1 × 0.504) + (1 × −0.497) = +0.007.* This straddle position would have a delta of +0.007. Its short-term exposure to the bond's price risk would therefore be minimal.
2. *Gamma = (1 × 0.086) + (1 × 0.087) = +0.173.* The trader, by going long the straddle, would benefit from any significant movements in the underlying bond's price, because the gamma is positive.

3. *Theta = (1 × −5.70) + (1 × −5.70) = −11.40.* This long straddle position, however, would be exposed to time decay. The call and the put would each go down in value by $\frac{1}{64}$th per day, so the overall straddle position would decrease in value by $\frac{1}{32}$nd per day, all other factors remaining the same.
4. *Kappa = (1 × 0.1875) + (1 × 0.1875) = 0.375).* The trader, having bought the options when their implied volatilities were trading at 9.90%, would benefit significantly from any increase in their implied volatilities. Should the implied volatilities increase by 1%, the straddle position would go up in value by 0.375, or $^{24}\!/_{64}$ths, points!

We have noted that for this trade to make money, the price of the underlying bond on March 12, 1989, would have to have fallen to [96.24] or less, or risen to [104.07] or more. This would mean a full three- to four-point move in one direction or the other. It is perfectly possible that the volatility of the underlying bond would rise, as the trader expects, over the 90-day life of the options, but that the final price of the bond would be close to its original price of [100.15+]. Volatility is a measure of variability; it says nothing about market direction or even the magnitude of absolute aggregate change over a given term.

There is nothing requiring the trader to hold the options to expiration, however. If volatility rises, as the trader anticipates, it is likely that the price of the underlying bond will *either* rise significantly *or* fall significantly *at some point* during the life of the trade. Moreover, since a rise in the actual price volatility of the underlying bond is very likely to be reflected in a rise in the implied volatility imputed by the options market (i.e., since the kappa exposure works in the trader's favor), the opportunity presented by any large bond price movement early in the life of the trade will likely be magnified by an acompanying relative increase in the market value of the options. For example, if the price of the underlying bond were to rise to [102.00] after 30 days, on January 12, 1989, and if the implied volatility at which the at-the-money options on this bond were trading on that date were to have risen to 11%, the 60-day put would then have a value of 2 and $^{42}\!/_{64}$ths, while the 60-day call would have a value of 1 and $^{6}\!/_{64}$ths, for a total value of 3 and $^{48}\!/_{64}$ths, a little more than the trader originally paid. Ignoring financing costs, this would assure a profit on the trade. Similarly, if the bond price were to fall to [98.24] on January 12, 1989, with the implied volatility still rising to 11%, the 60-day put would be worth 1 and $^{3}\!/_{64}$ths, while the 60-day call would be worth 2 and $^{44}\!/_{64}$ths, a breakeven result (again ignoring financing costs).

In summary, in a volatility play of this sort, the trader is not necessary betting solely on the probable position of the underlying bond price at option expiration; he or she is merely betting that at some point over the life of the trade the anticipated increase in actual, forthcoming volatility of the underlying bond will bring about the conjunction of a move in the bond price *and* an accompanying increase in implied volatility sufficiently large to assure a profit. The earlier a sharp move in the bond price occurs, the smaller it need be to bring about a profitable situation for the trader. This is because theta (time decay) works against the trader in this trade. The earlier any sharp move in bond price occurs, therefore, the better for the trader; not only does time decay work against the trader, but by taking the tradeoff early he or she saves on any financing costs, and assures a higher effective rate of return by shortening the actual holding period of the investment. Given the trader's opportunity to take profit *at any point during the 90 days* when circumstances are favorable, this volatility play beings to look more attractive.

Like a long option position delta hedged by the underlying security, such a delta-neutral long straddle position would have a positive gamma, negative theta, and positive kappa. We have seen some of the consequences of this qualitative combination of exposure parameters for the trader's prospects for taking profit over the life of the trade. In the next section, delta-neutral positions with different combinations of gamma, theta, and kappa characteristics are discussed.

CALENDAR VOLATILITY SPREADS

The trader in Example 9.1 sold the seven-day volatility because he or she believed that the bond's actual forthcoming volatility over the next seven days would be much lower than the call's 12.55% implied volatility. The trader's option position, delta hedged by the underlying cash bond, had a negative gamma, positive theta, and negative kappa. On the other hand, the trader in Example 9.2 bought 90-day volatility because he or she expected the bond's forthcoming 90-day volatility to be much higher than the option's 9.90% implied volatility. His or her long straddle position would have positive gamma, negative theta, and positive kappa, just the reverse of the exposure characteristics of Example 9.1. In this section, we will illustrate how option positions with different combinations of gamma, theta, and kappa characteristics can be constructed using combinations with different expiration dates.

Suppose that in the afternoon of December 12, 1988, the UST 9% bond of November 15, 2018, was trading at [100.15 +], and that (a) the 90-day at-the-money straddle on this bond traded at a price of 3 and $^{47}\!/_{64}$ths (implied volatility = 9.90%), with exposure characteristics (a_1) delta = 0.007, (a_2) gamma = 0.173, (a_3) theta = −11.40, and (a_4) kappa = 0.375, as in Example 9.2 above; and (b) the 7-day at-the-money straddle on this bond traded at a price of 1 and $^{25}\!/_{64}$ths (implied volatility = 12.55%), with exposure characteristics (b_1) delta = 0.002, (b_2) gamma = 0.435, (b_3) theta = −45.62, and (b_4) kappa = 0.125. If a trader were to buy $X million 90-day at-the-money straddles and sell $Y million 7-day at-the-money straddles, then the resulting **calendar volatility spread** would have the following short-term risk exposure:

1. delta = $0.007X - 0.002Y$
2. gamma = $0.173X - 0.435Y$
3. theta = $-11.40X + 45.62Y$
5. kappa = $0.375X - 0.125Y$

For example, if the trader bought $1 million 90-day and sold $1 million 7-day at-the-money straddles, he or she would have $X = Y = 1$, and the resulting option position would have delta = 0.005, gamma = −0.260, theta = 34.22 and kappa = 0.25. Unlike Examples 9.1 and 9.2, this nearly delta-neutral position has a very attractive positive theta, as well as a moderately negative gamma and positive kappa!

EXAMPLE 9.3: A PROFITABLE CALENDAR VOLATILITY SPREAD

What are the risk/reward characteristics of this calendar volatility spread, in which the trader buys $1 million 90-day at-the-money straddles at an implied volatility of 9.90% and sells $1 million at-the-money 7-day straddles at an implied volatility of 12.55% at, say, the 7-day horizon when the short straddle expires? Table 9.1 shows the values of the (then) 83-day options, and the cost to the trader of any component of the short straddle that may end up in the money, on December 19, 1988, under nine scenarios: implied (83-day) volatilities on that date of 9.90%, 11%, and 12.55%, and underlying bond prices for the UST 9% issue of November 15, 2018, on that date of [100.00], [100.15 +], and [101.00].

The trader's initial investment is $37,343.75 − $13,653.75 = $23,690.00. The position on December 19, 1988, is worth at least $31,093.75 ([3.03 +] times 1% times $1,000,000) in the *worst* of the nine scenarios in Table 9.1. Clearly, this is a profitable trade under any of the

Table 9.1 Scenarios for Calendar Volatility Spread on December 19,1988

	Vol = 9.90%			Vol = 11.00%			Vol = 12.55%		
	[100.00]	[100.15 +]	[101.00]	[100.00]	[100.15 +]	[101.00]	[100.00]	[100.15 +]	[101.00]
Put	[1.19 +]	[1.27 +]	[2,03 +]	[1.28 +]	[2.04 +]	[2.12 +]	[2.06]	[2.14]	[2.22]
Call	[2.00 +]	[1.23 +]	[1.16]	[2.09]	[2.00 +]	[1.25]	[2.18 +]	[2.10]	[2.02 +]
Cost	[−0.16 +]	0	[−0.15 +]	[−0.16 +]	0	[−0.15 +]	[−0.16 +]	0	[−0.15 +]
TOTAL	[3.03 +]	[3.19]	[3.04]	[3.21 +]	[4.04 +]	[3.22]	[4.08]	[4.24]	[4.09]

Values are given for 83-day put and call under each scenario. Cost is cost of any in-the-money component of the short straddle exercised Prices are in points and thirty-seconds of points.

above scenarios. This is essentially because we have assumed that the trader was able to accurately detect an opportunity for a substantial volatility arbitrage (playing off "volatility-rich" and "volatility-cheap" options of different terms against each other), *and capable of properly hedging away his or her delta risk.*

The fact that the trade is nearly delta neutral and has a healthy positive theta working in its favor is an indication of a solid arbitrage. What could possibly go wrong with this trade? If implied volatilities were to dive below even the 9.90% level, the value of the long straddle position would shrink, and the trader would take a loss. Alternatively, if the underlying bond price were to move dramatically before the short straddle expired, the trader would have to pay out a substantial amount when the 7-day put or call was exercised; this would be offset by an increase in the value of the (then) 83-day put or call, but because the corresponding 83-day call or put would then be worth far less, the premium value of the long straddle would be drastically reduced, leaving a net loss. If the underlying bond were to move to a price of [103.00] by December 19, 1988, for example, the trader would owe [2.16 +] on the short call, while the long 83-day put and call would be worth [0.27 +] and [3.09], respectively (at 9.90% implied volatility), for a total value of [1.20], or $16,250.00. Even if the implied volatility of the options were to rise, as it almost certainly would, the trader would still probably end up taking a loss. But neither of these scenarios is likely to occur within the critical seven-day investment window, so the down-side risk on this trade is quite limited.

By choosing appropriate values for X and Y in this example, a trader could eliminate any one risk exposure factor he or she chose. If a trader did not wish any kappa risk, for example, he or she could buy $1 million ($X = 1$) in 90-day at-the-money straddles, and sell $3 million ($Y = 3$) in 7-day at-the-money straddles; the resulting option position would have delta = 0.001, gamma = -1.132, theta = 125.46, and kappa = 0.00. Since there are four risk equations and only one unknown (the *ratio* of X to Y is what matters here!), only one of the risk factors can be guaranteed to be reduced to zero at a time (although, as our example illustrates, by choosing the right relative calendar spreads a trader can sometimes arrange that more than one of the risk factors simultaneously become negligible, as do both delta and kappa here.)

In general, by utilizing more options with different expirations and possibly different strike prices (strangles), a trader can achieve greater flexibility in hedging away different dimensions of risk. By choosing carefully the appropriate combination of options, traders can construct positions with a wide variety of qualitative exposure characteristics. Choosing a combination that achieves the desired degree of risk control while taking advantage of any perceived market mispricings (options trading above or below the actual forthcoming volatility anticipated by the trader) is both an art and a science. The examples given in this chapter are only intended to serve as an introduction. The practicing professional should have at his or her disposal a risk management system of the sort described in Chapter 7, incorporating the appropriate option pricing models, to evaluate the risk exposure parameters of real and hypothetical (scenario) positions.

REFERENCES

Discussion of option strategies and their risk/return characteristics can be found in many options texts, including Bookstaber (1987), McMillan (1986), and Natenberg (1988).

Bookstaber, R. M., *Options Pricing and Investment Strategies*, Probus Publishing Company, Chicago, 1987.

McMillan, L. G., *Options as a Strategic Investment*. Prentice-Hall, Englewood Cliffs, N.J., 1986.

Natenberg, S., *Option Volatility and Pricing Strategies*, Probus Publishing Company, Chicago, 1988.

10

Strategies Driven By Interest Rate Forecasts

As demonstrated in Chapter 9, options trading can be shown to be equivalent to betting on upcoming actual and/or implied volatility. The reason is that any option position can be hedged using either the underlying security or other options on this security to create a delta-neutral position that will have very little exposure to the security's price risk. Most experienced options traders are volatility traders and they therefore prefer delta-neutral strategies. There are, however, many market participants who like to use options as speculative and controlled-risk bets on interest rate movements. In this chapter, the risk/return characteristics of going long or short in naked option positions are described. An example of a bullish vertical spread trade is given, and the popular straddle strategy is revisited. As will be shown, many portfolio managers use the buy-write strategy to enhance the current income of their funds. The issues involved in choosing among strategies with similar risk/return characteristics will also be discussed in the last section of the chapter.

NAKED OPTIONS

A speculator, anticipating that the yield of the 30-year Treasury bond (T-bond) is going to rise (fall) significantly in the next month, can buy a 30-day put (call) on the 30-year bond. As the following example illustrates, his or her risk is limited to the price of the option, but the profits can be significant if his or her prediction turns out to be correct.

EXAMPLE 10.1: BUYING A NAKED PUT

In the afternoon of January 9, 1989, the U.S. Treasury (UST) 9% bond of November 15, 2018, was trading at a price of 99 and $^{13.5}/_{32}$nds and a yield of 9.054%. Thinking that the yield of this bond should rise as a result of inflation fears, a trader decided to buy a $1 million 30-day put, struck at the money (with a strike yield of 9.054%). The bond's 30-day implied volatility was trading at 10.2%, and the trader had to pay 1 and $^{5}/_{32}$nds, or $11,562.50, for the $1 million 30-day put.

If this put were held to expiration, and P were the price of the UST 9% issue of November 15, 2018, on February 9, 1989, the risk/return characteristics of this speculative investment could be expressed as follows:

Investment profit in points $(IPP) = -1\,^{5}/_{32}$, if $P \geq 99\,^{13.5}/_{32}$
$IPP = (99\,^{13.5}/_{32} - P) - 1\,^{5}/_{32}$, if $P < 99\,^{13.5}/_{32}$

The investment profit in dollars is equal to $1 million times 1% times the profit in points. For example, the UST 9% issue of November 15, 2018, actually had a closing price of 100 and $^{5}/_{32}$nds on February 9, 1989. The speculator would have lost $11,562.50 ($=$1,000,000 \times 1\% \times 1.15625$) on his or her interest rate bet. Speculators, however, do not always hold their option positions to expiration, especially if there are profit-taking opportunities. The short-term risk exposures of this investment were:

1. *Delta* = -0.498. If the bond price went down by 0.3 points, the speculator should expect to make a profit of only 0.1494 points (0.3 points $\times$ 0.498).
2. *Gamma* = 0.135. If the bond price went down significantly, say by two points, the speculator could expect to make more than 0.996 points (2 points $\times$ 0.498) because the put has a positive gamma. In fact, the profit would have been 1.25 points if the bond did go down in price by two points.
3. *Theta* = -11.40625. Besides delta risk, this speculative investment was also exposed to time decay. The put would go down in value by $^{11.40625}/_{365}$, or $^{2}/_{64}$ths, points per day, if all other market factors stayed the same.

4. *Kappa = 0.109375.* The trader bought this put when its implied volatility was trading at 10.2%. Should the bond's implied volatility drop by 1%, this option position would drop in value by 0.109375, or $7/_{64}$ths, points.

This naked put position, in summary, has a negative delta, positive gamma (and hence negative theta), and positive kappa. Its major exposure is to the negative delta risk; however, as the following case illustrates, its exposure to gamma, theta, and kappa risks cannot be ignored.

Case I: Importance of Volatility Assessment

Mr. S is a professional speculator in the U.S. bond futures market. When the March 1990 T-bond futures contract was trading at a price of 98 in late October 1989, he was very bullish and wanted to buy an at-the-money call on this futures contract. He called up his futures broker and was given a price of 2 and $^{10}/_{64}$ths for the call option, and he bought it. Mr. S had been using options on bond futures for over two years, and this author was very interested in knowing how speculators would value an option. The author, therefore, asked Mr. S the following questions:

1. Would he have bought the option if the price was 2 and $^{25}/_{64}$ths?
2. Above what price would he not buy the option?
3. How did he determine his cutoff price?

Mr. S's answers were not unexpected from a speculator. He bought the call because he was bullish. He knew the T-bond options market is very liquid—he did not think he could have gotten a cheaper price for the 98 call at the time he wanted to buy. He also did his *payoff diagram* analysis, and knew his breakeven T-bond futures price to be 100 and $^{10}/_{64}$ths. Since he expected the contract price would go beyond 101 by February 1990, he would have bought the call even if it was priced at 2 and $^{48}/_{64}$ths. Moreover, he really had no intention of holding this call till expiration. He knew this at-the-month call had a delta of about 0.5, and so he would make some quick profits should the contract price trade up in the interim, perhaps because of another stock market crash.

Mr. S's answers seemed logical, except that the gamma, theta, and kappa risks of his option position never crossed his mind! Suppose that the T-bond's actual forthcoming volatility was 10% and the fair value of the 98 call was 2 and $^3/_{64}$ths, which would also be the call's expected value on the expiration date. Suppose that, because of excessive speculation, the call actually traded at 2 and $^{47}/_{64}$ths (with an implied volatility of 13%), and Mr. S bought it anyway. It is easy to see that he would have an expected loss of $^{44}/_{64}$ths when he bought the call, because the forthcoming volatility was 10%. For instance, if the price of the T-bond on expiration date was 100 and $^{3}/_{64}$ths, Mr. S would end up losing $^{44}/_{64}$ths. It is important to note that this expected loss would not be due to bad speculation, but would be due to the high cost of volatility premium!

In the interim period before the option's expiration, the speculator could end up losing money even if the T-bond's price had gone up. This could happen if arbitrage traders began selling volatility at the 13% level, and the resulting drop in option value were not fully compensated for by the increase in the contract's price. For example, if the call's implied volatility dropped back to 10%, the contract's price would have to go up by more than one full point for the call to have a price of 2 and $^{47}/_{64}$ths. This is an example of how an option position's kappa risk can dominate its gains from favorable price movements.

Remarks

1. Interest rate speculators using options must bear in mind that options have gamma, theta, and kappa risks. They should have a proper framework to assess forthcoming volatility. They should buy a call not only when they are bullish, but when they also believe that the call's implied volatility is not greater than the bond's expected forthcoming volatility.

2. Speculators generally like to buy out-of-the-money options because these options are much cheaper (in absolute price) than near-the-money ones. At the same time, the percentage return on their speculative investment will be significantly higher if their prediction turns out to be correct.

3. Speculators using over-the-counter (OTC) options should work harder to search for the best bid or offer from the competing dealers. Because different dealers normally have very different order flows, the cost savings to the speculator can be substantial if he or she can consistently uncover the highest bid or lowest offer.

4. *Sellers* of naked options have unlimited down-side potential. Their option positions have negative gamma (positive theta) and negative kappa. Because of the high risks involved, U.S. pension funds, insurance companies, and mutual funds are not allowed to sell

naked calls or puts. In the last quarter of 1989, some Japanese financial institutions were interested in selling way-out-of-the-money puts on T-bond futures. The major reason was that their portfolio managers did not think these contracts would go down very much in price, because they were anticipating a slowing U.S. economy. The other reason was that these managers were expecting a steady inflow of new investment capital in the foreseeable future, and they decided that buying U.S. bonds at the strike price of the way-out-of-the-money puts they sold would be a very attractive "forward" investment for the incoming capital. On the other hand, by selling the out-of-the-money puts, they could gain some additional profits if the bond market were to go up in price and the puts were to expire worthless. They would have inferior results only if there were a significant drop in the market—an event that, according to their interest rate forecasts, was deemed unlikely to occur.

5. Instead of investing, for example, $10 million in a 30-year bond, a portfolio manager could purchase a 6-month $10 million call on the same bond, and use the remaining funds (about 97%) to invest in low-risk money market instruments. By rolling over both the long-bond options and the short-term instruments periodically, the portfolio manager could effectively synthesize a long-term investment vehicle with the following characteristics: (*a*) no capital risk, (*b*) increasing yield if short-term rate increases, (*c*) substantial capital gains when the long bond rallies in price, and (*d*) better (worse) performance than the simple bond purchase if the bond market is expected to be volatile (stable). Because the U.S. bond market has been extremely volatile in the past eight years, this type of low-risk, volatility-exploitation strategy is gaining popularity among pension funds and insurance companies (see Chapter 11).

VERTICAL SPREADS

As shown in Example 10.1 above, naked option positions have very significant exposure to nondelta risks. The following example will illustrate why many speculators prefer to use vertical spreads as a low-risk strategy to bet on interest rate movements.

EXAMPLE 10.2: BUYING A BULL SPREAD

In the afternoon of October 23, 1989, the 96 and 98 calls on the March 1990 T-bond contract (price $=$ 98 and $^{30}\!/_{32}$nds) were trading at 3 and $^{46}\!/_{64}$ths (9.19% implied volatility) and 2 and $^{34}\!/_{64}$ths (9.44% implied volatility), respectively. Thinking that the price of this T-bond contract should rise as a result of recession fears, a trader decided to buy a bull spread. He or she bought one 96 call and sold one 98 call and paid a net premium of 1 and $^{12}\!/_{64}$ths or $1,187.50.

If this option position were held to expiration, and P were the closing price of the March T-bond contract on February 16, 1990, the risk/return characteristics of this bull spread could be expressed as follows:

$$IPP = -1\ ^{12}\!/_{64}, \text{ if } P \le 96$$
$$IPP = -1\ ^{12}\!/_{64} + (P - 96), \text{ if } 96 < P \le 98$$
$$IPP = \ ^{52}\!/_{64}, \text{ if } P > 98$$

This spread trade would make a profit as long as the T-bond contract's price on the expiration date exceeded 97 and $^{12}\!/_{64}$ths. The profit in dollars would be equal to $100,000 times 1% times the profit in points. Spread traders, however, do not always hold their option positions to expiration, especially if there are profit-taking opportunities. The short-term exposure measures for this trade are:

1. *Delta = (1 × 0.698) + (−1 × −0.555) = 0.143*. If the bond price went down by 0.5 points, the trade should expect to lose 0.0715 points (0.5 points × 0.143).

2. *Gamma = (1 × 0.0625) + (−1 × 0.0715) = −0.009*. The speculator, by buying the bull spread, has a small negative gamma exposure. For example, if the T-bond price suddenly jumped one point to 99 and $^{30}\!/_{32}$nds, the 96 (98) call price would correspondingly increase to 4 and $^{29}\!/_{64}$ths (3 and $^{9}\!/_{64}$ths), and the trader would have made $^{8}\!/_{64}$ths, or 0.125 points if he or she liquidated his or her spread position. The trader would not have made 0.143 points, the profit according to the trade's delta, because this trade has a very small negative gamma.

3. *Theta = (1 × −5.7) + (−1 × −5.7) = 0.00*. This bullish spread also has very little exposure to time decay because both the 96 and 98 calls would go down in value by about $^{1}\!/_{64}$th per day.

4. *Kappa = (1 × 0.1875) + (−1 × 0.2109) = −0.0234*. With the T-bond contract trading at 98 and $^{30}\!/_{32}$nds, the 96 call's kappa is smaller than that of the 98 call because the 96 call is more in the money

than the 98 call. The bull spread therefore has a negative kappa. This kappa, however, has a very small magnitude.

This bull spread trade, in summary, has a positive delta and a very small negative gamma (positive theta) and negative kappa. Unlike naked option trades (see Example 10.1 above), its only significant exposure is to the positive delta risk. This is why many traders prefer to use vertical bull or bear spreads to make bets on interest rate movements.

REMARKS

1. In Example 10.2 above, if the trader sold one 96 call and bought one 98 call, he or she would have sold a bull spread, in which case the risk parameters would be the exact opposite of the values shown in the example. If the trader bought one 98 put and sold one 96 put, he or she would have bought a bear spread.
2. The two components of a vertical spread are always weighted equally (one to one). Buyers of vertical bull or bear spreads always have to pay some premium up front, when the trade is first executed.

STRADDLES AND STRANGLES

The widely used straddles and strangles strategies are discussed in detail in Chapter 9. While these strategies are normally used by professional option traders to make volatility bets, some market practitioners have viewed them as strategies driven by nondirectional interest rate forecasts, as shown in the following example.

EXAMPLE 10.3: SELLING A STRADDLE

Suppose that in the afternoon of December 12, 1988, the UST 9% issue of November 15, 2018 was trading at a price of 100 and $^{15.5}/_{32}$nds (yield = 8.952%), and its seven-day at-the-money options were quoted at 12.55% implied volatility. A speculator believed that the bond's price (yield) in the next seven days would trade between 99 (9.096%) and 102 (8.808%), and he or she therefore decided to sell a $1 million seven-day at-the-money straddle on this bond. Since he or she sold the seven-day call and put, respectively, at prices of $^{44}/_{64}$ths and $^{45}/_{64}$ths, the speculator received a total premium of $^{89}/_{64}$ths or $13,906.25.

If the options were held to expiration, and P were the price of the UST 9% issue of November 15, 2018, on December 19, 1988, the risk/return characteristics of this speculative investment could be expressed as follows:

$$IPP = (100 \; ^{15.5}\!/_{32} - P) + \; ^{89}\!/_{64}, \text{ if } P \geq 100 \; ^{15.5}\!/_{32}$$
$$IPP = (P - 100 \; ^{15.5}\!/_{32}) + \; ^{89}\!/_{64}, \text{ if } P < 100 \; ^{15.5}\!/_{32}$$

This option position would make a profit as long as the bond's price on the expiration date fell between 99 and $^3\!/_{32}$nds and 101 and $^{28}\!/_{32}$nds. The investment profit in dollars would be equal to $1 million times 1% times the profit in points. For example, the actual closing price of the UST 9% issue of November 15, 2018, on December 19, 1988, was 99 and $^{17.5}\!/_{32}$nds. The speculator would have gained $^{29}\!/_{64}$ths, or $4,531.25 (= $1,000,000 × 1% × $^{29}\!/_{64}$), on his or her "interest rate" bet, since he or she correctly predicted that the bond's price would fall between 99 and 102. The short-term risk exposures of this strategy were:

1. *Delta* $= (-1 \times 0.501) + (-1 \times -0.499) = -0.002$. Since the speculator did not make a directional bet on interest rates, his or her option position was effectively delta neutral.
2. *Gamma* $= (-1 \times 0.2185) + (-1 \times 0.2185) = -0.437$. The speculator, by going short on the straddle, had significant exposure to gamma risks. For example, if the bond price suddenly jumped one point to 101 and $^{15.5}\!/_{32}$nds, the call (put) price would correspondingly change to 1 and $^{10}\!/_{32}$nds ($^{9.5}\!/_{32}$nds), and the speculator would have lost $^{14}\!/_{64}$ths if forced to liquidate his or her straddle position.
3. *Theta* $= (-1 \times -22.81) + (-1 \times -22.81) = 45.63$. This speculative strategy would benefit from time decay. The call and the put would both go down in value by $^2\!/_{32}$nds per day, and the straddle position would therefore go up in value by $^{45.63}\!/_{365}$, or $^4\!/_{32}$nds per day, if all other market factors stayed the same.
4. *Kappa* $= (-1 \times 0.05469) + (-1 \times 0.05469) = -0.109375$. The speculator sold the options when their implied volatilities were trading at 12.55%. Should these implied volatilities increase by 1%, this straddle position would drop in value by 0.109375, or $^7\!/_{64}$ths, points.

REMARKS

1. Interest rate speculators often like to sell straddles and strangles because, most of the time, they end up making some small profits from their position's positive theta. However, because of their ex-

posure to negative gamma risk, they stand to lose a sizable amount of their capital if the bond market makes a big move.

2. Since sellers of straddles tend to hold their positions to expiration, they often overlook their positions' exposure to kappa risk during the interim period before expiration. They should not sell straddles and strangles if the options' implied volatilities are trading at levels well below the expected forthcoming volatilities of the underlying cash bonds or bond futures.

BUY-WRITE STRATEGIES

Options-writing strategies have been widely used to enhance a portfolio's current income. Several of the largest U.S. bond mutual funds, with billions of dollars in assets, are regular users of the buy-write strategy (see Siconolfi, 1989). The underlying premise of this strategy is to write calls against bonds held in the portfolio, thereby increasing the short-term income by the amount of the call premium. Since selling a call option is similar to preselling a bond at the call strike price, users of this strategy are willing to give up the bond price's up-side potential beyond the strike price in return for income enhancement. In a down market, the premium from the then-worthless call can be used to offset some of the portfolio depreciation resulting from the lower market price.

EXAMPLE 10.4: A 30-YEAR TREASURY BOND BUY-WRITE

Suppose that in the morning of September 9, 1987, the UST 8 ⅞% bond of August 15, 2017, was trading at a price of 93 and a yield of 9.588%, and its 30-day at-the-money options were quoted at 13% implied volatility. A portfolio manager decided to buy $1 million of the UST 8 ⅞% issue and simultaneously sold a $1 million 30-day at-the-money call on the same bond. Including accrued interest, the manager had to pay $939,021.29 for the cash bond. Meanwhile, he or she sold a 30-day call, struck at 93, on the bond for 1 and ⅜ths points, and received a premium of $13,750. The initial investment was therefore $925,271.29.

The holding period income generated by the cash bond was equal to $7,235.05 [$= \$1,000,000 \times (^{0.08875}\!/_{2}) \times {}^{30}\!/_{184}$]. In other words, the accrued interest of this bond on October 8, 1987, was $16,256.34. If the call were held by the buyer to expiration, and P were the price of the UST 8 ⅞%

issue of August 15, 2017, on October 8, 1987, the potential holding period return (R) of this buy-write could be expressed as follows:

$R = 100\% \times (930,000 + 16,256.34 - 925,271.29)/925,271.29 = 2.26\%$, if $P \geq 93$

$R = 100\% \times [(P\% \times 1,000,000) + 16,256.34 - 925,271.29]/925,271.29$, if $P < 93$

For example, on October 8, 1987:

    a. if the bond yield was at 9.838%, $P = 90\ ^{19}\!/_{32}$ and $R = -0.33\%$
    b. if the bond yield was at 10.088%, $P = 88\ ^{19}\!/_{32}$ and $R = -2.49\%$.

The actual price of the bond on October 8, 1987, turned out to be 91 and $^{9}\!/_{32}$nds, and the portfolio manager ended up with a 30-day return of 0.41%, compared to -1.06% if he or she had not written the 30-day call. It is clear that this buy-write combination would outperform an outright bond purchase as long as the bond price did not rally significantly.

REMARKS

1. Options writers generally sell 30-day one-point-out-of-the-money calls. However, some mutual funds managers prefer to roll over shorter term calls, especially if the one- and two-week implied volatilities are trading at relatively high levels, because shorter term options, especially the relatively expensive ones, have much faster time decay.

2. Insurance companies often have many bonds in their portfolios at any given time. Suppose a portfolio manager has decided to sell a certain bond should its price increase to P^*. He or she can enhance the portfolio's return by writing a call on the bond struck at P^*: (*a*) if the bond price never reaches P^*, the option premium will provide extra income to the portfolio; (*b*) if the call is exercised at P^*, the manager will happily sell the bond at P^*, knowing full well that he or she has also taken advantage of the call's time premium.

3. The buy-write strategy, with a positive delta, negative gamma (positive theta), and negative kappa, is similar to selling short a synthetic put. It is therefore exposed to significant down-side price risk. After the big fall in bond prices during the first half of 1987, buy-write mutual funds started to use out-of-the-month puts to protect against any future big drop in portfolio value. This insurance application of options is described in the next chapter.

COMMENTS

Various interest rate–driven strategies, including naked options, vertical spreads, straddles, and buy-writes, are described and discussed in this chapter. It has been demonstrated that vertical spreads are preferrable to naked options as a strategy if the trader does not want unnecessary high gamma, theta, and kappa risks. Users of naked options, straddles, and buy-writes are warned that they should not ignore their positions' kappa risks. In terms of their payoff diagrams and risk parameter values, however, different strategies may have similar risk/return characteristics.

A bullish trader, for example, has many strategies available. He or she can, among other choices, either (a) buy a call, (b) sell a put, (c) buy a bull spread, or (d) sell a bear spread. The trader's decision obviously depends on how bullish he or she is. If the trader believes the market is going to make a very big move upward, he or she should prefer (a) to (b), (c), or (d). To identify the most appropriate strategy, the trader should also make use of his or her volatility assessment skills. If the options' implied volatilities are all too high, the trader should prefer (b) to (a), (c), or (d); and if, for example, the 96 call's implied volatility is relatively cheap compared to that of the 98 call, he or she should use (c) to take advantage of the perceived mispricing. There are obviously many combinations of bullishness/bearishness and volatility levels possible, but the trader should not have difficulty sorting through these complications as long as he or she is familiar with the usage of payoff diagrams and the four major risk parameters.

REFERENCES

The basic option strategies and their payoff diagrams can be found in many standard texts, including Bookstaber (1987) and McMillan (1986). There are seven different articles on portfolio and trading strategies in the recently published "Handbook of Fixed-Income Options: Pricing, Strategies & Applications." For example, the various covered-call writing strategies are described in Jones and Krumholz (1989), while naked options, vertical spreads, and straddles are described in Kamphoefner and McKendry (1989).

Bookstaber, R. M., *Options Pricing and Investment Strategies*, Probus Publishing Company, Chicago, 1987.

Jones, F., and B. Krumholz, "Covered Call Writing Strategies," in Fabozzi, F.,
   ed., *Handbook of Fixed-Income Options: Pricing, Strategies & Applications*, Probus Publishing Company, Chicago, 1989, pp. 295–349.

Kamphoefner, J., and R. McKendry, "Trading and Arbitrage Strategies Using Debt
   Options," in Fabozzi, F., ed., *Handbook of Fixed-Income Options: Pricing,
   Strategies & Applications*, Probus Publishing Company, Chicago, 1989, pp. 225–
   263.

McMillan, L. G., *Options as a Strategic Investment*, Prentice-Hall, Englewood
   Cliffs, N.J., 1986.

Siconolfi, M., "Government-Plus Bonds Now Show Many Minuses," *Wall Street
   Journal*, August 30, 1989.

11
Portfolio Strategies Involving Options

To ensure that their investment objectives are met, many institutional investors have used quantitatively driven strategies to structure their fixed-income portfolios. The number of managers adopting portfolio strategies involving options has increased over the past few years. Most of these investors use options to hedge portfolio holdings. Bank and savings institutions also use options to hedge away interest rate risks during loan commitment periods. The idea behind this insurance-like option application is straightforward, but keeping the cost of this insurance low in practice often requires special execution skills. These issues will be addressed, and the dynamic hedging process for synthesizing a put option is also described. Pension funds and insurance companies generally have long investment horizons. Portfolio managers in some of these institutions have started using combinations of bond options and U.S. Treasury securities to synthetically create low-risk investment vehicles. These strategies, and their risk/return characteristics, will be described. An overall review of options trading and investing is presented in the final section, where the most widely used option strategies, and the institutions that employ them, are summarized.

PORTFOLIO PROTECTION USING PUTS

Bond options are widely used as hedges against adverse interest rate movements. Suppose that an investor or portfolio manager has a huge

Treasury bond portfolio, and fears that certain upcoming events may cause a short-term adverse move in interest rates. It would not be practical to sell all the securities in the portfolio; transaction costs may be high and the investor would still have reinvestment risks. Moreover, the dreaded interest rate move may never take place. To protect against a **contingent liability,** the investor should resort to a *contingent instrument:* options. Most simply, the investor can protect his or her portfolio by buying puts that will go up in value should interest rates rise.

EXAMPLE 11.1: A PROTECTIVE PUT

Suppose that on the morning of September 9, 1987, the U.S. Treasury (UST) 8 $\frac{7}{8}$% bond of August 15, 2017, was trading at a price of 93 and a yield of 9.588%. A portfolio manager was long in $100 million of this bond and expected bond yields to move lower. However, market participants were anticipating two major economic releases in the next two weeks that might cause violent swings of bond prices in either direction. The manager therefore decided to insulate his or her holding by purchasing $100 million in 14-day one-point-out-of-the-money puts at a price of $\frac{16}{32}$nds (implied volatility = 13%). If the puts were held to expiration, and P were the price of the UST 8 $\frac{7}{8}$% issue of August 15, 2017, on September 23, 1987, the potential holding period change in value (excluding the bond's accrued interest) of this put-protected portfolio could be expressed as follows:

$$dPV = P - 93 - 0.5, \text{ for } P \geq 92$$
$$dPV = 92 - 93 - 0.5 = 1.5, \text{ for } P < 92$$

where dPV is the holding-period change in portfolio value in percentage points.

For example, suppose that the price of the bond on September 23, 1987, turned out to be 93 and $\frac{13}{32}$nds with a yield of 9.544%. Excluding coupon income from the bond, the put-protected portfolio would end up losing 0.09375 points in value for the two-week period. This loss would occur in spite of a drop in the bond yield of 4.4 basis points; the put protection cost the portfolio manager $\frac{16}{32}$nds, which was a little more than the bond's actual price appreciation of $\frac{13}{32}$nds.

REMARKS

1. A put-protected bond portfolio has the risk/return characteristics of a call option. It has an absolute limit on down-side risk, while the potential gain remains unlimited, being reduced only by the

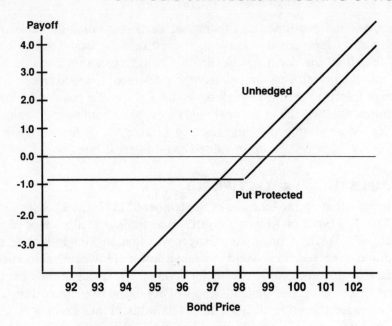

FIGURE 11.1 A put-protected portfolio.

"insurance premium" represented by the cost of the put (see Figure 11.1). The maximum loss occurs when the bond price drops to or below the put strike price. As in any option strategy, the user should select the strike price and expiration date to fit his or her investment outlook, objectives, and constraints. Moreover, such protection should not be bought if the put is trading at an implied volatility much higher than what the user expects the bond's actual volatility will be.

2. Pension funds and insurance companies generally have relatively long investment horizons, and are therefore most interested in using long-dated options in their portfolios. For example, a pension fund manager may want to buy a three-year put to make sure that his portfolio value is protected on the down side at the end of the three-year period. Such long-dated options, however, currently trade in a very thin market, with very wide bid-ask price spreads. Portfolio managers have therefore started using *dynamic hedging* or *portfolio insurance* strategies to replicate the payoffs of long-dated options. These strategies and their implementation issues are discussed in the following section, where the important role of short-dated options in such strategies is also discussed.

Creating Options through Dynamic Hedging

Puts are often used as insurance against a portfolio loss. Instead of buying expensive long-dated puts outright, portfolio managers can use **dynamic hedging** techniques to replicate the payoffs of a put. These techniques are therefore also known as **portfolio insurance.** Portfolio insurance in equities grew explosively from 1981 to October 1987. Because of a lack of liquidity associated with the stock market crash of October 19, 1987, portfolio insurers had trouble dynamically adjusting their equity portfolios, causing the concept of portfolio insurance to lose favor with a number of equity portfolio managers. Meanwhile, fixed-income portfolio insurance has been receiving more and more attention since late 1986, when portfolio analysts started recommending its use.

How Dynamic Hedging Works

It is possible to synthetically replicate the price behavior of an option on a given security by taking, and dynamically adjusting, an appropriate position in the underlying security. Because the value of the option changes by its *delta* when there is a unit change in the price of the underlying security, a portfolio holding this delta amount of the underlying security will have the same price sensitivity as holding the option itself. As the underlying security price moves, the option delta also changes, and the portfolio must be adjusted to hold the new delta amount of the underlying security. This dynamic process replicates the option payoff because the portfolio exposure is adjusted to mimic the option's price sensitivity. As long as the underlying security trades in a liquid market and its price moves continuously, the portfolio manager will be able to adjust the security holding sufficiently frequently, and this *synthetic portfolio* will be indistinguishable from the actual option in terms of its price behavior and sensitivity.

In protective-put or portfolio insurance applications, the portfolio is already long in a bond and the manager wants to dynamically synthesize a long-dated put. Since the put's delta is negative, ranging from negative one to zero, the portfolio insurer will sell an amount of the bond position equal to the put's delta at the start of the dynamic hedging process. If the bond price goes down (up), the put delta will get more (less) negative, and the manager will sell (buy back) more bonds. The market exposure of this put-protected portfolio will decrease as the price drops, as more of the position is sold off, thereby limiting its down-side exposure. But up-side potential remains unlimited, because market exposure will increase as the position is built back up (up to a limit of 100% of the original position) as the price goes up.

The process of dynamic hedging can be difficult and costly, however, especially when the market is very volatile. Even ignoring transaction costs, some losses are clearly incurred whenever an investor is forced to repeatedly sell in a down market and buy back in an up market! The sum total of such losses over the life of the synthesized option is the *cost* of the dynamic hedging strategy; it should, in theory, be close to the fair market price of the long-dated put option being synthesized, and can therefore be estimated using an appropriate long-dated option pricing model. The more volatile the market, the greater this cost will be, as would be expected.

In reality, of course, markets are not perfectly continuous, nor can a portfolio manager constantly be adjusting his or her position every time the market moves. Transaction costs alone would limit the frequency with which a manager would be willing to make such adjustments. In practice, therefore, there will always be some *slippage* in the value of the dynamically hedged portfolio as a result of transaction costs, market discontinuities, and the fact that adjustments are made only at discrete intervals.

Remarks

Model-Related Issues.
1. To use this dynamic hedging technique, a portfolio manager needs an option pricing model that can provide continuous updates of an option's delta. This strategy will fail miserably if the model gives incorrect results. (For a discussion of pricing models for long-dated debt options, see Chapter 4.)
2. The price of the put, and therefore the cost of the dynamic hedging strategy, depends on various input parameters, including estimates of future volatility and interest rate levels. The problem of estimating future volatility has already been addressed in Chapter 5. For a long-dated option, the actual volatility of the underlying security can vary drastically from week to week over the hedging period. But for periods of a year and over, the average volatility of the bond market tends to be more stable across time because there are bound to be *both* highly volatile and very quiet intervals within such a long period.

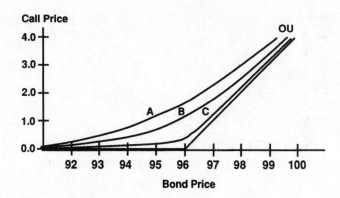

FIGURE 11.2 Convexity of option price as time to expiration decreases.

3. In dynamic hedging, every time the manager sells part of his or her portfolio, the proceeds are supposed to be invested in short-term risk-free assets such as Treasury bills (T-bills) and notes. The income from these assets varies with the prevailing short-term interest rate. Users should therefore select models that specifically and correctly take into effect possible yield curve shifts over time (see Chapter 4).

Hedge Adjustment. As pointed out in Chapters 3, 4, and 5, option models usually assume that the price movement of the underlying security is continuous, and that the option's delta can be continuously revised. This is, of course, impossible to do in practice. Generally, hedge adjustments are not performed at regular, daily or weekly time intervals. Instead, the portfolio is updated more (less) frequently in rapidly changing (stable) markets. Note that the portfolio insurer is short in gamma, while he or she is trying to replicate the payoff of a put. This is why portfolio insurers had problems during the week of October 19, 1987. For this reason, portfolio insurers often go long in some short-dated options to reduce their gamma risks and to match the put's price behavior better.

Using Short-Dated Options. The plot of an option's price, at any point during its lifetime, against the price of its underlying security is a convex curve. As shown in Figure 11.2, this "option price versus underlying security price" (OU) curve will increase in curvature as the option moves

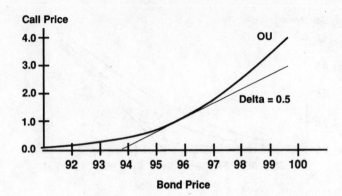

FIGURE 11.3 Delta hedging as tangent line (slope = delta).

closer to its expiration date; on that date, the OU curve is the option's payoff diagram. The option's delta is the slope of the OU curve at the current price of the underlying security. Using dynamic hedging to replicate the option's price behavior is like using a straight line (with a slope equal to delta) to approximate the OU curve in the neighborhood centered at the current price (see Figure 11.3). This approximation will be poor unless the security's price changes gradually and adjustments are made with every small price change. Because short-dated options' OUs are more highly curved than those of long-dated options, a more accurate way of approximating a long-dated option's price behavior would be to use a combination of (*a*) the underlying security and (*b*) shorter-dated options. By going long in some short-dated options, the gamma risk of the dynamic hedging process can be dramatically reduced.

Dynamic Hedging Versus Buying Long-Dated Options. Portfolio insurers have to work very hard: they need to constantly monitor and frequently update their portfolio holdings. The transaction costs involved are significant and they are short in gamma for the duration of the option's life! Buying a long-dated put outright would appear to be a much more convenient way of achieving the price protection for which these portfolio managers are looking. The seller of such an option, however, would become the dynamic hedger; for their hard work and for assuming the risk exposure, they normally charge a price that is somewhat higher than the option's theoretical fair value. With the development in time of larger and more liquid markets in long-dated options, however, this price premium may begin to shrink.

EXAMPLE 11.2: PORTFOLIO INSURANCE THROUGH DYNAMIC HEDGING

To illustrate the above remarks, consider a portfolio manager holding $110 million ($100 million face value) of the UST 9% bond of November 15, 2018, trading at 110 on May 15, 1992. Suppose that the manager's working investment horizon is a year, and that, while historical volatilities have been relatively low, the manager anticipates a more volatile market in the mid-term. (The U.S. presidential elections are approaching, as is European monetary unification.) What would a dynamic hedging strategy to take this manager through his or her one-year window look like?

The UST 9% issue of November 15, 2018, is trading at a price of 110. The portfolio manager's option pricing model tells him or her that the fair theoretical price of a one-year two-point-out-of-the-money put option on this bond is four points, with a delta of -0.418. Following the strategy outlined above, the portfolio manager will sell 0.418 of his or her position, leading to an initial hedged position consisting of:

$64.04 million in the bond ($58.22 million in face value)
$45.96 million in cash, assumed to be invested in, say, T-bills at 7.5%

One possible scenario for the evolution of the dynamically hedged portfolio position, with quarterly adjustments, is shown in Table 11.1.

In the scenario portrayed in Table 11.1, we have assumed that the bond undergoes a substantial, steady price decline over the entire holding period. The table shows the bond price, put price, and delta at three-month intervals; the proportions held in the bond and in cash, adjusted each quarter according to the new option delta; and the value of the bond holding, interest on the cash position, accumulated coupon income, and interest on coupon income. We have assumed a constant 12% annual volatility and 7.5% short rate throughout the holding period: although this is not strictly realistic, adjustments of these parameters would not

Table 11.1 Dynamically Hedged Position (12% Volatility, 7.5% Short Rate)

As of Date	Bond Price	Put Price	Put Delta	Bond Pos'n	Bond Value	Cash Pos'n	Interest	Cpn Inc	Cpn Int
5.15.92	110.00	4.004	-0.418	0.58219	64.041	45.959	0.000	0.000	0.000
8.15.92	108.00	4.260	-0.481	0.52634	56.844	51.991	0.868	0.000	0.000
11.15.92	106.00	4.659	-0.581	0.43541	46.153	61.630	1.850	2.369	0.000
2.15.93	104.00	4.989	-0.734	0.29379	30.555	76.358	3.015	2.369	0.045
5.15.93	102.00	6.000	-1.000	0.29379	29.967	76.358	4.410	3.691	0.089

materially affect the outcome of the scenario. We have used a Black-Scholes model to derive option prices and deltas; for greater accuracy, and especially for longer holding periods, appropriate long-term option pricing models should be used, since using a Black-Scholes model will lead to distortions.

The value of the final hedged position under this scenario's assumptions is $114.515 million. This is the sum of the value of the ending bond position ($29.967 million, or $29.379 million face at the ending price of [102.00]), the cash position ($76.358 million), interest on the cash position ($4.410 million), accumulated coupon income ($3.691 million), and interest on coupon income ($0.089 million). The ending value of the original portfolio of bonds *without* the put insurance under the same scenario assumptions would be $111.169 million, which is equal to the sum of $102.00 million (the value of $100 million face value bonds at the ending bond price of [102.00]), $9.00 million (coupon income), and $0.169 million (interest on bond income). The hedging strategy has thus successfully protected the portfolio against part of the loss. Incidentally, the value of a true put-protected portfolio—one consisting of the bond holding and a corresponding one-year two-point-out-of-the-money put option— would be $117.169 million. Adjusted for the initial cost of the put, 4.004, this gives an ending value of $113.165 million; actually buying the option appears to be *less* efficient than the dynamic hedge in this case! (In fact, if we were to adjust the bond volatility up as the bond price plummeted, our option deltas would be less negative, and the cash positions correspondingly smaller, and the final value of the dynamically hedged portfolio would end up closer to that of the put-protected portfolio adjusted for the initial option cost.)

As noted above, a dynamic hedging strategy can sometimes be improved by adding a long position in short-dated options to compensate for gamma effects. In the case of the above scenario, if we were to purchase six-month at-the-money put options on 10% of the value of the bond contract being hedged every three months, the result would be the modified scenario shown in Table 11.2

The purchase of the short-dated puts in Table 11.2 is financed out of the cash position, which slightly distorts the dynamic hedging strategy, leading to a smaller final bond position. Income from short-dated puts expiring in the money during the course of the holding period is added back into the cash position, as is the value of the remaining (three-month) put at the end of the holding period. The total value of the final position

Table 11.2 Dynamic Hedging with Short-Dated Option Positions

As of Date	Bond Price	Put Delta	Bond Pos'n	Bond Value	Cash Pos'n	Interest	Cpn Inc	Cpn Int	Short-Dated Put	Put Inc
5.15.92	110.00	−0.418	0.58219	64.041	45.599	0.000	0.000	0.000	3.602	0.000
8.15.92	108.00	−0.481	0.52300	56.484	51.636	0.861	0.000	0.000	3.550	0.000
11.15.92	106.00	−0.581	0.42872	45.445	61.674	1.861	2.354	0.000	3.557	0.400
2.15.93	104.00	−0.734	0.28753	29.904	76.411	3.002	2.354	0.044	3.468	0.400
5.15.93	102.00	−1.000	0.28753	29.329	77.174	4.398	3.647	0.088	0.000	0.764

is $114.636 million, which is slightly better than the result following a dynamic hedging strategy without the addition of the short-dated puts.

Of course, gamma effects will be most severe when the market is volatile and undergoes rapid shifts over intervals too short for the dynamic hedging strategy to cope with gracefully. For example, if we were to assume an even more dramatic fall in bond prices over the course of our holding period, the results of a pure dynamic hedging strategy and of such a strategy enhanced by the purchase of short-dated puts would be as shown in Tables 11.3 and 11.4. Note that here the short-dated puts have significantly improved the performance of the hedging strategy, with a final value of $114.149 for the enhanced strategy versus $113.459 for the pure strategy.

If bond prices had risen, rather than falling so dramatically, our short-dated puts would expire worthless, and the premium paid for them, about 1.41, would be lost. Of course, the portfolio manager could buy out-of-the-money puts and/or vary the proportions purchased to reduce the cost of this additional gamma insurance.

Transaction costs aside, more frequent adjustments will generally improve the efficiency of a dynamic hedging strategy. Since an investor is

Table 11.3 Dynamically Hedged Position (12% Volatility, 7.5% Short Rate) with Sharper Bond Price Fall

As of Date	Bond Price	Put Price	Put Delta	Bond Pos'n	Bond Value	Cash Pos'n	Interest	Cpn Inc	Cpn Int
5.15.92	110.00	4.004	−0.418	0.58219	64.041	45.959	0.000	0.000	0.000
8.15.92	109.00	3.795	−0.444	0.55984	61.023	48.395	0.868	0.000	0.000
11.15.92	105.00	5.265	−0.626	0.39427	41.398	65.780	1.782	2.519	0.000
2.15.93	101.00	7.416	−0.871	0.17473	17.648	87.953	3.025	2.519	0.048
5.15.93	100.00	8.000	−1.000	0.17473	17.473	87.953	4.632	3.306	0.095

Table 11.4   Dynamic Hedging with Short-Dated Option Positions during Sharper Bond Price Fall

As of Date	Bond Price	Put Delta	Bond Pos'n	Bond Value	Cash Pos'n	Interest	Cpn Inc	Cpn Int	Short-Dated Put	Put Inc
5.15.92	110.00	−0.418	0.58219	64.041	45.599	0.000	0.000	0.000	3.602	0.000
8.15.92	109.00	−0.444	0.55653	60.662	48.039	0.861	0.000	0.000	3.564	0.000
11.15.92	105.00	−0.626	0.38757	40.695	65.926	1.769	2.504	0.000	3.544	0.500
2.15.93	101.00	−0.871	0.16947	17.117	88.411	3.014	2.504	0.047	3.428	0.800
5.15.93	100.00	−1.000	0.16947	16.947	89.211	4.630	3.267	0.094	0.000	0.801

always buying in a rising market and selling in a falling one, it is generally advantageous to have made part of the necessary adjustment earlier, at better terms. On the other hand, if the market is simply oscillating around a stable level rather than trending up or down, the hedger actually *saves* money by missing intermediate adjustments for the temporary ups and downs. This is one way in which a dynamic hedging strategy may actually improve over true put protection, where such oscillatory movement is already incorporated into the price of the long-dated put by way of the volatility. In addition to determining a baseline frequency for adjustments to the hedged position, the portfolio manager engaged in dynamic hedging may wish to set a threshhold for market movement below which no adjustments will be made. There is certainly plenty of room for art and skill, especially in timing, to accompany the technical fundamentals of dynamic hedging.

CAPITAL PRESERVATION STRATEGIES

Risk-averse investors often prefer portfolio strategies that would specifically preserve their initial capital. There are various methods that an investor can use to preserve his or her assets. One simple way is to invest only in short-term U.S. Treasury bills (T-bills) and notes (T-notes); of course, other money market instruments can be used, but the higher yields of these instruments usually come with additional credit risks. The unappealing feature of these low-risk investment vehicles is that they do not provide *any* up-side potential. Because of their unique characteristics, options can often be used in capital preservation strategies, which also provide investors with substantial up-side potential.

Cash Bonds Plus Put Options

An example of such a strategy is a put-protected cash bond portfolio. Suppose that an investor has $10 million in capital to invest, and the 8.125% 30-year bond is trading at par (price = 100). A six-month at-the-money put on the bond is trading at 2 and $^{24}/_{32}$nds, with an implied volatility of just over 10%. To preserve his or her capital, the investor can buy about $9.725 million in bonds, and use the remaining funds to buy the same amount of six-month at-the-money puts. Since the bond has an income of 4.0625% every six months, while the put costs only 2.75%, the investor's minimum return for the six-month period is 1.3125%; if the bond market rallies, the investor can enjoy a sizable return on his or her investments.

Remarks

1. The user of this simple strategy should not simply buy and hold the cash bond and the put options for the entire six months. He or she should try to enhance the strategy's performance by exploiting any profitable trading opportunities. This can be achieved either by constantly seeking another bond that will outperform the one the user is holding, or by finding the cheapest way to buy the put protection.
2. For example, the investor could swap out of the 8.125% bond and into the 8.875% 29-year bond, if he or she believed that the latter bond was trading cheap relative to the 8.125% bond. Similarly, if the user thought the bond futures contract was cheap relative to the cash bonds, he or she could exploit the apparent mispricings to obtain a higher investment return.
3. To preserve capital, the user does not have to use at-the-money puts. The goal is to find the cheapest way to buy the protection that he or she needs. Since puts struck at different prices often have different implied volatilities (see Chapter 8), the investor can use his or her skills in assessing relative volatilities to lower the costs in getting the put protection.
4. During the course of the 6-month period, the 30-year bond could experience some wild price fluctuations, and yet settle back to its price at the beginning of the period. For example, the bond's price could have gone up to 106 by the end of the first three months, and come back down to 100 by the end of six months. In such instances, the six-month put option on the bond would expire worthless, and

the investor would have to be satisfied with the minimum possible return; meanwhile, if the investor had used two consecutive three-month puts, his or her return would have been substantially higher because of the rally in the first quarter. While there is no way to avoid this *timing* risk completely, the investor can diversify by using alternating six-month puts whose starting points are, for example, three months apart.

Money Market Instruments Plus Bond Options

A similar, but more flexible, capital preservation strategy involves the use of money market instruments and bond options. Suppose that the investor has $10 million to invest, and the six-month T-bill is trading at a discount yield of 7.46%, with a bond-equivalent yield of 7.86%. A six-month at-the-money call on the 8.125% 30-year bond is trading at 2 and ^{24}/$_{32}$nds, with an implied volatility of just over 10%. To preserve his or her capital, the investor can buy about $9.725 million (about $10.11 million face value) in 6-month T-bills, and use the remaining funds to buy $10 million 6-month at-the-money calls on the 30-year bond. Since the T-bills will be worth about $10.11 million at the end of the six-month period, the investor's minimum return for the six-month period is 1.0832%; and if the bond market rallies, the bond calls he or she owns will go up in price and give a very significant return on his or her investments.

Remarks

1. Many investors prefer to have their capital invested only in liquid investments. Because over 97% of the capital is invested in T-bills, this strategy is often presented as a highly liquid, low-risk investment product.
2. As mentioned in the previous remarks, the user of this simple strategy should try to enhance its performance by exploiting profitable trading opportunities in the money markets and in the bond options markets. This can be achieved by identifying a better yielding short-term security, or by finding the relatively cheapest calls.
3. For example, the investor can swap out of the six-month T-bill and into the six-month T-note, if he or she thinks that the T-note is trading cheap to the T-bill. Or, there may exist a T-bill with a different maturity, which has a very good chance of taking advantage

of the so-called *riding down the yield curve* effect (see Chapter 2), and hence may generate a superior return. Of course, other money market instruments, including repurchase agreements, U.S. government agency papers, short-duration CMOs or other mortgage-derivative products, commercial papers, and time deposits, can be used in place of the Treasury securities. The higher yields of these instruments, however, usually come with additional credit risks; in the case of mortgage derivatives, there are also some prepayment risks involved.

4. Again, the user does not have to use at-the-money calls. Since calls struck at different prices often have different implied volatilities (see Chapter 8), the investor should use his or her skills in assessing relative volatilities to lower the costs in getting the up-side potential he or she seeks. Moreover, to diversify away some of the timing risk (see above), the investor could use alternating six-month calls whose starting points are, say, three months apart.

OVERALL REVIEW

The U.S. debt option markets have grown significantly in the past few years. The Japanese Government Bond (JGB) optin market is just beginning to take off. Bond options are being used extensively by various institutional investors to meet their investment objectives: either to minimize risk for a specified return target, or to maximize profits for given risk constraints. The most widely used option strategies and the institutions that use them regularly are summarized here.

How U.S. Institutional Investors Use Debt Options

Financial institutions, including securities dealers, banks, and investment partnerships, use options arbitrage to make profits or to enhance their cash portfolio returns. Some of the relative-value trading strategies used by these arbitrage trading units, including *intrasector arbitrage* and the use of *implied volatilities*, are described in Chapter 8. One incidental but important consequence of these arbitrage activities is an improvement in the efficiency of the bond option markets.

Traders in various financial institutions, except those in pension funds and insurance companies, occasionally use options as highly leveraged instruments to speculate on (*a*) the bond's actual versus implied volatilities, by using delta-neutral strategies including straddles and strangles (see Chapter 9); and (*b*) interest rate movements, by using naked options and vertical spreads (see Chapter 10). Pension funds and insurance companies generally have much longer investment horizons. Fund managers in some of these institutions use combinations of U.S. government securities and debt options to synthetically create low-risk investment vehicles that also have significant up-side potential. Such strategies are described above.

The *buy-write* is one of the most widely used option strategies. Several of the largest U.S. bond mutual funds, with billions of dollars in assets, are regular users of this strategy. Some insurance companies, banks, and savings institutions also use this approach occasionally to increase short-term income in exchange for possible short-term capital gains. The issues involved in the practical application of this strategy are described in Chapter 10.

Finally, as discussed earlier in this chapter, most institutional investors use options to hedge away some of their portfolios' interest rate risks. Options are also used to provide upper (lower) bounds on the future buying (selling) prices of debt securities.

COMMENT

As in all investment activities, the benefits from buying or selling options do not come free. Naked option buyers often have to pay a steep time premium for their speculative bets, while buy-write users have to forego most of a bond's upside potential in exchange for additional short-term income. Portfolio managers use options because these instruments can change the risk/return characteristics of their investments to fit their market outlook. Any time an option is bought (sold), the buyer (seller) must believe that the market volatility is going to be higher (lower) than the option's traded implied volatility. Very few speculators would buy a call just because they think the price of the underlying security is going up; one would do so only if that call were also trading at a reasonable or relatively low implied volatility. Not everyone can be right about the direction of market volatility; the options market, like other markets, is a zero-sum game. Therefore, no single option strategy will work all the time, and an investment manager can add value only by using options judiciously, armed with appropriate quantitative tools and qualitative strategies. We have sought to lay out these tools and strategies in this book, but the exercise of judgment in choosing the appropriate strategy for a given investment setting is something the money manager will best learn by doing.

Figlewski (1988) concluded, after conducting a survey on the use of financial futures and options by major U.S. life insurance companies, that there may still be considerable growth in the U.S. options market because most of the second-tier insurance companies have not yet begun using options. The cited reason for the lack of usage is that options and their strategies are not fully understood! The expected growth in both the U.S. and Japanese bond option markets will therefore require a certain commitment to learning, especially learning how options pricing and computer technologies can be used in trading and investing in options. As Gastineau (1983) predicted: "... *in a few years, the fixed-income manager who does not understand risk-control and risk-adjusted enhancement with futures and options will be obsolete.*"

REFERENCES

There are several chapters on portfolio and trading strategies in the recently published "Handbook of Fixed-Income Options: Pricing, Strategies & Applications." For example, the use of options in total return portfolio management is discussed in Anderson and Amero (1989). Portfolio insurance has been receiving a lot of attention from academic researchers and Wall Street practitioners. Readers interested in the detailed mechanics involved in applying this dynamic hedging strategy should consult Sharpe (1985) and O'Brien (1988).

Anderson, K., and S. Amero, "Scenario Analysis and the Use of Options in Total Return Portfolio Management," in Fabozzi, F. J., ed., *Handbook of Fixed-Income Options: Pricing, Strategies & Applications*, Probus Publishing Company, Chicago, 1989, pp. 191–223.

Figlewski, S., "The Use of Financial Futures and Options by Life Insurance Companies," *Salomon Brothers Center for the Study of Financial Institutions*, Working Paper No. 469, New York University, New York, 1988.

Gastineau, G. L., "Futures and Options on Fixed Income Securities: Their Role in Fixed Income Portfolio Management," in Fabozzi, F., and I. Pollack, eds., *Handbook of Fixed Income Securities*, Dow Jones–Irwin, Homewood, Ill., 1983, pp. 871–872.

O'Brien, T. J. "Portfolio Insurance Mechanics," *Journal of Portfolio Management*, Spring:40–47, 1988.

Sharpe, W., "Portfolio Insurance," in *Investments*, Prentice-Hall, Englewood Cliffs, N.J., 1985, pp. 509–514.

Appendix
Derivation of Normal Price Model

To illustrate the derivation of closed-form option pricing formulas, we derive the normal price model formulas. The only mathematical prerequisite is elementary calculus.

As stated in Chapter 3, the price of a European call option with strike K and t years to expiration is expressed in this model by:

$$C = DF(\sigma[zN(z) + n(z)])$$

(3.3)

where $\qquad\qquad DF$ is the discounting function over the interval t

$z = (F - K)/\sigma$ is the normalized difference between strike K and forward (or future) price F

$n(z)$ and $N(z)$ represent the standard normal density function (mean = 0; standard deviation = 1) and the cumulative normal distribution function at z, respectively

σ is the absolute price standard deviation for the interval t in question

The absolute price standard deviation is:

$$\sigma = \frac{v}{100}F\sqrt{t}$$

where $\qquad\qquad v$ is the annualized percentage price volatility

248

> F and t are the option forward price and term in years, as be-
> fore

The option's delta or hedge ratio, which is just the derivative of the call price with respect to the underlying bond's forward price, is:

$$\delta C = DF(N(z)) \tag{3.4}$$

MATHEMATICAL DERIVATION

To derive these formulas, we assume that the price p of the underlying instrument is a *random variable* normally distributed at option expiration, centered at the forward price, F, with standard deviation σ. The fair value of a call option with strike price K is then the *expected value* of the option contract; that is, the probability-weighted average of its value in all possible outcome scenarios at the expiration date. (We will ignore the discounting factor DF throughout, to simplify the expressions.)

The expected value of a continuous random variable is the *integral* of the product of the values of that variable with the corresponding values of its probability density function. In our case, the price at expiration, p, has a normal probability density function $h(p)$ with mean equal to the forward price F and standard deviation σ.

Since the option expires worthless if the final price of the underlying security is less than the strike, K, and has value $p - K$ otherwise, we have for the value C of a call option:

$$C = \int_{p>K}^{\infty} (p - K)h(p)dp \tag{A.1}$$

where

$$h(p) = \frac{1}{\sigma}\, n\left(\frac{p - F}{\sigma}\right) = \frac{1}{\sigma\sqrt{2\pi}}\, e^{-[(p-F)/\sigma]^2/2}$$

is the probability distribution of prices p at expiration.

We can rewrite this as:

$$C = \int_{p>K}^{\infty} [(p - F) + (F - K)]\, h(p)dp$$

and hence:

$$C = \sigma \int_{p>K}^{\infty} \left[\frac{(p - F)}{\sigma} + \frac{(F - K)}{\sigma}\right] h(p)dp$$

Changing variables, we let:

$$z = \frac{(p - F)}{\sigma}$$

where z is now a random variable with the *standard* normal density function $n(z)$, with mean $= 0$ and standard deviation $= 1$. We have $p = \sigma z + F$, so $dp/dz = \sigma$, and $dp = \sigma dz$. We also let:

$$\bar{Z} = \frac{(F - K)}{\sigma}$$

Here $-\bar{Z}$ is the constant value of z corresponding to a price p equal to the strike price K. We then have:

$$C = \sigma \int_{z > -\bar{Z}}^{\infty} (z + \bar{Z}) n(z) dz \tag{A.2}$$

(Note that the factors $1/\sigma$ from $h(p) = (1/\sigma) \, n(z)$ and σ from $dp = \sigma dz$ cancel when we change variables from p to z.)

Rearranging the integrals, we have:

$$\begin{aligned} C &= \sigma \left[\int_{z > -\bar{Z}}^{\infty} z n(z) dz + \int_{z > -\bar{Z}}^{\infty} \bar{Z} n(z) dz \right] \\ &= \sigma \left[\int_{z > -\bar{Z}}^{\infty} z n(z) dz + \bar{Z} \int_{z > -\bar{Z}}^{\infty} n(z) dz \right] \end{aligned} \tag{A.3}$$

Now, by definition:

$$\int_{-\infty}^{x} n(z) dz = N(x)$$

where $N(z)$ is the cumulative standard normal distribution function. Therefore:

$$\int_{z > -\bar{Z}}^{\infty} n(z) dz = \int_{-\infty}^{\infty} n(z) dz - \int_{-\infty}^{-\bar{Z}} n(z) dz = N(\infty) - N(-\bar{Z})$$
$$= 1 - N(-\bar{Z}) = N(\bar{Z})$$

and Equation A.3 becomes:

$$C = \sigma \left[\int_{z > -\bar{Z}}^{\infty} z n(z) dz + \bar{Z} N(\bar{Z}) \right] \tag{A.4}$$

Since:

$$\frac{d(n(z))}{dz} = \frac{d\left(\frac{1}{\sqrt{2\pi}}e^{-z^2/2}\right)}{dz} = -z\frac{1}{\sqrt{2\pi}}e^{-z^2/2} = -zn(z),$$

we have, by the Fundamental Theorem of Calculus:

$$\int_{z>-\overline{Z}}^{\infty} zn(z)dz = \int_{-\infty}^{\infty} zn(z)dz - \int_{-\infty}^{-\overline{Z}} zn(z)dz$$

$$= -n(\infty) - -n(-\overline{Z}) = n(-\overline{Z}) = n(\overline{Z})$$

(A.5)

Finally, combining Equations A.4 and A.5, we obtain:

$$C = \sigma[n(\overline{Z}) + \overline{Z}N(\overline{Z})]$$

This is precisely Equation 3.3 given in Chapter 3, except for the discounting factor *DF*.

The option delta is just the *derivative* of this expression with respect to the forward price *F* (where $\overline{Z}$ and *F* must now be treated as variables). Since:

$$\overline{Z} = \frac{(F - K)}{\sigma} \text{ and } \frac{d\overline{Z}}{dF} = \frac{1}{\sigma}$$

we have:

$$\frac{dC}{dF} = \frac{dC}{d\overline{Z}} \times \frac{d\overline{Z}}{dF} = \sigma \times [-\overline{Z}n(\overline{Z}) + \overline{Z}n(\overline{Z}) + N(\overline{Z})] \times \frac{1}{\sigma} = N(\overline{Z})$$

which is just Equation 3.4, again ignoring the discounting factor *DF*.

Derivations of other, related closed-form option pricing formulas sometimes require more advanced mathematical techniques, but the general principle is the same: one is evaluating a probability-weighted average of outcomes (payoffs) at option expiration, which boils down to evaluating an integral expression similar to Equation A.1.

Index

Over-the-counter option, 10–11
  cash bond, 46
  terms, 11

Path independence, arbitrage-free rate
    movement model, 94
Performance analysis, scenario-
    driven, 182–183
Perturbation function, arbitrage-free
    rate movement model, 93
Portfolio insurance. *See* Dynamic
    hedging
Portfolio management
  dynamic hedging, 235–242
    hedge adjustment, 237
    mechanism, 235–236
    model-related issues, 236–237
    short-dated options, 237–238
    vs. long-dated options, 238
  put, 232–242
    risk/return characteristics,
      233–234
  relative-value analysis, 198–199
Price, defined, 2
Price sensitivity, lattice-based option
    pricing model, 73
Pricing model
  bond option, 58–116
    analytical approximations,
      114–115
    analytical models, 61
    binomial, 61, 70–83
    Black-Scholes model, 65–68
    common closed-form, 62–70
    delta, 59
    hedge ratio, 59
    known elements, 59
    lattice-based, 70–83
    lognormal price model, 65–68
    lognormal yield model, 69–70
    multinomial model, 88
    multiple factors, 114
    multistep arbitrage opportunities,
      87–88
    need for sophisticated, 86–90
    normal price model, 62–65
    path dependence, 89–90
    put-call parity, 59–61
    sensitivity measures, 59
    simulation model, 106–113
    stochastic model, 62
    term structure-based, 90–106

    uncertain strike prices, 89
    unknown elements, 59
    variable interest rates, 87
    variable volatilities, 88–89
    variant distributions, 114
    varieties, 61–62
    yield-based model, 68–69
  put-call parity, 141
Pricing model selection, 118–124
  bond future, 119–122
    long-dated options, 122
  cash bond, 122–124
    long-dated options, 124
  short-dated American options,
    120–122, 123–124
  short-dated European options, 120,
    121, 122–123
Primary dealer
  advantages, 28
  bid-ask spread, 30
  Federal Reserve Bank of New
    York, 28
  functions, 28
  information from, 29–30
  inventory risk, 30
Probability, lattice-based option
    pricing model, 74
Profit-taking, delta-neutral trading,
    165–166
Proprietary analytics, computerized
    trading system, 178–179
Put option
  cash bond, 243–244
  defined, 2
  payoff function, 5
    written, 5, 6
  portfolio insurance, 16
  portfolio management, 232–242
    risk/return characteristics,
      233–234
Put-call parity
  bond future, 141–146
  defined, 141
  pricing model, 141

Quality option, embedded option, 42

Rate movement model, 97–102
  basic interest rate process
    generation, 98

22.4.91
474.50